College of the Overwhelmed

The Campus Mental Health Crisis and What to Do About It

Richard Kadison, M.D.
Theresa Foy DiGeronimo

JOSSEY-BASS
A Wiley Imprint
www.josseybass.com

Published by Jossey-Bass
A Wiley Imprint
989 Market Street, San Francisco, CA 94103-1741   www.josseybass.com

Jossey-Bass books and products are available through most bookstores. To contact
Jossey-Bass directly call our Customer Care Department within the U.S. at 800-956-7739
or outside the U.S. at 317-572-3986, or fax to 317-572-4002.

Jossey-Bass also publishes its books in a variety of electronic formats. Some content that
appears in print may not be available in electronic books.

Library of Congress Cataloging-in-Publication Data

Kadison, Richard, date
   College of the overwhelmed : the campus mental health crisis and what to do
about it / Richard Kadison, Theresa Foy DiGeronimo.
      p. cm.
   Includes bibliographical references and index.
      ISBN 0-7879-7467-6 (alk. paper)
   1. College students—Mental health—United States.   2. College
students—Mental health services—United States.   I. DiGeronimo, Theresa Foy.
II. Title.
      RC451.4.S7K336 2004
      378.1'9713—dc22

                                                                    2004006656

Printed in the United States of America
FIRST EDITION
HB Printing   10 9 8 7 6 5 4 3 2 1

Contents

Acknowledgments   v

Introduction   1

Part I
The Problems: Why Are Some Kids So Unhappy at College?   5

1. Normal Developmental Issues   7
2. Pressure and Competition: Academic, Extracurricular, Parental, Racial, and Cultural   35
3. Financial Worries and Social Fears   65
4. Crisis on Campus: Feeling Hopeless and Helpless   89

Part II
The Solution: For Colleges, Parents, and Students   153

5. What Are Colleges Doing About the Crisis? And What More Should Be Done?   155
6. What Can Parents Do?   183
7. For Students Only   213

Appendix A: The 2002 American College Health
    Association Survey Results   239
Appendix B: Everything You Need to Know About
    Medications   243
Appendix C: Checklists for Colleges and
    Counseling Centers   261
Appendix D: Resources   267

Notes   275
About the Authors   285
Index   287

Acknowledgments

I thank my wife, Maria, for her ongoing support and her understanding about our lost vacation and family time. I also thank my son, Will, for his patience during the writing of this book, which cut into our Lego time and soccer games. Thanks go to my father, Elmer Kadison, for pushing me to consider medical school despite my reluctance. I also thank my cowriter, Theresa DiGeronimo, and our editor, Alan Rinzler, for creating the opportunity to write this book and for keeping me on track.

There are many people who have helped me write this book. I am indebted to all who have taken the time to share an opinion, offer expertise, or just listen as I thought out loud. In particular, I thank:

Irv Allen, psychiatrist, Harvard Mental Health Service

Roseanne Armitage, professor of psychiatry and director of the Sleep and Chronophysiology Laboratory, University of Michigan, Ann Arbor

Sally Donahue, director of financial aid, Harvard University

Yvonne Jenkins, psychologist, University Health Services, Boston College

Malcolm Kahn, University of Miami

Sharon Ladd, director, Harvard University International Office

Susan Marine, director, Office of Sexual Assault Prevention and Response, Harvard University

Mary Tinkham, assistant director, Harvard University International Office

Ling-Chi Wang, professor of Asian-American studies and ethnic studies, University of California, Berkeley

John Winkelman, M.D., Ph.D., assistant professor of psychiatry, Harvard Medical School, and director, sleep lab at Brigham and Women's Hospital, Boston

Bill Wright-Swadel, director, Career Services Office, Harvard University

I also thank the students I have seen over the years who have taught me so much about the trials and tribulations of college life. I especially thank the students who took the time to share their stories so that other students may learn from their experiences. I will not list their names in order to protect their privacy, but you each know who you are, and you have my deepest thanks.

And special thanks to our editors, Carol Hartland, Catherine Craddock, and Bev Miller, who skillfully shepherded the manuscript through the editorial process.

Richard Kadison
Cambridge, Massachusetts

*To my son, Will, now just five years old. Writing this book
has taken away some time from us, but he is
the light of my life and the inspiration for the book.
I hope the ideas here will help him and others lay the groundwork
for a more positive experience preparing for and experiencing
education with openness and trust, and the freedom
to explore the infinite opportunities before them.*

Introduction

This is a book about the extraordinary increase in serious mental illness on college campuses today and what we can do about it. If your son or daughter is in college, the chances are almost one in two that he or she will become depressed to the point of being unable to function; one in two that he or she will have regular episodes of binge drinking (with the resulting significant risk of dangerous consequences such as sexual assault and car accidents); and one in ten that he or she will seriously consider suicide. In fact, since 1988, the likelihood of a college student's suffering depression has doubled, suicidal ideation has tripled, and sexual assaults have quadrupled. The information on student mental health presented throughout this book is shocking—yet it is the elephant in the room that no one is talking about.

I have written this book for parents, students, and college counselors and administrators to open a dialogue, get us talking, and suggest ways we all can face these facts and do something about them.

Having worked in student health for twenty-five years, I've have been blessed with the opportunity to be involved with young people during the most exciting time of their lives—a time full of potential, dreams, and infinite choices. But over the years, I've seen the pressures and expectations increase and more and more students struggling with severe mental health issues. I've also seen frustrated parents who feel shut out and unsure of how to help. This book is my response to this increasingly common situation.

In Part One, "The Problems: Why Are Some Kids So Unhappy at College?" we explore the varied stresses that cause so many college students to suffer mental health problems. I hope that realizing what these students are facing will help you better understand how the push and pull of dependence and independence can sometimes be overwhelming. In the chapters in this part, we take a close look at developmental issues such as identity development, relationships, sexuality, and roommate problems. Then we explore the effects of academic pressures, extracurricular demands, parental expectations, and racial and cultural differences that affect self-worth. We examine the enormous financial pressure to pay the college bills and compete for postgraduate employment and graduate school admission. And finally, we'll see how the culture of fear created by the terrorist attacks of 9/11/01 have affected college-age children.

Those on college campuses across the country who feel hopeless and helpless respond with a variety of dysfunctional coping mechanisms. Part One concludes with a discussion of the warning signs and symptoms I see most often: depression, sleep disorders, substance abuse, anxiety disorders, eating disorders, impulsive behaviors (which include out-of-control sexuality and cutting/self-mutilation), and suicide. I also share the personal stories of students who have experienced these problems. I am grateful to the students who had the courage to come forward and talk about their experiences so that other students may not have to suffer in the same way .

In Part Two, I ask you to consider the roles that college personnel, parents, and the students themselves play in balancing academic and mental health needs. College mental health service programs are under the same pressures as other units of academic institutions and must lobby for limited budgetary resources. Rapid changes in health care and the diminishing public resources for referral add to the crunch. The number of psychiatric hospital beds is shrinking, as is funding for public clinics. Medication utilization has gone up dramatically, and the cost of this medication can be prohibitive.

This situation has created a dilemma for college administrators: How does students' emotional well-being fit into the academic picture? With the highly publicized suicides and lawsuits at schools like Massachusetts Institute of Technology and New York University, institutions must choose between trying to ignore or minimize the serious emotional challenges students face in college versus seeing emotional development as part of the intellectual, developmental, and spiritual growth that is integral to the college experience. Most have chosen wisely.

But even with the increased awareness among college administrators of their role in nurturing students' mental health, there is only so much that college counselors can do. Mental health services are often underfinanced, understaffed, and generally unequipped to handle the number of students who desperately need help. Many of these situations are hidden and never known: students suffer silently, drop out, or return home. Mental health directors on college campuses across the country are beginning to seek help, raise public consciousness, and gain parental support, but the problems remain.

That is why Part Two includes an important how-to chapter for parents. It's ironic that just when you feel you are setting your children free they often need your support and attention more than ever before. Although you cannot solve all the world's problems for your young adult children, you can still be involved and proactive in guarding their mental health. To start, you need to consider the chosen school's attitude toward and resources for providing emotional growth and stability in their students. Then you need to become aware of the problems that college students face so you can be attentive to the warning signs of emotional distress and prevent major emotional breakdowns. You must also know how to intervene if an emotional crisis strikes.

And finally, I turn my attention away from college administrators and parents and speak directly to those living in the midst of this high-pressure environment: the students themselves. The final chapter provides checklists, tips, and advice pertinent to the day-to-day life of all college students. It offers "do-this-now" suggestions about things that students can do in order to maximize their potential and lower their risk of developing common emotional and psychological problems. It discusses specific and simple steps that the students can take to avoid becoming overly stressed, to recognize signs of trouble, and to address real problems when they arise.

I've also included an appendix of resources and contacts. These will help you find further information on the many topics explored in this book.

All of our sons and daughters attend the college of the overwhelmed. I hope that the information in this book will get us talking about that. We all can be part of the solution if we learn to recognize the symptoms associated with being overwhelmed, take steps to ensure that students have access to appropriate care (especially since most of the problems are very treatable), and do our part to reduce the sources of stress that push too many college kids to the edge.

Part I

The Problems
Why Are Some Kids So Unhappy at College?

Many parents of college students whom I speak to are very much aware that the undergraduate years can be stressful. They realize that being away from home for the first time and meeting high academic expectations is a situation loaded with tension. But from an adult point of view, many of these parents also wonder how college kids can suffer serious emotional or mental problems. After all, they seem to have it made. They've made the grade and been admitted, and for the most part to the college of their choice. Some students, moreover, have all their bills paid for them; they have free lodging and food (whether living at home or in dormitories), and they ordinarily have very active social lives. So what is there to be so upset about?

What these parents don't realize is that despite this appearance of comfortable status, secure environment, and a pleasant social world, a multitude of hidden problems have caused a steady and alarming rise in the severity of students' mental health problems across the nation in colleges and universities large and small, public and private.

The chapters in Part One examine the root of this crisis, which can begin with developmental issues such as identity development, relationships and sexuality, conflicts with roommates, and the competition for grades and other achievements, all problems that can be fueled and exacerbated by powerful parental pressure and cultural expectations, as well as major economic anxiety in an era of financial downturns and a shrinking job market, and social anxiety in this post-9/11 culture of fear.

I hope that these chapters, which are based on my experience and that of many colleagues at other universities, and on personal experiences shared by students, will give you some insight into the lives of college students that will help you better understand why the college years are ripe for serious and potentially major self-destructive behaviors.

Normal Developmental Issues

When young adults begin college, most have one foot firmly planted in the security of home and family while the other foot is moving rapidly into the unexplored world of adulthood. For some, the jump from dependent to independent living is an easy move, accomplished with great aplomb. But for many others, the shift can be too sudden and too drastic, leaving them stuck between two worlds in a state of uncertainty, bewilderment, and acute anxiety. Consider Kristen, for example:

> Kristen was a straight A student who had been very active in her small, suburban high school. She was thrilled to be accepted into a large, urban university and couldn't wait to kick the dust of her "hokey little town" off her shoes. She entered college with the clear-cut goal of earning high grades and going on to a prestigious law school. But by the end of her first semester, she was begging her parents to come home. When Kristen's parents pressed her to explain why she wanted to give up all her plans and dreams, she insisted, "I just don't like it here. I want to come home."
>
> Although Kristen couldn't (or chose not to) explain the details of her feelings, it's very likely that her inability to make the transition to independent living had less

to do with the university and more to do with the internal process of change, ranging from mild stress caused by fear of the unknown to the first episode of a more serious problem such as depression.

The most common developmental issues that affect college-age kids and that will be covered in this chapter are identity development, relationships and sexuality, and interpersonal issues. Your child may face none, some, or all of these issues. I believe that knowing about them and understanding how they can affect personal development and academic success will give you the information you will need if your child seems unhappy at school or calls home and says, "I just don't like it here."

IDENTITY DEVELOPMENT

Late adolescence is a time of transition, a period of reflection on family values, career aspirations, and lifestyle experimentation. Before heading off to college, kids' developing sense of self is formed within the context of their family and immediate social experiences. The values and the academic and career expectations of the child and parents are often in line (at least on the surface). Even kids who attend boarding schools are closely supervised and molded by their teachers and parents. By the time they leave high school, many teens have a strong sense of self and purpose and feel confident about who they are and what they believe in.

But things change when they go off to college—as they should. Part of the function of college is to give young adults the freedom to explore their world. They will meet other students whose life views will challenge their previous assumptions—students with different backgrounds and values, with cultural differences, and with new philosophical and political ideas (more conservative or more liberal than their own). They'll be thrown into a world with ready access to sexual freedom and experimentation, along with alcohol and drugs. During this time of exploration, the question, *Where do I fit into life?* becomes more difficult to answer. Now the young adult may begin to define herself by new experiences and relationships, and this can change, challenge, and sometimes clash with the identity she left home with. Although this is a normal developmental process, it is a source of great anxiety for many college students.

"We're Not in Kansas Anymore"

In college, the model for living changes. These young adults are now exposed to many and varied life structures. They live with other students and learn about different lifestyles, backgrounds, cultures, races, and values. No longer do many of these young adults look to the family structure for direction and guidance. Rather, they stand in bewilderment like Dorothy in Munchkin Land whispering to Toto, "I have a feeling we're not in Kansas anymore."

For some young adults, this may be the first time that they have the freedom to recognize the differences between their own upbringing and others. They may see that other college-age kids have more or less financial freedom, or are more or less sexually mature and experienced, or are more or less bound by religious beliefs. Or they may see that other styles of clothing and body art are forms of personal expression rather than rebellion against parental rules. There is a tension between feeling unique and special versus fitting in and being part of the group. This is an opportunity for growth, but also fuel for confusion and anxiety.

When the new life model clashes with the child's family model, it can cause great internal upset. If the child chooses to shift and adopt new values and lifestyle, he or she may feel the stress of separation and parental disapproval—for example:

> Anya is an eighteen-year-old first-year student from Indonesia who was raised in a single-parent home by her mother. Her mom came from a poor, conservative family where the cultural expectation was to get married by

age eighteen and raise a family. Before sending her daughter off to college, Anya's mother confessed to Anya that she had been an "accidental" pregnancy and that she had considered an abortion. But she added that although it had been very difficult to raise a child alone, she was glad she did not have the abortion and was very proud of Anya and her accomplishments.

At school, Anya had a difficult adjustment period. She wanted to be accepted by her American classmates. She was very attractive but shy. She started using alcohol to relax in social situations, and one night she went home with someone she was dating, had sex without a condom, and got pregnant.

Anya told her boyfriend, who said he wasn't ready to commit to her and that she should have an abortion. She felt tremendous shame and guilt, as you can imagine. She couldn't bring herself to discuss this with her mom, but decided to speak with a counselor to sort out what would be right for her. Part of her felt that she should go home, have the baby, and make the same choice as her mother had, while a stronger part knew she had this opportunity for an education that she could not turn away from to live the same kind of difficult life her mother had led. Since leaving home, her beliefs and values had changed.

Other young adults cling to family values and beliefs for security, but on some deeper level they realize that not all of the old values and beliefs fit anymore. This pull of loyalties can cause great personal discomfort. Here's another story to illustrate this:

Karen, who came from a staunchly Republican family, learned in a political science class that her parents' belief that Democrats were all a bunch of bleeding-heart liberals looking for government handouts was not entirely true. But when she went home on holidays and during semester breaks, she couldn't bring herself to challenge their narrow beliefs. She seethed inside as she listened to their dinner conversations that tore into all Democrats with equal contempt, but she sat in silence rather than risk parental disapproval.

By assuming that their grown daughter held the same political beliefs as they did, Karen's parents were unknowingly pushing their daughter away emotionally. She couldn't agree with them, but she couldn't disagree either. And so she felt stuck in silence and internal conflict.

Leaving home to explore the broader world is an exhilarating experience, but don't be surprised if your child also starts to talk or behave in an entirely new way like someone you don't completely know any more—someone who disagrees with you about just about everything.

Broken Life Lines

Personal connections sustain all of us in our day-to-day lives. It is the connections we have with others that provide security and a sense of safety and that reinforce our sense of who we are. Unfortunately, I have found that these personal connections have an often underappreciated role in maintaining the mental health of college students.

In his book *Aging Well*, George Vaillant asserts that connections and relationships are the best predictors of happiness and satisfaction in life, ranked higher than career or financial success or even good physical health.[1] That's why some children who go to college will find themselves in a very vulnerable place if they can't immediately (or ever) establish personal connections.

When this happens, some undergraduates will not tell anyone that they feel socially isolated. They don't want to complain to their parents, and they don't want to seem needy or "uncool." They want an identity that appears to be strong and independent, even when it is actually insecure and painful. So they may withdraw and become anxious or depressed. That's what happened to Kisha.

> Kisha chose a beautiful small college on the East Coast because she loved the ocean and felt a small school would give her the emotional support and sense of community that she wanted. But after only two days on campus, Kisha knew this wasn't the place for her. As she later explained, "Everybody in that college was a science geek. When we would go to the beach, all they wanted to do was look for algae and scum! There was no one like me who just wanted to relax and sunbathe."
>
> At first Kisha went out socially with her roommate, but soon she stayed behind in her dorm room alone. She kept in touch with her high school friends by e-mail, but because they were full of stories about their social activities and new friends, she was embarrassed to admit her loneliness. Her parents assumed she was happy and active because that's what she told them. But when it came time to return to school for her sophomore year, Kisha began to cry and finally told her mother that she was miserable at school and did not want to go back.

When kids go off to college, society expects that their identity will shift from being dependent children to being responsible adults, but as students like Kisha find out, this expectation and the reality of the experience often clash—and for a good reason. The societal pressure to become more autonomous and independent comes at a time when college students are entering a new world where they need extra support and guidance. They many resist asking for help or even expressing their anxiety and confusion to their parents because they don't want to seem childish or weak. But the reality is that they don't yet have other sources of comfort and guidance, and so the stress of being "grown up" is magnified. Without personal connections, many young adults will eventually break down.

This breakdown can have the same impact as a jab to the gut, according to a 2003 study from the University of California, Los Angeles. Researchers there have found that social exclusion may cause as much distress in a pain center of the brain as an actual physical injury. "There's something about exclusion from others that is perceived as being as harmful to our survival as something that can physically hurt us," said lead author Naomi I. Eisenberger. "These findings show how deeply rooted our need is for social connection."[2]

There are other students who don't mind leaning on their parents at all; in fact, they have no need to create new relationships and connections because their parents remain their source of security. Kids like Bradley go to classes at college but look to home for personal connection:

> Bradley goes to a university 150 miles from his home, yet his father makes the trip every Friday night to bring him home and again on Sunday night to take him back. Bradley calls home daily and tells his parents every detail of his day. He keeps in close touch with his high school friends and spends his evenings chatting with them on his computer. Bradley knows he should make some friends at college, but it just doesn't seem to happen. Although he seems relatively happy, Bradley's habit of family dependence interferes with the ability to develop a necessary sense of autonomy.

It's difficult to find the right balance of home connection: too much or too little makes the development of the adult identity a difficult challenge.

Lost Glory Days

The college years are a time of identity crisis for many young adults who have defined themselves by their high school activities. What happens to the high school star athlete, for example, who is no longer playing sports? This student has spent the past ten years or so spending untold hours practicing athletic skills and living securely within the camaraderie of his or her teammates, and all of a sudden—bam!—that life is over. In the same way, the student who was very active in a music, dance, or drama program but is now pursuing a more academic curriculum may have trouble leaving that part of the self behind. And there are many students who were popular class leaders in high school who find themselves lost among the college masses and unable to distinguish themselves. These kids often have trouble adjusting to their new lives. This was the case for Mark:

> In high school, Mark had been class president, captain of the football and baseball teams, and prom king, and he had been voted most likely to succeed. His parents were sure he would do very well at the large public university that offered him an academic scholarship. But at the end of his sophomore year, Mark became severely depressed and dropped out of school. His parents were shocked when Mark explained that he just didn't fit in there. He had tried to join the newspaper staff, but was told all the positions were filled. He went to a debate club meeting and found that there were fifty students on the waiting list in front of him. He had had a new roommate each semester and had not made any close friends. Mark just couldn't find a way to feel important or accomplished, both important factors in the formation of his former identity.

If Mark holds too tightly to the "glory days," he will have trouble creating a new identity that gives him a feeling of purpose and achievement. Letting go is not easy, and it is often the root of emotional problems. One of the key factors that makes a difference for students is flexibility—the ability to adapt one's coping skills and develop new ones in a different setting. In Mark's case, being too focused on his past identity made his transition difficult, despite efforts to create new opportunities and experiences.

For other young adults, letting go is a desired goal, but it can be difficult to accomplish. Some students hope to wipe away their unpopular high school image and make a fresh start in college. But in reality, they usually bring personality and psychological baggage with them, and the problems they've had in making and keeping relationships don't disappear just because they're in a new environment. This can be a major disappointment for students who expected college to give them a clean slate and a brand-new start.

Changing the Best-Laid Plans

When stressed, we all search for things that are familiar and comfortable. So when college-age kids enter a new environment, it is comforting for them to know who they are and where they're going. For this reason, many first-year college students arrive with definite career goals. They immediately declare a major in business management, for example, and happily envision themselves working in the corporate world. Some follow through and earn their business degree without pause. But as the course work progresses, others find themselves terribly bored with their math and economics classes but enthralled with, say, their psychology courses. This can cause a strong identity struggle. There's often a tension between wanting to hold on to the plan, even if it doesn't feel right, but it is familiar and it is a part of who the student thought he would be.

Letting go of the original plan leaves many students in a place of uncertainty, and that can be a very scary experience. It is an especially difficult situation if the student is in a small college with a strong institutional identity that no longer fits the student. That would be the case, for example, with a student who attends MIT to become an engineer and instead falls in love with oil painting. In these cases, changing majors can mean changing schools, losing credits, and starting over. This is a highly stressful process that, as discussed in Chapter Three, is even more difficult if the change of career plans will upset the student's parents.

A Joy and a Challenge

The degree of identity issues students must grapple with vary depending on the college environment they enter. Some will encounter the shock of leaving a conservative home to enter a liberal college, while others will commute to a local college where they feel at home. But whatever the situation, all college-age kids are engaged in the developmental process of reshaping their identity. For parents, it can be both a joy and a challenge to stand by and watch it happen.

Additional Resources

Since its inception in 1920, the American College Health Association has been dedicated to the health needs of students at colleges and universities. It is the principal leadership organization for the field of college health and provides services, communications, and advocacy that help its members to advance the health of their campus communities. You can find additional information on college health services at its Web site, www.acha.org.

RELATIONSHIPS AND SEXUALITY

Although college kids will say that they can't wait to exercise their new sexual freedom when they get to college, there is a lot of anxiety among undergraduates surrounding their sexuality. Some will experience their first intense sexual relationship. Others will feel pressured to engage in sexual behaviors that push against their beliefs and values. And many will get their hearts broken when they confuse attachment and sexuality.

Boy Meets Girl

The ways in which many college kids meet potential partners are changing, and this alone can be stressful for students. It would be nice if your son fell for his physics lab partner and spent his evenings at the library with her doing homework together, but that's not the way it usually happens in the college dating scene. Today many students are clubbing, taking drugs like Ecstasy, going on spontaneous "booty runs" (sex dates), and partying until dawn.

These students are very intelligent young people, but they often have unrealistic feelings about the potential impact of their behavior. Some think they're invulnerable or at least don't stop to consider the consequences of their actions. They have unprotected sex, don't worry about getting HIV/AIDS, and put themselves at risk for contracting more than twenty other sexually transmitted diseases that affect some 3 million teenagers in the United States every year.

Today's college kids have heard all the lectures about club drugs, date rape, and safer sex, but many do not think it applies to them— until they face the fallout. When college students face date rape, sexually transmitted diseases (STDs), pregnancy, abortion, or any of the other negative consequences of careless sex, they are unlikely to look to their parents for help. They had been warned about the dangers of these behaviors, and now they feel stupid—and worried. Once their emotional or physical health is compromised by the consequences and disappointments of their sexuality, they find it extremely difficult to concentrate on schoolwork. Some flounder or drop out.

Peer Pressure

We are all bombarded by the media with the message that casual recreational sex is the norm. But many students come to college having limited experience with their sexuality and are surprised to hear their peers boasting of their latest sexual conquests. They often feel pressure to be sexually active as a way to find intimacy and a sense of connection in a new environment.

For students whose families have stressed abstinence, this contrast and pressure is even more severe. Because the number one goal of new college students is to establish connections, many find it hard to say no to sex without worrying that they will be isolated. Because they believe that "everybody is doing it," they are more likely to "do it" too, but then may feel terrible for betraying their own beliefs and their family's trust.

The striking data about perceived sexual behaviors versus actual sexual behaviors fuel the myth. A National College Health Association survey of 29,230 college students in 2002 points out how strongly the "everybody's doing it" mentality is entrenched in these young people. The survey found that the students' perception of peer sexual behavior was not on track with reality. The surveyed students assumed that only 2 percent of their peers were not sexually active, yet the reality was that 24 percent of their peer group who responded to the survey fit that classification as sexually inactive. They also assumed that 85 percent of their peers had had two or more sexual partners, but the reported data found the actual percentage to be a much smaller 28 percent.[3] These distortions of fact push college kids to bend to peer pressure that in reality doesn't even exist—but they don't know that.

The Link Between Alcohol, Sex, and Emotional Disorders

There is a persistent link between alcohol abuse and sexuality on college campuses. These young adults are anxious about being sexual, and so they drink to relax and lower their inhibition level. But this frequently leads to unwelcome trouble.

Females especially face negative consequences when mixing alcohol and sex. One study found that 50 percent of the females involved in college campus acquaintance rapes had been drinking when the sexual assault occurred.[4] Because alcohol impairs judgment and reduces inhibitions, Mara's case is far too typical:

> Mara was a virgin when she began college. She had had several boyfriends in high school, but her family and religious values were strong, and she chose abstinence. In October of her freshman year, Mara and her girlfriends were thrilled about being invited to an off-campus fraternity party. After hours of carefully preparing their outfits, hair, and makeup, the three set off, hoping to shake off the tension of their school studies and meet new friends. When they arrived, the frat house was packed with handsome young men; the dim lights and pulsating music charged the night with anticipation and possibility, and the alcohol was free and abundant. This was going to be the best night ever.
>
> When Mara woke the next morning at 5 A.M., she was stunned and dazed. She was lying naked on the floor of an unfamiliar bedroom with the unconscious nude body of a boy she didn't even recognize lying heavily across her legs. Looking around, she saw several more naked bodies tossed about in the frozen stillness of sleep. As she frantically tried to collect her thoughts, the last

thing Mara remembered was leaving the frat house with someone who offered her a ride home because she looked too drunk to drive. With her heart and head pounding, Mara stared up at the ceiling as her tears gave voice to her shame and embarrassment. This was not how she had planned to have her first sexual experience.

Mara's embarrassment soon turned to panic as she thought about the possible consequences of her black-out: pregnancy, possible abortion, and STDs. On top of her fears came a tremendous sense of regret and guilt for letting her family and herself down.

Unable to talk to their families about this life-altering situation, many young women try to handle the guilt, pregnancy, or abortion alone and suffer tremendous emotional pain. Some drink even more to stop feeling so bad. (See Chapter Three for more information on date rape.)

Men too sometimes suffer emotional pain when mixing alcohol and sex, but for very different reasons. Under the influence of alcohol, men may have difficulty getting and maintaining an erection. When they start to worry about performance, the problem compounds itself (the brain, after all, is the largest "sex" organ). The problem then becomes associated with shame, embarrassment, and fear. Men especially have great difficulty talking about their fear of sexual failure, and this fear soon becomes a self-fulfilling prophecy. Nineteen-year-old Dan is a typical example:

To ease his fear of appearing foolish or inexperienced, Dan would have a few beers to take the edge off before becoming sexual with his girlfriend. But because alcohol is a depressant of the central nervous system, it interfered with Dan's ability to get a good erection. When that happened, he panicked. To calm the terror, he began to drink even more before a potential sexual encounter, setting up a vicious cycle of sexual dysfunction. Dan was unable to talk about this problem to a counselor or to his girlfriend, and certainly not to his parents. Soon he couldn't sleep, eat, or concentrate on schoolwork. No one knew why Dan was so unhappy at school, and he wasn't about to say.

Alcohol also plays a large role in almost every sexual assault case seen on college campuses. These sexual assault cases consist almost entirely of "he-said/she-said" scenarios about what happened behind closed doors when both were drunk and neither memory is clear. The accused feels there was a clear message that the accuser was interested in being sexual and is now making unfair accusations. The victim never feels satisfied that the complaints are taken seriously because the accused is rarely expelled from school based on this fuzzy picture without witnesses. The resulting anger can lead to ongoing psychological difficulties for both parties.

Quite clearly, alcohol and sex don't mix well for college-age kids.

Gender Differences

A common problem in college relationships is the different views that men and women have about the meaning of their sexuality. For many women, there is a heightened expectation of intimacy following the beginning of a sexual relationship. They are more likely than men to have sex with a partner they expect to have a long-term relationship with. They often assume that sex signals a commitment.

Some young men, in contrast, have very strong libidos but fears of intimacy and commitment. They may not be looking for a long-term relationship and expect that their females partners feel the same, though they often don't.

These are clearly stereotypes, but they are common occurrences and causes of tension and disappointment for both males and females.

Tips for Mental Health

Just as in the general population, many "couples" issues arise for college students. Some students seek couples counseling when there are domestic violence or other physical altercations, which sometimes escalates to restraining orders and legal action. Others look for premarital counseling. It is very helpful for young couples to consider the ways in which their values and preferences will affect their long-term relationship.

College couples should consider a number of issues when they find themselves in a serious relationship. Issues such as living together before marriage, religious differences, having children or not, and deciding whose career will take priority are all better discussed before tying the knot. For all couples, sex and finances are the other common areas of tension. The frequency of sex and attitudes about spending and saving money often cause problems when young couples begin to think about a life-long commitment. Sometimes religious-based counseling is helpful when the student has a strong spiritual or religious belief system.

Same-sex couples also find it helpful to talk about their feelings and needs, especially if each partner is in a different place in the coming-out process. Usually brief therapy to identify the areas of potential tension and to create a process for discussion is very helpful and all that is needed.

Female Sexuality and Body Image

Like their male partners, women too struggle with a fear of sexual failure, but their form of failure is quite different. Society gives females the message that in order to be attractive to the opposite sex, they must be pencil thin. In 1984, the decidedly unscientific *Glamour* magazine conducted a survey through the department of psychiatry at the University of Cincinnati that asked thirty-three thousand women of college age questions about their body image. The survey found that only 25 percent of these women felt comfortable with their bodies; 75 percent felt they were physically flawed. And 96 percent said that their weight affected how they felt about themselves. *Glamour* repeated the survey in 1998 and found that "far from making progress, we actually lost ground."[5] Connection between body weight and self-image too often leads to eating disorders:

> Suzanne started therapy for her eating disorder when she was sixteen years old. She was five-feet, six inches and weighed about ninety-eight pounds. After she went off to college, she would return and tell me that she was in great shape. "You say anorexia is dangerous to my health," she would say, "but I go to the gym for two hours in the morning; I run four miles in the early afternoon, then I go back to the gym at night and work out for two more hours. I'm in far better shape than you are. How can you tell me I'm killing myself?" This college routine went on for about six months. Then one day, Suzanne was climbing the hill to her dormitory, and without warning, she just couldn't go on. She didn't have the energy or the muscle strength to continue the climb. Yet even after this physical breakdown, she was still convinced that she needed to lose weight in order to be attractive.

Your daughter may be taking this kind of body image with her to college. With this negative self-image, she is at risk for suffering anxiety, depression, or an eating disorder if her attempts to form an intimate relationship are not immediately successful. (These symptoms of college stress are explained in detail in Chapter Four.)

The Male Body Image

Don't overlook the possibility that your son may have body image problems that can lead to depression, anxiety, or eating disorders. Young men too are subject to societal pressures to be "hunks" and to have "six-pack" abs. There are plenty of males putting in excessive hours in the gym and following ritualistic diets in their drive to calm their insecurities about personal appearance.

Confusion over Sexual Orientation

Concerns over sexual orientation frequently rise to the surface during the college years and cause intense emotional pain, often unnecessarily. Sexual experimentation is quite common in this age group; for some, experimenting sexually with friends of the same sex is nothing more than satisfaction of a curiosity.

My colleagues at the Harvard School of Public Health and researchers at the Center for Health Policy Studies in Washington found that 20.8 percent of American men and 17.8 percent of women surveyed reported homosexual behavior or attraction.[6] Considering that only about 10 percent of the population define themselves as homosexual, these numbers show that many heterosexuals experiment with a same-sex relationship, and some define themselves as bisexual. But still, the experience can upset the fragile sexual identity of some, causing severe anxiety.

Other college students will discover, perhaps for the first time, that they are homosexual. A person's reaction to this awareness can vary from relief, to finally feeling at peace with one's sexuality, to horror at the thought of the reaction from family and friends. A student who reacts with fear and upset is at great risk for emotional distress. In fact, the frequency of depression and suicide attempts is much higher among homosexual students—not due to the sexual preference itself but to the reactions of family and societal pressures that accompany this label.

As an only child growing up, Pat was her dad's constant companion, and he was her biggest fan, following her to her many sporting activities over the years. "My dad was always so proud to call me his little 'tomboy,' " says Pat with a soft laugh. It was with great pride that Pat's dad brought her to college where she had earned a softball scholarship and where the two continued to stay in touch with frequent telephone calls and visits.

While at college, Pat continued to make her dad proud. She excelled in the classroom and on the softball field. "But gradually," says Pat, "I came to accept something about myself that I wasn't sure my dad would approve of. It was something I had long suspected: I was a lesbian." This acknowledgment was good for Pat because it freed her from the uncertainty and anxiety that had plagued her high school years. She now had a loving partner; she was happy, relaxed, and fulfilled. But still she worried about how this would affect her relationship with her father.

Over semester break in her junior year, Pat brought her friend home to meet her parents and to tell them of her sexual orientation. "Mom and Dad," began Pat, "I know this will surprise you, but Kate and I love each other. We're lesbians, and we're hoping you'll be able to accept that."

After a few seconds of excruciating silence, Pat's dad said, "You don't know what you're talking about. This is just a phase you're going through." And he walked out of the room and refused to discuss the subject any further.

Pat returned to school heartbroken. "My dad still won't talk to me," she says with her head bowed. "He's uncomfortable even being in the same room with me. I've hurt him deeply because I've killed off the daughter he thought he had. So mostly I just stay away and I cry a lot because I miss his friendship and because I love him and I know he can no longer love me back."

For all college students, whether heterosexual or gay, lesbian, bisexual, or transgender, the developmental process of becoming comfortable with one's sexuality can be an exhausting and overwhelming experience that too frequently gets wrapped up in silence, shame, embarrassment, and denial.

Additional Resources

Parents, Family and Friends of Lesbians and Gays (PFLAG) promotes the health and well-being of lesbian, gay, bisexual, and transgendered persons and their families through support, education, and advocacy. The organization has 450 chapters and affiliates in communities across the United States. For more information, log on to the Web site at www.pflag.org, or look for further contact information in Appendix B.

INTERPERSONAL ISSUES

For students who live away from home during their college years, adjusting to shared living with one or two roommates is both an opportunity and a challenge. When things go right, life-long friendships develop. But one of the most common complaints heard by college counseling services is roommate problems. The students' solution to the bad-roommate problem is to request a different roommate, but many colleges grant that request only in exceptional circumstances. Administrators know that if they let all students who don't get along move, they would spend the entire year playing musical rooms.

One of your child's developmental tasks while away at college is to learn how to get along with others, how to problem-solve differences, and how to live in less-than-perfect surroundings. Some do this very well; others find themselves in situations that seem unbearable, and they feel much anxiety over the question of whether to deal with it themselves or ask for their parents' help. This uncertainty, combined with the problem itself, leaves many kids disturbed and unhappy.

Learning to Share

In many cases, roommate problems are a simple matter of learning to share and compromise. Our kids' first lesson in sharing usually comes in kindergarten, but their second and biggest lesson comes in college. For some kids, this is the first time they have lived in crowded conditions. Many homes today have enough bedrooms for each sibling to have his or her own room and also have several bathrooms. Many kids have their own TV, computer, stereo, and phone. College throws them into a small, often scruffy or antiseptic room where they suddenly have to adjust to another person's constant presence, as well as that person's preferences in music, TV programs, friends, and sleep and study habits. Eventually most adjust and learn the valuable lesson of how to agree to disagree. That's what happened to Erin:

> "I came to college from a high school with absolutely no diversity," Erin says with a shrug of honesty. "So I subconsciously gravitated toward people who looked like me and dressed like me. That made me feel more at ease— more at home. But then in my sophomore year, I was randomly assigned to room with a girl who was my polar opposite: flip-flops versus shit-kicker boots; Dave Matthews Band preppy versus a punk rocker."

Erin was sure it was going to be a terrible year. She did not want to live with someone she had nothing in common with. But one night, while they were walking along a beach, Erin learned that there was more to a person than first appearances. "Although we grew up in different worlds," says Erin, "we were not so very different after all. I learned that she had a deep love and respect for animals. So do I! She also loved music that related to her life; it was a different kind of music than I listened to, but we suddenly realized that our lives were kind of like different songs singing the same message."

Erin admits that if she had not been forced to live with her roommate, there is little chance that they would have become friends. "I would never have approached my roommate in the cafeteria or during a class," she says, "but ironically, now I know that out of all the people I've met at college, the one who looked the least like me turned out to be the one most like me both spiritually and morally. My experience with this wonderful person has given me a new outlook on my own life and a new respect for the differences in other people."

Significant Problems

In some circumstances, the pressures caused by mismatched roommates are enormous and not easily ignored or solved. Following are a few examples of roommate situations that can disrupt the emotional and mental health of college students.

Psychological Disorders

Some students arrive at college with diagnosed disorders that make it virtually impossible to room with certain types of people. Steven, for example, has an obsessive-compulsive disorder and cannot sleep or study in a messy room. When he was paired with a roommate who littered the room with old food wrappings and wet towels, he suffered great anxiety, and this interfered with his ability to focus on academic work. He requested a single room, but it wasn't available. Sometimes a school disability coordinator can help in these circumstances.

Many schools make an effort to match the likes, dislikes, and needs of their students when assigning roommates. When that's the case, the student must be honest about any psychological disorders or other personal quirks that would interfere with comfortable living. Students with certain psychological disorders can make life very difficult for their roommates.

> This was the case for Maya, whose roommate, Katlyn, suffered from anorexia. It wasn't long before their dorm room became a sort of halfway house where Maya spent much time and energy nurturing Katlyn. She would bring her small meals several times a day and encourage her to eat; she made sure Katlyn went to all her classes and helped her to complete her assignments when lack of nourishment made Katlyn too exhausted to concentrate. Maya didn't like playing nursemaid, but she couldn't turn her back on someone in need. When Maya's parents heard the whole story, they were very upset because they felt that this was detracting from their daughter's educational and social experience. They were not paying top dollar so their daughter could be someone else's keeper. But Maya felt responsible for Katlyn and didn't know where to draw the line. Soon she had not only the stress of caring for her roommate but also the stress of fighting with her parents over the situation.

Like the population at large, many college students have psychological disorders. Coping with their problems while sharing a room with someone else can be an overwhelming challenge.

Overnight Guests

It's not unusual for college kids to invite off-campus friends for a visit and allow them to stay in their rooms overnight. When this happens on an occasional basis, their roommates learn to be accommodating and patient. But some kids let their friends practically move in, and that is a major imposition on the roommate whose space is invaded and whose sleep is constantly disturbed. All dorm students want to get along and want to be liked by their roommates, so many put up with behaviors and activities that bother them, but after awhile, they have to decide if the friendship is worth the trouble. Reporting a roommate who breaks the overnight rules is a big step fraught with fear and anxiety, but that's part of learning to stand up for one's rights. Not all college-age kids are ready to take that step.

The overnight situation gets even more difficult when the overnight guest is a sexual partner. It's hard enough for young adults to sort out their own sexuality, but dealing with the sexual exploits of a roommate can be more than they can handle. It's not unusual for resident life administrators to hear complaints like Tim's who said, "It was bad enough when my roommate kept bringing his girl-friend into the room during the day to have sex and expected me to get lost for an hour, but now she's staying overnight. I can't sleep with them making all that noise, but where am I supposed to go?"

Roommates may notice what appears to be out-of-control sex-ual behavior: bringing different partners home several times a week, sometimes associated with out-of-control drinking. It is very diffi-cult for students to confront one another about these issues for fear of rejection, when in fact, the roommate really needs a direct con-versation about the impact of the behavior from someone who cares. This situation calls for strong interpersonal skills and self-confidence that not all college-age students have.

Alcohol and Drug Use

It's no secret that some college kids abuse alcohol and recreational drugs. But when a roommate turns the dorm room into the corner bar or crack house, this is a serious situation. If the bystander roommate turns in the offender, he risks being isolated and shunned as an informer and "goody-goody." But the consequences for having alcohol or recreational drugs in a dorm room are often severe, so ignoring the situation also puts the roommate at risk for being busted along with everybody else. So what's the innocent party to do? Whether he or she turns in the roommate or not, the innocent party will live with tension and fear, always fuel for major emotional problems.

The Hard Facts

Here are some of the results of a survey of 29,230 college students conducted by the American College Health Association (the full survey results are available in Appendix A).* These numbers highlight the reason it's so important for parents to understand the stress and anxiety their college-age children struggle to cope with:

- 15.3 percent said they had relationship difficulties within the last year.

- 9.8 percent felt that alcohol use had affected their academic performance.

- 33.6 percent did something they later regretted while drinking.

- 16.4 percent had unprotected sex while drinking.

- 45.4 percent did not get enough sleep on many of the previous seven days to feel rested upon waking.

*Reprinted from the report *American College Health Association. National College Health Assessment: Reference Group Executive Summary Spring 2002* (Baltimore, Md.: American College Health Association, 2003).

IT'S A GENDER THING

The way your child adjusts to college life depends in part on gender, because the coping methods of males and females are generally quite different. Although there have been some specific scientific studies done in this area, my beliefs are based primarily on personal observances of college students over the past twenty-four years.

I have found females to be far more emotionally mature when they arrive at college. They are more tuned in to their feelings and tend to see the connection between the stresses of college life and their feelings. Therefore, they are the ones who more often seek help, although they may not be the ones with more problems.

In the important work at the Stone Center at Wellesley College, researchers have found that women's development and satisfaction with life occurs in and through relationships.[7] If women find and develop satisfactory support networks and feel a sense of connection, they have a greater sense of well-being. When they do not, their emotional intuitiveness makes them more vulnerable to psychological pain, and their coping mechanisms can be very negative. Some find their comfort in eating disorders, depression, or sexual promiscuity (as discussed in Chapter Four).

Men tend to create their relationships in more competitive, adversarial ways—in sports, academic accomplishments, or sexual prowess, for example. When they fall short of their own expectations, they have no real sense of why they feel so miserable. Rather than explore these feelings (as females will do), they avoid even thinking about their feelings and turn instead to counterproductive coping behaviors—commonly alcohol and drug use. The American College Health Association study found that 11.4 percent of responding males said that in the two weeks before the survey they had had five or more alcoholic drinks on three to five occasions; only 6.9 percent of females gave the same response.[8]

Males use mood-altering drugs and alcohol to make themselves feel more socially comfortable, and if that doesn't work, they use them to numb to the pain. Alcohol use is a common male response to the stress of developing relationships and the hurt of not fitting in. This is not to suggest that females don't abuse alcohol and drugs as well. But it is more common for males to become involved in substance abuse in order to dull the pain of struggling through developmental issues.

————————

Before the college years, you were able to organize your children's lives and supervise their activities. Now they are on their own and face the developmental task of learning how to balance their lives so they can feel confident in who they are, become fully engaged socially, learn what they are able to do and what they can't or shouldn't do, and be academically successful. These tasks are all normal developmental issues that cause crisis only when they get out of balance.

The adjustment to college and adult life causes many college-age kids exceptional stress, but it is not the only disruptive factors in their lives. In the next chapter, we'll take a look at how the demands to be the best, do it all, meet parental expectations, and deal with cultural and racial pressures lead some kids to the brink of disaster.

Pressure and Competition
Academic, Extracurricular, Parental, Racial, and Cultural

It seems to me that college students today are more driven to succeed than any generation before them—and more likely to break down. Certainly, it's still true that the college years are a time of unbounded intellectual, emotional, and social growth. But as Chapter One noted, the journey can be fraught with the developmental pressures of fitting in, getting along with roommates, exploring sexuality, and addressing the myriad of questions that come with the transition from adolescence to adulthood. And as if that weren't enough to handle, the pressure-cooker atmosphere on campus is intensified by academic, extracurricular, parental, and racial and cultural pressures. This chapter looks at these forces, which are all part of the college experience.

ACADEMIC PRESSURES

The kids whom I see entering college today are not strangers to academic pressure. With record numbers of high school seniors applying for a finite number of spaces at public and private colleges and universities across the country, the institutes of higher learning have become far more selective than in the past. And many kids get the message early on that being good isn't good enough.

Consequently, during their high school years, these ambitious students have taken college-level courses and SAT and ACT preparation classes. To boost their transcripts, they have participated in internships and attended corporate and political conferences and workshops; they have led the student government, joined after-school clubs, competed in varsity athletics, and volunteered their time in community and humanitarian projects. They have taken the tough job of doing well in school and getting into college very seriously.

Finally, the college acceptance letter arrives in the mail, and the pressure is off. With the prize in hand come feelings of relief and exhilaration, but they are short-lived. After arriving at school, a new set of pressures and expectations appears. Now comes the push to earn top grades and distinguish one's self in order to get into graduate school or secure a good job in a very competitive market. Some students face this task with a clear agenda and plan; others arrive with a blank slate. Most begin with a combination of enthusiasm, uncertainty, and a paradoxical desire to be unique and to fit in. Without strong coping skills to face these internal and external pressures, today's college students are walking combustibles, and the competitive college environment is often the igniting match.

Gotta Get All A's

In high school, it wasn't too difficult for the best students to rise to the top and for even average students to get exceptional grades. But college often changes all that, striking a blow to kids whose total sense of self-worth is tied to academic achievement (and this seems to be the case more and more often).

I get a lot more calls lately from faculty saying, "I received an e-mail from a student saying that if she fails this course, she's going to kill herself." The reason for this desperate feeling is not so much the objective stress (such as fear of doing poorly in the class) but the subjective stress. Too many students who get a B on a test overgeneralize and assume that this one misstep will lead to a disastrous life. They feel deeply that they are failures who will never get into graduate school or be successful in their careers. There is a complete loss of perspective, especially for the brightest students. They were tops in their high schools, but now find themselves in the middle of the pack surrounded by other "perfect" students. Because this is a time of developing autonomy, they face a challenge to their preconceived view about life—*I'm supposed to be smarter and stand out.* This confusion affects their identity as they struggle with the question, *If I'm not the best, who am I?* Sadly, some decide, *I'm a failure and a disgrace.*

College kids who are very focused on grades in order to get into graduate school or grab top jobs tend not only to feel more stress than other students, but I believe that they also get less out of their education than those who allow themselves to be less focused and less perfect. Grade-obsessed students are less willing to explore courses that are not directly related to their major. Students have told me that they do not want to "waste" their time or risk getting a low grade in an area they are not entirely comfortable with. They don't give themselves the freedom to enjoy learning for learning's sake. (Ironically, even some students in liberal arts colleges resist a liberal education.)

This is not a problem at top-tier schools only. Students at schools of lesser renown may feel even greater pressure to prove themselves. They may feel they are already at a disadvantage to students at the Ivies and need to achieve even more and accomplish even greater feats in order to compete for a place in graduate school or in the job market.

This situation robs these students of a chance to enjoy learning, which in itself is a wonderful antidote for academic stress. They won't let themselves work off tension through the fine or performing arts or put things in perspective through philosophy, religion, or psychology courses. They also miss the opportunity to delve more deeply into themselves and figure out who they are and what they really want to do with their lives.

The students who suffer the most academic stress are often the very ones least willing to admit to anyone at college that they are suffering. They fear that conceding even the slightest struggle will kill their chances of getting a good recommendation for graduate school or jobs. With an eye still on the prize, they try to deny the problem but pay the cost in suffering.

The Hard Facts

The American College Health Association survey of 29,230 college students found these impediments to academic performance (the full survey results are available in Appendix A):[*]

- Stress—29.3 percent

- Sleep difficulties—21.3 percent

- Concern for a troubled friend or family member—16.6 percent

- Depression, anxiety disorder, seasonal affect disorder—11.6 percent

- Death of a friend or family member—8.8 percent

----

[*]American College Health Association, *National College Health Assessment: Reference Group Report* (Baltimore, Md.: American College Health Association, 2002).

Gotta Work Harder

Other students are quite resilient when they get their first "unacceptable" grade and vow to work even harder. For many students, however, this response makes the situation even worse:

Ted was a business student who came from a small, rural high school. He entered a large university and immediately felt that he did not have the educational background that others students brought with them. But Ted did not despair over his first C on a term paper; he was determined to prove that he could succeed. He confronted the challenge by increasing his study time, gobbling up every free second. He gave up his morning jog, barely grabbed a snack during the day, stopped "unnecessary" socializing, and stayed up to the wee hours of the morning studying.

Ted thought he was doing a good thing. He did not realize that in addition to studying, daily exercise, nutritious food, adequate sleep, and good friends are also absolutely necessary to academic success. By studying too much and too long, Ted was soon studying less and less efficiently. This increased his need to study more, setting up a dangerous cycle: the more kids study and give up exercise, food, sleep, and social interactions, the more susceptible they become to depression.

Tips for Mental Health

Exercise and food feed the body and the brain so they can function at peak levels. Early stages of sleep allow us to feel rested and restored, and the later stages allow us to integrate cognitive functions so we can remember what we studied the day before. Friendships give us necessary comfort and support.

Walking a Thin Line

The colleges your children attend should demand academic excellence. You should hope that their course work is challenging. But we must all be aware of the very thin line your children walk between feeling challenged and feeling overwhelmed. If they get stuck on the wrong side of that line, they will need us to be nearby to pull them back over.

THE EXTRACURRICULAR JUGGLING ACT

For some students, college is a three-ring circus, and they are the jugglers. In one hand, they juggle the balls representing the demands for high academic performance; in the other, they twirl the hoops of social relationships; and in the air, they spin the pins of their extracurricular activities. Some manage to maintain the delicate balance without dropping any of the load, but for others, the act is just too difficult, and balls, hoops, and pins eventually collide.

Undergraduates who must master an especially difficult balancing act are the student athletes. They are often engaged in time-intensive and demanding sports activities while trying to survive the pressure all other students face as well. They try to keep up with studies while practicing their sport seven days a week. Then they scramble to keep the pieces together when their team goes on trips to away games during long seasons, causing the athletes to miss classes. Practices sometimes run through the dinner hour, adding another level of challenge in finding good nutrition and getting adequate calories to regenerate the fuel spent during practice.

In addition to their desire to perform well in the classroom, these students may have the added pressure of performing well on the athletic field or arena. There is usually intense competition for spots in the starting lineup. One poor practice session, a fumbled football, a bad at-bat, or poor shooting on the basketball court can quickly erode the athlete's sense of self-esteem, his or her identity as an accomplished star (which they all were in their high schools), and the ability to stay mentally strong in the midst of all the other college pressures.

I'll share a recent story of a football player who is a good example of how things can so easily go wrong for college athletes:

> As a high school player, Harry had won numerous division and state honors. He was heavily recruited by college coaches and decided to take an athletic scholarship to a powerhouse school three hundred miles away from his home. At the end of his first freshman semester, he packed his bags and quit school. His friends and family were shocked and wondered what could have happened to such promising talent.
>
> Harry's coach wasn't so surprised; he's seen this happen many times before. "Harry was a good player," he says. "But he wasn't the best on my team. No matter how hard he tried, he wasn't going to be in my starting lineup as a freshman. But I have to admit, he was a hard worker. In fact, Harry put in too much time on his own in addition to our grueling team schedule. And that hurt his studies. I was told in October that he was failing two classes, and I immediately put him on mandatory study time, but that didn't help. This was a young man who was obsessed with what he saw as his failure on the field and just couldn't keep his mind on the books. I also think Harry was homesick. His dad had been his number one supporter, and without him on the sidelines, maybe Harry just felt too alone out there." Put all these factors together, and it's no longer shocking that this young man headed for the security of home.

Athletes like Harry are not uncommon. Even the ones who make the starting team struggle with pressures and expectations that can make it very difficult to balance the demands of school with those of their coaches.

I recently heard of a soccer star who loves the sport and her team and coach, but she finds herself under tremendous pressure during the long soccer season. She travels nearly every weekend for Division 1 games up and down the East Coast, often leaving on a Thursday (missing classes) and not getting back until late Sunday night or even Monday. She is exhausted upon her return, and she still has homework to do. That's a tough schedule for anyone.

Also notable are the disruptive schedules of members of the band, orchestra, glee clubs, student drama productions, student government organizations, debate clubs, feminist and political activities, and other activities that demand not only a lot of practice and rehearsal but extensive travel time to distant and time-consuming events. Many students take their involvement in these activities very seriously, and sometimes to the breaking point. This was the case with one ambitious news editor:

> Larry had a high-achieving personality, and he tried to do it all. Larry took over as editor in chief of his college newspaper after the former editor abruptly left school. Larry knew the editorial staff was a bit disorganized and that the quality of articles had taken a dive over the past year, but he thought it would be easy to get the paper back on track. That naive assumption almost cost Larry his college degree.
>
> "The reporters had no idea what 'deadline' or 'journalistic integrity' meant," Larry recalls with a sad shake of his head. "I would end up writing half the pieces myself and doing major rewrites on the pieces that 'borrowed' information right out of the New York Times. I was spending hours and hours every day (often until three or four in the morning) in the newspaper office. School work? What was that? Friends? I had no time for them, and because I was so tired and cranky, they had no time for me either. By the end of the semester, I had

almost single-handedly saved the paper from disgrace, but the price was awfully high. I no longer wondered why the previous editor dropped out of school. My GPA plunged, and I ended up on academic probation. I want to be a journalist when I graduate, and so I thought this was an important life experience for me. Now I think I'll get my degree first and then jump into the real world of newspaper reporting."

A new editor took over for Larry the following year and no doubt is holed up somewhere right now, trying to keep the presses rolling, but at what cost?

PARENTAL EXPECTATIONS

In the 1960s and 1970s, sons and daughters openly rebelled against parental expectations. With peer support behind them, they had no trouble speaking out against their families' views of politics, religion, and moral values. But it seems to me that the children of the new millennium are not as outspoken about their own needs and goals and pay the price in increased stress.

Many in this college generation have been raised in a culture of conformity and high expectations. Parents have given their children every opportunity to enrich themselves, to excel, to become superkids. In highly structured and supervised environments, they give and give and give more than any generation before them. This is a positive situation in one sense: today's children have had far more exposure to after-school and Saturday morning classes in dance, art, science, politics, and computers and greater specialized focus and training in athletics and music. But as the bar continues to be raised higher and higher and the academics become more and more challenging, this culture of high expectations sets up a classic situation for stress and early burnout.

The situation can be particularly stressful in immigrant families. In these cases, some hopeful and ambitious parents push their kids hard to move up from just-off-the-boat working-class status to middle-class professionalism. This syndrome leaves no time or tolerance for exploring life or self.

It is with the best of intentions that parents raise the bar on minimum expectations. But a large number of sound studies have found that the results of this increased pressure from home have a part to play in the epidemic of mental health issues on campus.

Expecting Top Grades

You have a right to expect your child to get good grades in college. Parents who know their child is goofing off, partying too much, or dedicating far more time to perfecting video game skills than studying have good reasons to demand better. Although socializing is an important part of the college experience, the goal, after all, is to get an education.

Parental pressure for good grades becomes a problem when it is unrealistic. Some parents are convinced that a child who earned all A's in high school should do the same in college, but this often does not happen. The reality of a higher education finds students who earned all A's in high school quickly wracking up B's and C's in college even though they're working hard and giving full effort to their classes. They may find that the study skills and level of work that rewarded them in high school are inadequate for college studies. They need time to acclimate to the higher expectations. They need support from home that assures them that doing their best is all they can do—that sometimes the grade is not the most important thing.

But this message is hard to believe, never mind deliver, if your child has always been at the top of his or her class. And it's also hard for parents to judge if their children who are earning those B's and C's are really working hard:

> Geta and her parents are caught in this argument over grades, and neither side is able to concede to the other.

Geta had been in the top 5 percent of her high school class in Florida. When she entered an elite college in the Midwest, she says she was unprepared for the academic rigors she faced and ended her first year with a B– average. Geta's parents were angry and threatened to pull her out of the college if she did not raise her grades the following semester. They had come to this country from eastern India and worked hard seven days a week in their own restaurant so that their daughter could have a good life in a profession like computer engineering or medicine. They expected Geta to focus on her studies and graduate at the top in her college class. There were no excuses to do otherwise.

Geta, who had been having trouble adjusting to the academic demands of her school, found that adding her parents' demands to her stress load was more than she could handle. She failed out of school her sophomore year and returned home with an eating disorder that seemed to successfully divert her own and her parents' attention away from her academic failure and the underlying reason of unrealistic expectations.

Expecting to Share the Same Goals

At his graduation from Harvard Law School, my friend's joy was momentarily dimmed when his mom came up to him and said quite seriously, "It's still not too late to go to medical school." The parental expectation that children choose a certain career can be direct, as in this case, or more subtle, as in my own case. When I was in college, I became interested in Buddhism and religious studies. Although my parents didn't order me to drop those classes, I knew they didn't like the idea. My dad grew up quite poor in Chicago and worked hard to get to medical school and then send his own son to an Ivy League school. I'm sure that to him, the idea of spending time studying religions seemed like a waste of time and money. It could not possibly contribute to my ability to earn a living when I graduated.

Fortunately, my parents remained calm while I explored subjects that were nonmedical, but today many parents are more vocal in their plans for their children. On campus after campus, counselors tell of students doing poorly in courses required for medical or law school, for example, in a conscious or unconscious effort to escape from the career expectations of parents.

Some parents steer their sons and daughters toward certain careers and assume they will follow that lead without question. We all have heard the stories about the young adults who are disowned when they refuse to join the family business. We've heard about the families who pressure their children to choose occupations with social status in fields like law, medicine, or business. We all also know stories about young people who bend to the pressure to please their parents and then live with regret and personal disappointment for the rest of their lives. Some young adults do both: they earn the college degree their parents insist on and then turn away and follow their heart into another field. In many of these situations, the pressure on the young adults is more than they can handle, and soon they find themselves struggling with anxiety disorders, eating disorders, substance abuse, or depression. It is very difficult to live knowing you must choose to please those who love you or please yourself.

Expecting Close Communication and Family Togetherness

Your child will feel additional stress if there is disagreement over how much you two should communicate. Certainly, just because your child has entered college, you don't expect to be cut off from information. Whether your child is living at home or in a dorm room, you expect to hear how he is doing, how his classes are going, what kind of grades he is getting, what friends he's making, how his professors are, and so on. But these perfectly natural expectations are notorious for causing tension between parents and their college-age children.

The college student is struggling to become autonomous and may not feel like communicating much or often. Some are just too busy to stay in touch. Others find that too much communication triggers loneliness and homesickness, and so they avoid it. And some say it pulls them back into the parent-child lectures and arguments they've grown out of. For whatever reason, it is quite common for college students to either intentionally or unintentionally put distance between themselves and their parents. Although this is their choice, they still feel the stress of parental complaints.

This disagreement over sharing one's self spills over into family togetherness time as well. Parents often tell me that because they are still supporting their child and consider her a member of the family, they naturally look forward to seeing her occasionally. The students I talk to don't always feel the same but do feel the guilt associated with this differing view.

> Max confided to me that he was very excited about visiting his roommate's family over the Thanksgiving break, but had not yet told his parents about this plan. "They're going to be so angry that I'm not coming home for Thanksgiving," he admitted. "But it's a five-hour car ride from campus to my home, and Jim's house is only one hour away. But as long as my parents are paying the bills, there's no way I can make them understand that I'd rather not make the trip; they always try to guilt me into doing what they want." Max's plan was to spring this news on his parents at the last second and take off before they had a chance to make him change his plans. Obviously, he did, indeed, feel guilty.

Canceling visits home may be a coping mechanism to fight off homesickness, or it may be done in the rush of a self-centered life, but either way, it is always the cause of family tension that adds on more layers of daily tension.

What Parents Don't Expect

Of all the many things parents tell me they expect from their children at college, I have never heard parents say that they expect them to develop emotional or mental problems. They would never think that they could be the parents of one of the 38 percent of students who say they have been so depressed in the past year that they couldn't function. They can't imagine that their kids will be the ones involved in binge drinking at college, and yet we know that approximately two-fifths (44.5 percent) of college students reported drinking five drinks in a row (or four in a row for women) within the two weeks previous to the survey.[1] Your child may be the one who is studying hard, feeling happy, and accomplishing all goals—but maybe he is not, and your expectation that all is well makes it harder on your child to speak up.

Many parents also don't expect their children to seek counseling for psychological problems. Students who come to our mental health services center tell us that their parents would be upset if they found out. Their parents have given the clear message (whether stated or unstated) that their children should not talk about their background or family life to "strangers." They don't want counselors digging in to the details of what goes on at home, and their children know it. In these cases, students struggling with mental health issues are in a troublesome bind: either respect their parents' feelings and stay away from mental health counseling services or seek relief from their pain, but they can't do both. That's a lot of stress. (We'll take a look at what parents can do when these mental health problems occur in Chapter Six.)

RACIAL AND CULTURAL PROBLEMS

Minorities, immigrants, and foreign nationals face exceptionally tough challenges at college. They frequently face cultural and racial differences that can interfere with their personal, social, and academic growth. In some cases, the family identity conflicts with the emerging new identity of the young adult away from home. In other cases, family expectations based on the culture of their country of origin cause the student to feel guilt and shame during this time of self-exploration and growth. These students are especially vulnerable to the emotional tug-of-war between new opportunities and family expectations. And most important, they very often feel tremendous pressure to fulfill the expectations of parents who have struggled very hard to reach this country, provide a safe and secure home for their families, achieve a level of economic success sufficient to send their kids to good schools (often as the first in their families to attend college), and now assume their hopes and dreams will be fulfilled by this new generation of more educated, accomplished, high-achieving candidates for professional careers.

My experiences with a diverse student population have shown me firsthand how difficult it can be for even the most dedicated and hard working of these students to stay mentally and emotionally healthy while navigating the often treacherous terrain of a college campus whose culture is far different from the one at home.

Discrimination

Minority and immigrant students face the typical identity issues facing all college students: *Who am I? Where do I fit in?* But for these students, the issues are compounded. Their identity as a minority or immigrant on campus can add tremendous strain to their daily lives, especially on predominantly white campuses.

For various sociological reasons, immigrants and minorities are often looked down on in the United States. Some groups (specifically black and Hispanic) have not had equal access to higher education in years past. They have integrated so-called white colleges in any significant numbers only in the past twenty-five years, and this backdrop of not being a traditional part of these institutions is still very dominant.

Irving Allen, a psychiatrist to the Health Services at Harvard University, says, "Unfortunately, college campuses are microcosms

of the larger society and cannot reliably offer these students supportive safe havens from the profoundly ambivalent stance of this
society toward them."[2]

When you consider the affirmative action cases and the pas-
sionate debate around those issues, it is still apparent that there are
negative feelings about minorities and immigrants on campus, especially at top-tier schools. Here, minority and immigrant students
don't often face blatant discrimination or prejudice, but they know
that they are suspect in the minds of the white student population.
They know their admission is perceived as being tainted by the
belief that they do not have to meet the same qualifications as white
students. They know many of their peers think they have gotten
special advantages and don't deserve to be in their classes. And
there are further charges that minority students are the cause of
grade inflation by professors afraid to fail students of color and risk
the charge of racism. These erroneous assertions put a burden on
these students to prove they belong, while at the same time erod-
ing their self-esteem.[3]

My colleague Yvonne Jenkins, Ph.D., who is now a psychologist
at Boston College's University Mental Health Services, recalls two
stories about black students that clearly show the kind of attitude
that makes our children of color feel out of place:

> In one instance, Jannine, a young woman of color, was
> sitting in the common room of her dorm with a number
> of white students when a black woman on the housing
> staff walked through, stopped, and asked to see Jannine's
> student ID. The suspicion that Jannine didn't belong at
> the college because she was black (which was the only
> explanation for what happened since none of the white
> students present were asked to show their ID) was an
> insult that was magnified for Jannine because it was
> another woman of color who challenged her. She was
> saddened and angered by this powerful example of the

internalization of oppressive perceptions by another woman of color.

In a separate instance, another young woman of color was also subject to an interrogation that she believed was sparked by her color. Theresa's brother came to the school to give her a ride home for a long holiday weekend. Because she wanted to work on a college paper while at home, she asked her brother to take her computer out to the car for her while she packed up her overnight bag. Theresa was puzzled when she left her dorm a few minutes later and saw two police officers outside the dorm. Then she was mortified to find that her brother was being questioned on suspicion of stealing a computer.

These are examples of what Jenkins calls microaggressions. Over time, these daily assaults wear down the pride of minority and immigrant students and cause them to question if in fact they do belong in college. It can cause them to doubt their dreams and aspirations. And some begin to buy into the idea that they are less worthy of a good education than others.

Although many minority and immigrant students have experienced bias assaults before arriving at college, the hurt can be especially acute in the academic environment. Often these students expect things to be different in what they think will be an educated and unbiased college community, and so they are especially hard hit by the reality of continued prejudice. This huge disappointment can lead to self-doubt and emotional difficulties.

Coming from a Culture of Anti-Intellectualism

Most sadly, it is not only the prejudice of white peers that leads to these problems, but also the burden of an anti-intellectual culture from within the minority and immigrant communities that adds to the college student's identity confusion.

"Acting white" is a charge often levied against children of color who earn high grades and achieve academic success. This is an insult that also targets standard speech, clean-cut clothing, mainstream music and art, as well as social activities such as tennis or chess. This charge may come out of a college student's old neighborhood or even from other students of color on the college campus. It is an insult that keeps many young men and women from reaching their full potential.

In their article "Black Students' School Successes: Coping with the Burden of 'Acting White,'" authors Fordham and Ogbu relate the experience of the great college and professional basketball player Kareem Abdul-Jabbar, who transferred from a predominantly white to an all-black high school. His experiences are mirrored on college campuses all over the country when students of color appear to be "acting white" to their peer group: "It was my first time away from home, my first experience in an all-black situation, and I found myself being punished for doing everything I'd ever been taught was right. I got all As and was hated for it; I spoke correctly and was called a punk. I had to learn a new language simply to be able to deal with the threats. I had good manners and was a good boy and paid for it with my hide."[4] This dumbing-down phenomenon hurts all students of color as they struggle to maintain their family and cultural identities while growing in positive directions.

Most painfully, this jealously sometimes comes from the child's own family. Although the family feels proud of the academic accomplishments of the child who goes off to college, some are not able to tolerate the change that the college experience brings to the family:

> Kashif noticed this problem when he came home from school for the semester break in December of his freshman year. He was eager to tell his older brother about his college experiences. Although his brother did not go to

college, Kashif always looked up to him. But the first time he started talking about a professor he especially liked, his brother shot him down: "I don't care about no professor," he spat out. "You think I want to hear you talk all uppity about your white-ass teachers who think they can turn you into their little servant boy? You're no better than anybody else around here, and no college classes is gonna change that." Kashif was stunned. He didn't understand why his brother was so angry. He had encouraged him to go to college, to get out of the neighborhood. Now he seemed almost resentful.

Kashif's mother added to his distress. While helping his mom put away the groceries one afternoon, Kashif confided to her that he sometimes felt lonely on campus—that he hadn't yet made any close friends. His mother's reaction was swift and sharp: "I'm working overtime to pay your bills. I have to worry about getting mugged in this neighborhood every night when I come home. I can't afford to see a doctor about this pain in my back. And you're complaining that you have no friends while you're hanging around living a life of leisure at college? Boy, you don't have any idea what troubles are."

Kashif's academic and personal life were devalued by his family's reactions. Soon he withdrew from them, never talked about his concerns or fears, and eventually stopped coming home at all if he didn't have to. He felt isolated at school and at home, and by the middle of his sophomore year he was suffering from depression.

Whether it's friends, classmates, siblings, or parents who try to keep the college student from changing and growing, it is extremely stressful and cause for painful soul-searching for students who want to belong but don't know where they fit in.

Additional Resources

You can gather more information about battling discrimination on college campuses through these two organizations (see Appendix B for more contact details):

- National Association for Equal Opportunity in Higher Education, www.nafeo.org

- United Negro College Fund, www.uncf.org

Family Expectations

As discussed in Chapter One, all college students feel a strong need to fit in with their peers. To do this, minority and immigrant students sometimes look for ways to be more like white American students and less like themselves and their families. To adapt to their new environment, these students often feel they must change who they are and turn away from where they come from. This denial of background and self, which can be riddled with profound guilt, is compounded by family expectations.

Incredibly, I've observed students who come from families that do not expect their children to engage with the prevailing culture on campus. They expect their children to get an education but not grow away from the family traditions. They expect them to date only those of their own racial, ethnic, or religious background. They expect their children to continue practicing the tenets of their religion. They even expect that their diet and social activities will remain culturally pure. These expectations are unrealistic and unfair:

> When I first met Irena, she was seeking help for symptoms of depression. As we talked, it became clear that Irena's daily struggle was with her Dominican family's expectations. She was torn between three possible actions: she could follow her family's wishes by dressing very conser-

vatively, dating only other Dominicans, and taking the two-hour drive home every weekend to go to church with the family. Her second option was to lie to her family while secretly dating her white boyfriend, dressing stylishly, and creating an imaginary Dominican Catholic church nearby. Her third, and most difficult, option was to openly disobey her parents and hope they would eventually understand her need to grow and change and become more "American."

Any one of these three options would present Irena with a no-win situation: she would either feel tremendous guilt for weakening her connection to her family, or she would feel unfairly constrained and limited in her traditional (but now outgrown) family role. Until Irena could find a way to blend her changing identity with her parents' expectations, there was no doubt that her symptoms of depression would continue.

Family Hopes

Students from minority and immigrant families are frequently the first generation to seek a higher education. This is a wonderful advancement for these families, but also a powerful load of pressure on the children. Too often, the family has high hopes that this child will be the family savior in many different ways. This will be the child who gets out of the old neighborhood. This will be the child who brings honor to the family. This will be the child who ends their financial struggles—who sends money back home to family, sends siblings to college, gets Mom out of the projects. This is enormous pressure to succeed that middle- and upper-class kids don't have to deal with.

There is also pressure attached to the mantra that these children hear from their families: "You are so lucky. We're so proud of you. You've made all my struggles worthwhile—all these hours and days and weeks and years of work. All the money we saved to send you to college." That's a lot of family pride to live up to. The implied message is, "Don't mess up. We're all counting on you." This external pressure to be successful in college keeps many immigrant and minority students on track, but it pushes just as many over the edge.

This is especially difficult to handle when the young adult's parents have no college tradition or experience to offer as guidance. And no one is able to give appropriate advice or guidance to help the college student fulfill these high hopes.

Absence of Role Models

There is a profound absence of role models for minority and immigrant students on college campuses. Either consciously or unconsciously, minority and immigrant students (especially students of color) notice that there are not many people on the faculty who look like them. Certainly, this contributes to feelings of isolation and estrangement; it's hard to feel that necessary sense of connection when the people around you cannot relate to your background, experience, or appearance.

This lack of diversity among faculty members can make it difficult for minority and immigrant students to feel comfortable on campus. After all, role models who look like you make you feel welcomed and at home. They make you feel as if you belong and are a part of things, and they help you believe that you too can strive for success. Without this, the minority or immigrant student may feel like an anomaly who is no more than an affirmative action quota filler. And even when an all-white faculty does not have a direct or conscious effect, it is my belief that this is one more assault that in time can wear down the confidence and self-esteem of our minority and immigrant children.

Prejudice Against Asian Students

Other immigrant groups arrive at college with a reputation of advantage and face the prejudice this brings. This is especially notable among Asian American students who arrive on campus labeled as "brains." For reasons not clearly understood, Asians, whether born abroad or in the United States, are exceptionally high achievers in school. Phil Kaufman, lead author of a study on Asian students published by the National Center for Education Statistics, says the key ingredient seems to be that Asian parents have higher expectations than American parents for their kids.[5] It is interesting to find that parental expectations do actually push college-age young adults to achieve academic success, but in the Asian college student population, this push for success has caused a new brand of pressure and prejudice.

From within their own families, Asian students face the now famous "Asian parents syndrome." This is a parental style that accepts no excuses for not being the best. It demands excellence and is powered by extremely high expectations. Young Asian kids know exactly what it is and even post comments about it on-line, with egregious examples, mutual complaints, and occasionally a bit of humor.

From outside the family, Asian students also face unique pressures. As changes in affirmative action laws make it more difficult for youth of color to find a place in top-tier universities, the demise of the quota system opens the door to more qualified Asian students. This, some predict, will cause an overflow of Asian students who, oddly enough, will feel exposed and vulnerable as a result of their success.

Ling-Chi Wang, professor of Asian-American studies and ethnic studies at the University of California at Berkeley, has predicted that soon Asians will make up more than 50 percent of total undergraduate enrollment on the eight University of California campuses, the nation's largest public university system, if the same merit-based criteria continue. As this begins to happen, Wang has observed a backlash against these students that has sometimes made them feel marginalized and ignored. For example, he has seen many people, including faculty, become intolerant of Asian students' weaknesses in reading and writing.

"Although Asian students generally perform 40 to 50 points higher than other American students on the math portion of the SATs," he says, "they score 30 to 40 points lower on the verbal sections because of their immigrant backgrounds." This language deficit causes some on college campuses to feel these students who are "taking over" don't really belong there. The Asian students know they are not always wanted and that their language difficulties make their admission status suspect.

There is also a degree of resentment from both the faculty and fellow students against the Asian American's drive to excel academically. Wang notes, "From the time they are born, Asian Americans tend to be under a lot of parental, community, and family pressure to perform well, and so the students flock to the college's academic support services to maintain their instinctive competitive edge. But other students feel they are 'soaking up' all the available services." This resentment makes it more difficult for Asian American students to feel wanted and at home on the college campus.

Although Asian students have a reputation for being exceptionally smart, many have an exceptionally difficult time in college adjusting to a rigorous academic climate and learning style that they are not familiar with. Wang has observed this in his students: "In elementary school and high school, these students do very well because they are responsible, obedient, docile, and respectful. They are good at regurgitating facts, playing the game to manipulate the system, and getting high test scores, good grades, and letters of recommendation. When they get to college, however, they have great difficulty adjusting to the critical and creative thinking that is expected of them. I give my students take-home final exams that ask them only two open-ended questions that challenge their analytical abilities—and they hate it. They would prefer to sit in the classroom for two hours and give back objective, memorized information rather than go home and have to think critically about questions that challenge them to question the facts."

The expectation of family and peers that they perform exceptionally well in the classroom clashes with this foreign learning style and causes many Asian American students to feel distress that too easily can lead to depression, anxiety disorders, and other mental health problems. Wang notes, "When faced with such problems, they frequently find college counselors generally insensitive, unsympathetic, and unable to understand their predicament and offer appropriate advice."

INTERNATIONAL STUDENTS

Foreign nationals who come to the United States with temporary student visas face the same adjustment conflicts as all other college students regarding developmental, academic, and parental pressures. They may also experience many of the same difficulties faced by immigrants and minorities such as racial discrimination and language problems. If these factors aren't enough to wear them down, they also must deal with unique problems that can additionally contribute to loneliness, anxiety, confusion, and depression.

Although most international students arrive in the United States feeling euphoric at the prospect of living and learning in a new country, it often doesn't take long for culture fatigue to set in. Even for those who are reasonably fluent in English (if it is their second language), it can be a daily struggle to think, speak, read, and write in a second language and to decipher the many American idioms, expressions, and euphemisms that they did not learn in their English-language classes back home.

At the same time, these students are facing the challenge of getting through the day, intent on thinking about every move: *Which bathroom faucet gives hot water and which cold water?* (Americans always put the hot faucet on the left.) *How do I choose from two dozen different laundry detergents, and how do I turn on this washing machine?* Conscious living gets very tiring and stressful over time and eventually may make these young adults feel as if they just can't cope.

Learning Styles

The differing classroom culture is also a major issue for international students. This is most evident in the relationship between students and faculty. In many foreign countries, the professor is the

The Hard Facts

- After five years of steady growth, the number of international students attending colleges and universities in the United States in 2002–2003 showed only a slight increase over the prior year, up less than 1 percent, bringing the 2002–2003 total to 586,323, according to Open Doors 2003, the annual report on international education published by the Institute of International Education (IIE) with support from the State Department's Bureau of Educational and Cultural Affairs.

- For the second year in a row, India surpassed China as the leading sending country and now represents 13 percent of the total number of international students in the United States. India was followed by China (64,757, up 2 percent) and Korea (51,519, up 5 percent).

- The University of Southern California continues to be the leading host institution in the United States, with 6,270 international students, and California is the leading host state. The New York City Metropolitan Statistical Area continues to host more foreign students than any other metropolitan area in the United States, with 36,086 total, as the home of both New York University (with 5,454) and Columbia University (with 5,148), the nation's second and third leading host campuses.

- Students from the Middle East were down 10 percent from the previous year, with decreases of 25 percent each from Saudi Arabia (4,175) and Kuwait (2,212) and 15 percent from the United Arab Emirates (1,792). The combined total number of students coming from all countries in the Middle East is just 34,803, down from 38,545 in the prior year.

- Asian students comprise over half (51 percent) of all international enrollments, followed by students from Europe (13 percent), Latin America (12 percent), Africa (7 percent), the Middle East (6 percent), and North America and Oceania (5 percent).

- The most popular fields of study for international students in the United States are business and management (20 percent) and engineering (17 percent). After two years of very large growth, the number of international students studying mathematics and computer sciences has decreased by 6 percent, although these students still make up 12 percent of the total.*

*Institute of International Education, *Open Doors 2003: International Students in the US* (New York: Institute of International Education, Nov. 3, 2002).

[http://opendoors.iienetwork.org/].

authority. Students are not allowed to challenge, question, or disagree with the instructor; they cannot offer their own opinions, and they do not discuss issues. In these countries (particularly in Eastern Asian countries), class participation is unheard of; students are often seen as sponges: they are expected to absorb information and squeeze it back.

But in the United States, students learn from a very early age that expressing their opinions is valued and is often a significant part of their grade. In Harvard Business School, for example, 50 percent of the grade is based on class participation. This can be a devastating adjustment for students who are not accustomed to speaking out in class and is particularly difficult if English is not their first language and they are worried about a strong accent or misuse of words. This difference in learning styles can be very intimidating.

Informality in the classroom, which American students find relaxing, is another daily occurrence that causes stress for many international students. These students have never been in a learning environment where the teacher sits around casually with the students, where students drink soda and coffee in class and walk in late or leave early. They have been raised to sit in straight rows and take notes from formal lectures. Also, they are sometimes confused by the American concept of group work in which students work together toward a common mutual goal. Often they do not understand where the line is between legitimate sharing and plagiarism. The concept of plagiarism, which is heavily stressed in American secondary schools, may not be taught at all in the educational systems of other countries.

Additional Resources

The Institute of International Education helps students and scholars worldwide with all aspects of international study, including testing and advising, scholarships, information on opportunities for international study, and emergency financial assistance. For more information, use the on-line site at www.iie.org.

The Effects of Terrorism

Since the terrorist attacks on the United States on 9/11/01, it has become more difficult for students from any Muslim country to get a student visa. Students from the Middle East, Indonesia, Pakistan, India, and elsewhere are scrutinized more closely.

For these students, getting to the United States is only half the battle. The lucky few who get a visa frequently find an unwelcoming campus environment. They may be harassed by local law enforcement agencies and sometimes even by campus authorities. This is a difficult, stressful, and tension-packed time to be a visiting Muslim student.

Daily Life Dilemmas

Even outside the classroom, where they should be able to relax, life is a challenge for many international students. Some find it difficult to socialize because the social cues used to get along with others can be so very different. For example, Americans are very hands-on communicators. But in other cultures, it may not be acceptable to shake hands or touch another person while speaking. Also, the amount of space between one person and another that is comfortable in one culture may be more or less for another. For example, some international students are accustomed to standing very close to the person they are talking to, causing Americans to avoid social contact with these students.

Casual comments can be easily misinterpreted; for example, when a classmate says, "See ya later," an international student may expect that that person will actually get in touch later in the day. When it doesn't happen, he will wonder why and worry that he did something wrong.

Even eating is not always easy. Because food is a source of comfort, international students frequently miss the foods of their homeland and find American dietary customs hard to follow. When I asked one Korean young man, for example, what he missed most, he said, "Rice for breakfast." A German student answered, "Good bread." Longing for a bowl of rice and a chunk of bread from home are troubles unique to these students.

Legal Issues

Aside from daily life, international students also live within legal confines that can be quite limiting. For example, those in the United States on temporary student visas must be full-time students. This means that they can't drop a class even if they are having difficulty passing it. It also means that they can't lose too much time

to illness, take a leave of absence without permission from a designated school official, or fail out.

International students are restricted in their ability to earn
money. They can work part-time on campus, but unlike their American counterparts, they cannot work longer hours or get a job off-
campus. They also may be limited in their ability to visit their
homeland. Especially since 9/11, students are very aware that if they
leave the United States, they may face visa delays on their return
trip. They want to go home between semesters, but worry about not
being back in time to start classes.

Resistance to Help

When the worries become overwhelming, international students are
the last to seek help. It seems that talking about stress and its effects
on health is an American phenomenon that many international students do not understand. In some cultures, it is unacceptable to talk
to strangers about personal feelings. Some may feel that mental illness
brings shame to their families. Many have no idea that disorders like
depression and anxiety can be cured. And so they suffer alone, far from
home. For these reasons, I often don't hear about the problems of
international students until they are in crisis with nowhere else to turn.

For all of these reasons, minority, immigrant, and international
students sometimes shoulder an even heavier emotional load than
other students on college campuses. Like all our children, they too
need strong, understanding parental support to remain mentally
healthy throughout this time of adjustment and transition.

———————

As a university therapist, I have seen hundreds of students struggling under the burden of academic, extracurricular, parental, or
cultural pressures. Year after year, I have seen these factors severely
interfere with the ability of intelligent and ambitious students to do
well in college. In the following chapter, I explain how these problems can be compounded by financial difficulties and social fears.

Financial Worries and Social Fears

So far, we've looked at a wide range of daily stress factors that our college-age children grapple with. They face difficult developmental tasks involving identity, relationships, sexuality, and roommate issues. These exist alongside academic, extracurricular, parental, and cultural pressures. And now to round out the picture that illustrates why so many of our children face mental health crises on campus, we can add financial worries and social fears. These two can weigh the heaviest on some students, who worry over both the practical concern of paying for college and the subjective fear for personal safety.

FINANCIAL WORRIES

College is expensive. Whether your child goes to a public or private school, commutes or resides, the college bill in almost all areas of the country is severely painful to the pocketbook. To some parents, this comes as a shock because when they went to college back in the 1970s, the cost was usually less than $5,000 per year for a private college and less than $2,000 per year for a public college. But the fees began to jump in the 1980s. In fact, between 1981 and 1994, costs increased 153 percent at public universities and over 200 percent at private universities. During this same period, median family income in the United States increased by 75 percent, only half of the public university cost increases.[1] Today, the tuition climb continues, with no slowdown in sight. The College Board has reported that college costs in 2003 rose 9.8 percent at public schools and 5.7 at private schools, the largest increase in thirty years. That's an especially big jump considering that inflation, as measured by the consumer price index, rose just above 2 percent that year.[2] Today, parents face paying a whopping $40,000 a year at top-tier private universities and about half that at public institutions. That's not out-of-pocket affordable for many people.

The second shock comes when the extras are added in. The figures printed in the college guidebooks do not include the hidden costs of a college education; things like computers, books, lab fees, activity fees, health services fees, laundry, clothing, transportation out of the region or across the country in some cases, and the cost of socializing drive up the bottom line even further. It is no wonder that student anxiety and guilt are commonly associated with the price tag of today's higher education.

If the student's family is paying the bill, even if there is some financial aid in the form of grants or student loans, there is generally some personal sacrifice involved. Some parents take on second jobs or second mortgages, and give up personal pleasures such as vacations, restaurant dinners, and new clothing. In some cases, the sacrifices are silent and subtle; in other cases, they are loud and very apparent. Either way, the young adult is well aware of the family situation and often feels an overwhelming sense of guilt.

Money is a touchstone for all kinds of family issues that come tumbling out when the bill is due:

> Anthony was blindsided by this reality when he called his dad from college asking for a personal computer. Anthony knew his parents had to take out loans to pay his college bills, but they never complained or mentioned that it was causing a financial hardship. So he didn't think it would be a big deal when he told his

father that it was much easier for his friends to get their research and writing done on their own computers right in their dorm rooms, compared to the hassle of using the school's computer lab, which was always crowded and was far from his dorm.

Anthony's dad exploded at the request. "How can you be so selfish? Your mother and I are working overtime so you can focus on your studies and not have to work. But that's not good enough? Now it's too far for you to walk across the campus to use the school computer? Well, when you start chipping in to help pay the bills, you can have your own fancy laptop!" The phone went dead with a bang. Anthony probably caught his dad after a hard day at work or on a day when he was worrying about the pile of unpaid bills on his desk. But the accusation that he was selfish for taking their money and asking for more hit Anthony hard. Their financial arrangement remained a sore point throughout Anthony's college years (during which he says he never asked for anything extra again).

Children of Divorce

Students from divorced families are commonly caught in a highly stressful financial situation at home that spills over and affects their college experience. Most colleges have a financial aid policy requiring both parents to contribute to the cost of education, even when one or both are unwilling. This means that the student must gather financial aid application forms and tax forms from both parents. Sometimes the noncustodial parent will not cooperate, and the tensions of the divorce are reignited, with the young adult at the center of the dispute.

Even when children of divorce manage to get these forms from both parents, they must go through the process repeatedly because they must reapply for their aid each year. If at any point they are unsuccessful in getting the cooperation of both parents, the financial aid package may change dramatically and push them out of school. This is the harsh reality that these students live with.

Other students face the stress of financial problems when their family situation changes after they enroll. I have seen a number of students who come to our mental health services center suffering extreme stress and anxiety after a parent has left the family. Not only is their worry over the family unity profound, but these students also realize that this situation can affect the custodial parent's ability to pay the college bill, and they worry incessantly about the likelihood of their returning the following semester.

Brandy is typical of college students caught in the middle of divorce battles. At the end of her freshman year, Brandy's parents separated. Brandy says that they both told her that because she was now "out on her own," they expected that she wouldn't be much affected by their decision. But when the term bill for the fall semester of her sophomore year arrived, it became very obvious that Brandy's life might drastically change. There was no official divorce settlement yet, and so there was no court order requiring either parent to pay the cost of higher education. Brandy's father claimed that he never wanted his daughter to go to a private college and that if she insisted on staying there, she and her mother could figure out how to pay for it.

Brandy did return to her college in the fall after her mother took out a substantial loan, but she was very aware that if the divorce settlement did not order her father to help pay the next term bill, she would have to transfer to a commuter college near her home. Of course Brandy was upset by the changes in her family life, but she was especially upset by the way her parents' problems were affecting her life. "How," she complained, "can I

concentrate on school work when it is very possible that
I won't even be in this school next semester?" She had a
good point.

The Working Student

Hundreds of thousands of student juggle a full academic load and a
job either on or off campus. Many of them learn the hard way that
their academic record suffers when the job drains away too much
study time. But many are in a situation in which they know that if
they work too much, they may flunk out of college, but if they don't
work too much, they won't be able to afford college. And so they
continue to juggle with all fingers crossed.

Students who work in local jobs to pay the bills also worry about
the loss of opportunities for future job placement:

> Suzan wanted to take advantage of a summer internship
> offered at a publishing house in a nearby city; she felt it
> would improve her resumé when she graduated and set
> out to find a job as a magazine editor. But the internship
> was unpaid, and Suzan needed to work full time over the
> summer as a lifeguard at the town pool to help her fam-
> ily pay her college bills. Suzan didn't even bother to
> apply for the internship.
>
> Dan faced a similar dilemma when his biology profes-
> sor offered him a part-time, low-paying job in his lab.
> This job would give him experience he wanted in his
> field of study, but it would not pay nearly as much as his
> job working at the local supermarket. His instructor
> couldn't understand why Dan turned down such a good
> opportunity.

When students are forced to choose between the mundane jobs
that reduce their indebtedness and those that pay little or nothing

but are valuable learning and networking opportunities, they stand in the proverbial spot between a rock and a hard place: no matter what decision they make, it's going to hurt.

Loans: The Good and the Bad

When a financial aid officer assesses a family's ability to contribute to the cost of education, there is an assumption that education is right up there at the top as a spending priority. But that is not always the case in many families. Ours is a society of spenders, not savers. Many families spend what they make—and more. And so the amount of money that the federal government and the college expect a family to contribute is often far more than the family can pull out of current income. Savings from past income is just not there or is designated for other purposes such as retirement or emergencies.

A 2003 survey by the Investment Company Institute found that of all parents saving for college, those with children between the ages of eleven and fifteen had saved a median of only $15,000, barely enough to pay for one year at a public college or university.[3] In many families, current income leaves nothing extra after paying the monthly bills, and so that leaves only future income on which to borrow from. And that's why the majority of parents today take out loans to pay the cost of tuition, room, and board. At Harvard, for example, at least 70 percent of students receive financial aid (slightly higher than the 60 percent of undergraduates nationwide who receive some form of aid).[4] According to loan provider Nellie Mae, the average undergraduate leaves school with a debt of $18,900, up 66 percent from five years ago.[5]

The Nellie Mae survey found that over half of all graduates with debt feel burdened by that debt.[6] In fact, apparently the burden of college loans strongly influences the plans of many graduates. "There's no way I can go to grad school after I graduate," says Joyce with a laugh tinged with regret. "My parents owe so much money already; I can't ask them to borrow any more. And besides, I think they'd kill me if I even hinted that I wanted to stay in school." The results of a 2002 National Student Loan Survey found that many students are facing the same dilemma: 42 percent of college graduates who did not go on to graduate school said their student loans had a major influence on their decision to head toward the job market rather than toward graduate school.[7]

Uncertain Economic Times

The National Center for Education Statistics projects that there will be 1.22 million graduates from the class of 2004.[8] That's a lot of students entering a job market that proved very tough for the class of 2003, many of whom are still looking for a job. In addition, salary offers in some fields are lower than they were just one year ago, according to the summer 2003 issue of *Salary Survey*, a quarterly report published by the National Association of Colleges and Employers (NACE). "With fewer jobs available—meaning less demand—some majors are seeing lower starting salaries," says Marilyn Mackes, NACE executive director of the National Center for Education Statistics. "Overall, it [2003] was a difficult year." In fact, NACE's fall 2003 *Salary Survey* report shows that few disciplines posted increases in their starting salary offers, and among those that did, the increases were, in general, modest.[9] I have seen this dismal employment situation throw some students into a panic as they approach graduation.

This is not how it was supposed to be. The plan was to get a college degree and move easily into a high-paying job that would justify the high cost of education and pay back college loans. Without lucrative job offers, graduating seniors sleep with nightmares of being able to get only a low-paying job in a fast food restaurant.

Bill Wright-Swadel, director of career services at Harvard University, has a broad view of this situation from his experience at six different colleges, from community schools and state universities to two Ivy League schools. He realizes that today's students are graduating at a difficult time. "In the short term," he says, "today's graduates are coming into a very weak job market that does not offer the same financial opportunities as it did to their older siblings and which their parents may still be expecting. Right now, it is much more difficult to get an internship while still in school and more difficult to secure a high-paying position in jobs where the greatest growth was just a few years ago, including jobs on Wall Street, or in investment banks, or consulting or technology firms."

> Catherine found this out the hard way. Her brother, Earl, graduated from college in 1998 when the job market was booming for computer science majors. Right after graduation, Earl took a $15,000 signing bonus and a six-figure salary from a high-tech computer company expanding into dot-com enterprises. As Catherine entered college in September 1998, she expected to follow in her brother's footsteps and gladly took on college loans to finance her studies at a highly touted institute of technology. With Earl's success in this field already established, Catherine's parents gladly cosigned her loans. But by graduation day in May 2002, the dot-com bubble, along with Catherine's plans, had burst. She had no job and was $80,000 in debt. Instead of celebrating her graduation, Catherine moved back home, drew the shades, and stayed in bed for weeks. Her parents finally coaxed her out long enough to see a doctor, who quickly diagnosed severe depression, a common symptom of a syndrome some are now calling "postgraduate crisis."

Wright-Swadel says that in a poor job market, he sees more students going on to graduate school rather than into the job market where they would have to buck the tough economic climate. However, this solution to the problem brings new problems of its own. This extension of their education increases the new graduates' indebtedness, and although it gives a boost to their credentials, that does not necessarily boost their earning potential. Whether they enter the job market with an undergraduate or graduate degree in business, they are still considered an inexperienced employee, and often the pay is the same. "Around the country," says Wright-Swadel, "we can see that credential building doesn't necessarily change a student's portfolio as much as he or she might hope." As undergraduates see their older peers suffering through this job market maze, their own anxiety over financial security in the future can build. After handling all the other pressures through the college years, for some this can tip the scales of mental health.

Cost of Peer Approval

The college your child attends may be a good academic match, but when there is an awareness on campus of class issues related to finances, it may not be a good financial match. This is especially true in top-tier schools with expensive price tags. There is an assumption that the students who attend these schools are rich, but that couldn't be further from the truth. Harvard financial aid adviser Sally Donahue says that 50 percent of the students at Harvard receive an average college scholarship of over half the cost of attendance. "This gets complicated," she says, "because students who receive financial aid often feel further stigmatized when they look around and see other students spending a lot of money. They go out to eat, or buy clothes, or go to movies in town (never mind the vacation trips to ski in Aspen!), and the students who don't have this kind of ready cash feel great pressure to keep up."

Lack of financial status brings with it powerful emotions. When faced with this kind of financial inequity, some students remain isolated from peers or drop out of school completely. But others find a solution to the problem by getting one (or more) of the credit cards that are advertised all over campus. As adults, we are generally able to say, "I'm not going out tonight because I just can't afford it." But the need to belong is so strong at college, and the credit card is so easy to acquire and use, that many students remain socially popular—and get in way over their heads.

College students are prime targets for credit card companies, which set up tables on campus and entice students to sign up for new cards with promises of free tee-shirts or other enticements. An average college freshman is offered eight credit cards in his or her first semester. The average graduating senior has six cards in his or her name, and 31 percent of these seniors carry a balance of $3,000 to $7,000.[10] These kids know they're in financial trouble, but don't know how to pay down the debt and still keep up appearances.

> Matt's parents were shocked when he told them about his first credit card bill. "Matt charged $400 in his first month as a freshman," remembers his mom, Tracy. "My first question was why any bank would give this boy a credit card!" Matt explained to his mom that when he was buying his books, he was told that if he filled out a credit card application, he could have a free dictionary and thesaurus. So he figured, "Why not?" Then with his new credit card in hand, he felt free to decorate his dorm room, buy some CDs, and treat himself to a new pair of sneakers. Tracy was not amused. "I took his card and cut it up with scissors and placed it in an envelope with the $400 payment. I explained that when my son had a job and a bank account, I was sure he would be happy to have their credit card, but until that time, he would not be using the card again."

The Need for a Financial Return

Post-9/11, there is an exceptional sense of patriotism that still lingers on many college campuses. As events in the world unfold in full color on television, students are immersed in conversations about their roles in the emerging global state. Many feel strongly

Additional Resources

If you find that your young scholar is having trouble handling finances and is charging more than he or she is able to pay, these resources may help:

- National Foundation for Credit Counseling, 1–800–388–2227, www.nfcc.org. This counseling program has more than thirteen thousand community-based agency offices across the country. They provide consumer counseling and education services on budgeting, credit, and debt resolution. They offer free or low-cost confidential services.

- Association of Independent Consumer Credit Counseling Agencies, 800–450–1794, www.aiccca.org. The AICCCA has affiliates in all fifty states that offer counseling services for individuals over their head in debt.

that they would like to do something to improve the world; some feel they should direct their energies to some field of public service, education, environmental protection, government, or military service. But then comes the financial reality that even in a bad job market, those types of jobs do not pay as well as corporate jobs. The cold fact is that career choices are often influenced by the student's degree of indebtedness. Students have told me that they need to sell their souls to feed the bank.

Parents too are part of this push to sell off ideals to the lure of profit. Facing bills of $20,000 to $40,000 a year, parents are growing hard-nosed about what they expect, and their children know it is the duty of a good son or daughter to justify the tremendous financial investment that is riding on them. Many of these parents who see education as a financial investment in their child's future hope for payback in a high-earning career. Given the high cost of college, when their children take classes in subjects such as photography or philosophy that do not contribute to practical marketable skills, they see it as a frivolous distraction. Some refuse to pay $30,000 a year so their son or daughter can take a low-paying job as a teacher or an artist. Even when parents don't verbalize any career expectation, students are well aware of the financial sacrifices their parents are making and the subtle push to find an entry-level job with a paycheck that will justify these sacrifices.

In some families, the pressure for college training for high-paying jobs is self-serving. In many poorer families (especially immigrant families), the parents make sacrifices to put their children through school with the expectation that on graduation, their children will get high-paying jobs that will then help support the family and perhaps put their siblings through college. It is an entrenched expectation that today's students often feel is an unfair burden.

The issue here is not whether you should exert pressure on your children to balance the cost of the education with a high-salaried job after graduation. It is instead the fact that many college students feel the pressure to give their parents a financial return on their educational investment, and this adds to the stress load they carry. Recognizing the sacrifice and feeling a strong need to succeed, they experience this stress both internally and externally.

SOCIAL FEARS

When colleges do surveys to find out what parents look for in a college, personal safety always comes out very near the top of the list. At informational sessions, parents want to know how campus security personnel keep nonstudents off campus, how the dorms are secured against unwanted visitors, how the pedestrian paths are lighted, and how the campus is routinely patrolled. They want the statistics on campus violence, robberies, rapes, and brawls. They try to help their children choose a college that cares about their safety.

Additional Resources

Check out these Web sites for information that will help you alleviate the anxiety that comes with high debt and dwindling savings:

- Federal Student Aid offers "The Student Guide to Funding Your Education." www.ed.gov/studentaid.

- "Student Gateway to the U.S. Government" provides reliable links to students for information on planning for their education and paying for it. www.students.gov.

But even when a campus appears secure and safe, as in life anywhere else on earth, there is always a risk of danger, and all college students know this. The attack on fellow students at Columbine High School in 1999 made random and senseless acts of violence a very real part of their world. The terrorist attacks of 9/11 further obliterated any pretense of living safe and sound. Intense media coverage of these kinds of violent events hammers home the reality that the world is a violent and an unpredictable place. And colleges across the country are not immune to the ripple effect of these fears. There's no doubt that this social climate in which our children live makes it all the more difficult for them to accomplish the developmental task of moving from dependent childhood to independent adulthood.

Fears common among college students discussed in this section include campus violence, post-9/11 terror, and fear of sexual assault.

Campus Violence

Today's students know that the college campus is no longer a refuge from harm. Firsthand experience with crime on campus and the national news coverage of problems on campuses around the country quickly shatter the myth of invulnerability among this age group. In addition to common dorm room robberies and fistfights, news headlines of campus murders and assaults in 2002–2003 alone make them very aware of the latest campus tragedies—for example:

"College Shooting Spree." In October 2003, Jeffrey Wilinski was arrested and charged with a bizarre plot to massacre students inside the computer science building at the University of Maryland. His threats had been communicated on the phone and through the mail.[11]

"Fraternity Brawl Results in Critical Injuries." In October 2003, two Rutgers University students in New Jersey were critically injured at an off-campus brawl that involved members of a Rutgers fraternity, a social club, and some members of the school's wrestling team.[12]

"Graduate Nabbed in Case Western Shooting." In May 2003 at Case Western Reserve University in Cleveland, a graduate student armed with two high-powered handguns killed one person and wounded two others, while holding police at bay for seven hours. During the rampage, ninety-three people were trapped inside the building, hiding in offices, classrooms, and closets.[13]

"Student Slain in College Shooting." In April 2003 at Louisiana Technical College, Terome Silvie was shot to death by a fellow student while sitting in an electronics class. Another student in the class was wounded in the leg.[14]

"Three Professors Killed at University of Arizona." In October 2002, students taking a midterm exam at the University of Arizona College of Nursing watched fellow student Robert Flores shoot and kill two professors after being barred from taking the test. Another professor was found dead in her office on another floor of the building. Flores then killed himself.[15]

"Catawba College Shooting." In January 2002, a cross-city rivalry in North Carolina turned deadly when a Livingston

College student fired a bullet into the chest of a Catawba college student. This murder rocked a town still reeling from the random shooting of faculty member Dr. Randle Frink two weeks earlier and a fatal campus fire earlier in the year.[16]

"Two Die in Community College Shooting." In January 2002, word about a murder-suicide quickly spread around Broward Community College in Florida. The two young students were found dead on the path between the college's performing arts building and the English Department offices.[17]

Fortunately, despite these headlines, violent incidents like these are rare given the hundreds of thousands of students on college campuses each day, and so it is unlikely that your child spends her days worrying that she will be shot down as she walks to class. But every time there is a campus tragedy like these, the ripple effect touches thousands of college students and makes them feel insecure and vulnerable, even if only momentarily. They suddenly see the frailty of life and the random nature of death. This realization that the college campus is not protected from life's horrors adds to their already heavy burden of maturation.

Additional Resources

For more information on how to prevent and respond to crime on campus, log onto this Web site: National Center for Victims of Crime, www.ncvc.org.

Post-9/11 Terror

Many young adults are especially sensitive to the fear associated with random crime in the aftermath of 9/11, the war in Iraq, and the bombing of trains in Madrid in March 2004. They know that there is a higher level of uncertainty in the world today and the United States no longer feels like a haven from these worries. Leaving home and moving into major cities or into towering dorms brings fears that students didn't have to think about only a few years ago. The concern that they or their families back home will be hurt by a terrorist attack can be far down their list of worries, but it is there in the psyches of some students and adds to the overall stress of becoming an independent adult in an uncertain world.

The lingering effects of the terrorist attacks in 2001 also affect certain groups of students more than others. We take great pride in the fact that the United States is an ethnic melting pot, but in this age of terror, there is new pressure and concern on anyone who looks Middle Eastern. In the aftermath of 9/11, there were heated debates on college campuses about the U.S. response. Some Middle Eastern students were afraid to go out after the attacks, for fear of being taunted on buses or told by drivers yelling out car windows to "go home." Others reported painfully predictable searches every time they got on an airplane. For some of them, it became so frustrating that they chose to return to their home countries for employment rather than put up with continuing harassment. Today, the overt prejudice has calmed down somewhat, but many students say they still feel that there is a lingering distrust of anyone who looks Middle Eastern:

> Jim transferred in his junior year to an Ivy League college and was feeling pretty good about the way his life was going when his world dramatically changed on 9/11/01. "Suddenly," remembers Jim, "I was a suspicious character because I look Middle Eastern." Jim's mom is from Lebanon and his dad is from Egypt, and Jim became a target of discrimination. "I knew every time I wanted to fly home to see my family, I would be stopped in the airport and searched," Jim says. "I knew my carry-on luggage would be inspected, and I knew that I would face

the embarrassment of being singled out." Oddly enough,
Jim didn't feel more than a vague sense of annoyance. "It
was men who look a lot like me who blew up the World
Trade Center, so I can understand why people get nervous when I board a plane. But I do regret that this experience has hurt the pride I felt when I first arrived at
school. Instead of feeling good about myself when I walk
across campus, now I feel ashamed and embarrassed."

It is very difficult for any of us to feel wholly secure in this uncertain world. The insecurities brought on by the national fear of terrorism add one more degree of difficulty to the young adult's
developmental task of feeling comfortable in this new stage of life.

Fear of Sexual Assault

A survey of 3,472 undergraduate and graduate students enrolled at
twelve randomly selected colleges and universities in the United
States found this remarkable result: "Rape is a crime most feared by
women, even more than the fear of being murdered."[18] What an
incredible burden of fear our young women carry as they leave
home! Unfortunately, this fear is often well founded.

The U.S. Department of Health and Human Services has
reported that the number of students seeking help after a sexual
assault at the counseling center at a large midwestern university
quadrupled in 2003.[19] This rise in the number of reported sexual
assault cases is typical of colleges across the country and reflects
both the growing willingness of young women to seek counseling
after such an attack and also the rising prevalence of sexual assaults
in society at large. The numbers are frightening. In 1998, the U.S.
Department of Justice funded a national survey of eight thousand
Americans called the Violence Against Women Survey. It found
that 17.6 percent of women and 3 percent of men reported having
been raped.[20] (Although it occurs less frequently, men can also be
the victims of rape.)

Although rape is the most publicized form of sexual violence against women and men, the fear of many other forms of sexual assault also adds a tremendous psychological strain to college students' lives. In addition to rape, attempted rape, and sodomy, sexual assault includes any unwanted sexual contact or threats. Some types of sexual acts that fall under the category of sexual assault include unwanted touching, groping, fondling, or kissing; forced masturbation; or forced exposure to sexually explicit pictures. Basically, almost any sexual behavior that a person has not consented to that causes that person to feel uncomfortable, frightened, or intimidated is included in the sexual assault category.[21]

Fear of sexual assault lingers not only in dark alleyways but in the light of daily life as well. In the vast majority of cases, the assailant is not a stranger. A Violence Against Women Survey found that a whopping 76 percent of women raped or otherwise physically assaulted after age eighteen were attacked by a current or former husband, a cohabitating partner, or a date. Acquaintance rape (also called date rape) is coming out of the closet, so to speak, and men and women are beginning to understand the risk and their rights. Nevertheless, this type of sexual assault is the kind that is least likely to be reported and least likely to be taken seriously when it is. Quite often the evidence depends on the victim's word against the rapist's, and this kind of defense is very difficult to prosecute. This is especially true when alcohol is involved, as it often is. As mentioned in Chapter One, one study found that 75 percent of the males and 50 percent of the females involved in college campus acquaintance rapes had been drinking when the sexual assault occurred.[22]

Equally chilling is the recent highly publicized epidemic use of date rape drugs. These are sedatives (such as Rohypnol and GHB) that cause sedation and amnesia. The small pills or powder are slipped into an unsuspecting person's drink, allowing a sexual assault to occur without the victim's being able to remember what happened. In many of these cases, the crime cannot be reported or prosecuted because it is difficult for the victim to remember the details or prove the encounter was nonconsensual and forced.

Although an acquaintance rape is difficult to prosecute, the trauma caused by such an assault is just as severe as that associated with rape by a stranger. In fact, it can be more difficult to bear because the assault victims so infrequently reach out for help. Because the assailants are known to the assaulted person, many hold themselves responsible for not having better judgment of a person's character, for drinking too much, or for allowing themselves to be in the situation in which the rape occurred. These victims are also usually in the difficult position of having to see their attacker in daily life afterward, causing distress, fear, and humiliation.

Whether a stranger or an acquaintance rape, the assault on the psyche can be especially cruel for the approximately 70 percent of sexual assault victims who do not report the crime. In these cases, there is no justice or retribution—no opportunity for vindication and no relief from the fear of a repeat attack. The reasons for non-reporting are many, most of which are based on a need by the assault victim to protect himself or herself from further victimization through media exposure and from a legal system that often puts the victim's behavior and history on trial.[23]

Given this statistic, the sad truth is that if your child is sexually assaulted on campus, he or she may not tell you. But psychological changes you can observe may leak the truth. Of course, the emotional and psychological effects of a sexual assault vary from individual to individual, but college health counselors see similar patterns. These include social withdrawal, depression, nightmares, difficulty concentrating, loss of self-esteem, loss of appetite, substance abuse, insomnia, panic attacks, eating problems, sexual dysfunction, and self-mutilation.[24] In addition, according to the National Women's Study, nearly one-third of all rape victims develop rape-related post-traumatic stress disorder. Posttraumatic stress disorder is a mental health disorder primarily characterized by chronic anxiety, depression, and flashbacks that develop after experiencing significant trauma—in this case, sexual assault. Although these are serious symptoms, they are easily missed. (Chapter Six provides more information on how to recognize personality changes that cry out for help.)

Karen's daughter was raped at the end of her freshman year, but because it took Kaylee three months to tell anyone about it, the trail has gone cold, and it is unlikely that the attacker will be found. "I never thought my daughter would keep something like this from me," says Karen. "I was just shocked when she finally opened up." Karen was shocked because she and Kaylee had been exceptionally close. Kaylee usually confided in her mother about intimate health issues such as problems with her monthly period or vaginal infections, and she felt comfortable talking about personal subjects like her boyfriend, Ben. Kaylee had been dating Ben for about six months and was always full of information about what Ben said and what Ben was doing. Then suddenly Kaylee stopped talking. When Karen asked her how Ben was doing, Kaylee snapped abruptly, "I'm not seeing him any more, and I don't want to talk about it." Karen assumed Kaylee needed time to get over a broken heart and gave her some time and space.

But over the summer break, Karen started to think that there was more to Karen's quiet mood than the breakup. Karen had become exceptionally withdrawn and quiet. She didn't go out with her girlfriends anymore, and she was losing weight. Whenever Karen asked her daughter if she was feeling all right, Kaylee would fire back with anger, "I'm fine. Stop asking and leave me alone." Karen knew it was hard to get over a broken relationship, but she had a gut feeling that something else was going on, so she did not leave her daughter alone. Karen continued to be kind and loving and frequently reminded Kaylee that she was there to help and support her. She told her often that she wanted her daughter to be able to talk to her about anything—anything at all.

Finally, two weeks before the new semester was to begin, Kaylee sat down to talk to her mother. She started to explain that she didn't think she wanted to go back to her college. Maybe a different college would be better for her. When pressed for a reason, Kaylee started to cry, and the truth tumbled out. Karen learned that her daughter had been raped in the woods behind her dormitory in the last week of the spring semester when walking back to her room from a late class. She didn't recognize the attacker and didn't know if he was a student. She explained between heaving sobs that she had run to Ben and told him what happened, expecting help and support. But instead, Ben got angry. He said terrible things that made Kaylee feel dirty and somewhat responsible. Ben warned her not to tell anybody else about what happened if she didn't want to embarrass him and be shunned by her friends and family. So Kaylee kept quiet and suffered alone. Ben never called her again. In this case, the young woman was victimized twice: once by the rapist and then again by someone she trusted to give her good advice.

Tips for Mental Health

Susan Marine, the director of Sexual Assault Prevention and Response at Harvard University, has these tips to parents whose sons or daughters have been assaulted:

- Believe them.

- Do not judge them.

- Listen to them.

- Return control to them, and let them make all of their own decisions about how to handle the assault.

- Be aware of what the college or university offers in the way of support and counseling so the student can feel empowered to take action on his or her own behalf.

Chapter Six offers more tips on what parents can do to support their children through times of crisis.

Additional Resources

For more information on the symptoms and treatment of posttraumatic stress disorder, contact the National Center for Post Traumatic Stress Disorder, Web address: www.ncptsd.org.

The effects of a crisis can lie in the psyche for a long time. A young adult who experiences a traumatic event may appear completely recovered after a time, but the deep feelings of the emotional assault can be reawakened by a variety of life events. In my own life, 9/11 sparked memories of a traumatic event that I had experienced twenty years earlier. When I was on vacation in Barbados with a girlfriend, someone jumped out from behind some bushes and assaulted and robbed us. I thought the incident was forgotten in my past, but the tragedy on 9/11 triggered memories of what it was like to be so terribly frightened and so vulnerable. Students who think they are leaving behind personal traumas to start anew at college may find themselves reliving the terror if they face another world or campus crisis.

These threats to personal safety are all around our children. They can't turn on the TV or pick up the newspaper without seeing world violence, national disasters, and campus dangers. To balance this bombardment to their sense of security, some students try coping strategies that can be dysfunctional and even dangerous. The next chapter explores various kinds of risky coping behaviors that include substance abuse to dull the fear, sexual promiscuity to create a sense of connection, and eating disorders to gain a sense of control.

4

Crisis on Campus
Feeling Hopeless and Helpless

The previous chapters have clearly answered the question, *What do college kids have to be so upset about?* In fact, they illustrate why this period of time may be the most difficult life passage of all. Now the question is: *How will your child handle these stressful situations?* Some students tackle developmental issues, parental and societal pressures, and economic hardships with incredible strength and resilience. But many resort to dysfunctional and even dangerous coping methods that make it much harder to navigate this rite of passage.

This is a time of growing autonomy when students value making independent decisions above all else. As parents have pointed out to me quite frequently in parent orientation meetings, their children don't talk to them much about their college experience, but it doesn't mean parents can't and shouldn't play an active role at this important time in life.

The key here is that we must listen closely for signs of problems and be gently persistent in inquiring about our child's new life and experiences. Of course, we must respect boundaries, but we can do that while listening carefully, offering advice when asked, and, most important, being open to new ideas and interests without judging and leaping in to give advice that isn't requested. I know this is easier said than done, but the importance of giving it a good try will become clear as you read this chapter and get an insider's view of the problems common on college campuses today, and sadly, they are common.

This chapter takes a close look at several of the harmful consequences of coping mechanisms gone awry that are quite commonly seen in young adults facing the many stresses of growing up, meeting expectations, and finding a comfortable place in the world. In order of common occurrence, these harmful consequences are

- Depression

- Sleep disorders

- Substance abuse

- Anxiety disorders

- Eating disorders

- Impulsive behaviors, including sexual promiscuity and self-mutilation

- Suicide

Undoubtedly, some of the students who experience these symptoms are at higher risk than the general population to experience psychological and emotional difficulties simply by the draw of the genes, but after heredity, the leading risk factor is stress, and there's plenty of that in college.

By now, you must be wondering: *What can I do about any of this when my child is in the process of separating from the family, telling me less and less about personal problems, and rarely around to observe?* In Part Two of this book, I suggest some very specific things you can do to prevent a college meltdown, but the first step in proactively parenting a young adult is to have a clear understanding of the negative ways some kids cope when the going gets tough.

You are the first and best judge of your child's mental health, especially because the number of college students who seek help from mental health counselors at colleges across the country is quite small. That is why your child needs *you* to be paying attention. Far too many kids in psychological pain don't reach out, and even those who do, wait too long. College counselors repeatedly tell me that the saddest thing they see each year is the many students who have suffered for months before seeking help. These kids have symptoms, but they're vague and hard to explain—they're not sleeping, can't concentrate, eat too much or too little—and they don't associate them with either a medical or psychological problem. They need someone who has known them all their life, who can see the differences in their behavior, and with whom they have regular contact to ask, notice, and know what the symptoms mean. They need you.

The information in this chapter is not meant to scare you or to imply that psychological dangers lurk around every corner of the college campus waiting to jump out and attack your child. For the majority of kids, college is a wonderful time filled with opportunities for positive growth and development. But the fact is that it is an overwhelming experience for many. This chapter gives you the information you'll need to spot potential trouble. It tells you what you need to know to better observe and evaluate your child's behavior (even from afar) and know when to intervene before your child finds himself or herself in a crisis situation.

This role puts you in a very difficult position. Your child wants you to be proud of his developing independence and needs the opportunity to make mistakes and learn from them, but he also needs your guidance and wisdom to recognize problems and address them. You walk a fine line to balance these two tensions.

The balancing act becomes even more difficult with problems that developed in the past. Sometimes students and parents do not mention these issues on college health forms or talk openly about them in hopes of gaining a fresh start. Coming to college *is* a fresh start, but the burden of having these problems and keeping them secret ironically often makes them worse. The student feels more isolated and gets the sense that she is different, and she worries that if friends knew what was really going on, she wouldn't be liked. This is another example of needing to find a balance between being truthful and protecting one's private life.

DEPRESSION

Depression is not just about feeling sad. It is an illness that also affects the ability to think and reason and can cause insomnia, sexual dysfunction, and weight loss or gain. It is associated with other psychological problems, including anxiety disorders, eating disorders, substance abuse, and suicide. It is a disease that affects every body system and many functions of the brain. And it is rampant on college campuses. The following story of Darrell's long fight with depression clearly illustrates how this problem affects so many aspects of a student's life:

> By the time Darrell realized he was suffering from major depression, he had already left one university and transferred to another, only to find himself still discontented and lonely.
>
> It all started back in his senior year of high school. Darrell noticed that he felt unhappy, lethargic, and tired, but he put it off without complaining and looked forward to feeling better when he began college. However, after only a few weeks at college, he knew something was very wrong. "I was having difficulty making friends," he says, "and I felt so lonely. I spent most of my time secluded in my room feeling terrible that other people around me were having a good time and enjoying campus life, but I just couldn't. I figured it was the wrong college for me—just a bad fit—and so I started looking for another school where I wouldn't feel like this."
>
> Darrell's parents had no idea he was so unhappy. Darrell made sure of that. "I pride myself on always appear-

ing to be in control, and I didn't want my parents to think I couldn't handle school. In fact, my depression probably helped me academically because good grades were my anchor. I could focus on my schoolwork to distract me from my loneliness. So here I was at one of the nation's top twenty-five schools and getting excellent grades. How could I tell my parents that I wanted to leave because I wasn't having a good time?"

Darrell told his parents he wanted to transfer to an even better school for purely academic reasons. He applied and was accepted for admission the following year. While waiting to transfer, Darrell first visited a college counseling center at the school he was leaving. "I filled out a form that asked me to explain what was bothering me," remembers Darrell. "I wrote down that I needed help with stress management. Although the possibility of depression wasn't mentioned at that time, the counselors let me talk about all the stuff that was on my mind, and it felt really good. These were things I couldn't say to family or friends (not that I had many) because I was still trying to hold up the image of being someone who had it all together and I didn't want to admit that there might be some cracks in that image."

After transferring, Darrell's hopes for a new beginning were quickly dashed. "I was unhappy right away," he says. "A new environment didn't change the way I was feeling at all. I still felt the disconnect between my internal and external world. A month later, I went to the mental health counseling center where I talked about the symptoms that had been plaguing me. I couldn't get out of bed in the morning. Every movement took so much effort. I didn't have the energy to walk across campus and then sit through an hour-long lecture. And when I did, I couldn't wait to get back into bed. I felt very unhappy all the time and spent far too much time thinking about death (although I never had a specific plan for suicide). I had this feeling of hopelessness and now realized that if I couldn't shake the feeling in either of these two very good schools, it probably wasn't the school that had the problem."

Darrell was diagnosed with major depression along with social anxiety, given a prescription for Prozac, and referred for regular counseling sessions with a therapist.

This helped Darrell, but did not suddenly turn him into a new man. "I'd say I felt less depressed, but I wouldn't say I felt happy. I still didn't feel excited about being at such a good school, and I still didn't feel like making any effort to make friends. But I felt better, and that was something."

During his therapy sessions, Darrell learned more about depression and began to understand why he felt the way he did. Along the way, he also learned that it was not always necessary to hide his pain. After joining a mental health awareness advocacy group, Darrell met other students who were also struggling with mood and anxiety disorders. "This made me feel more comfortable in my own skin," he says with obvious relief. "And it helped me to realize I was not alone with this."

Feeling more comfortable with his mental health issues during his junior year, Darrell wrote a paper for school about his experience with depression. At that time, he also decided to tell his parents. "All along, we had had a good relationship. We talked for an hour at least two times a week, but I worked very hard to keep this problem from them. But then I realized that it was more of an effort to put on the show all the time than to tell the truth." So Darrell shared this paper with his parents. "I think they were surprised and rattled," he admits, "but ultimately it strengthened the bonds we have and it's become easier to talk with them about the issues that until now I had been hiding." That alone has helped Darrell move forward with greater confidence.

As Darrell's experience shows, just because our kids say, "I'm fine," doesn't mean they really are. We need to learn how to listen to the silence and be attentive to the signs of depression they may try to hide.

An Epidemic of Depression

Darrell's story is all too typical. A 2003 study conducted by researchers at Kansas State University examined the kinds of problems counselors at its counseling center had addressed over thirteen years. Among other findings, the percentage of students seen with depression nearly doubled, and these findings reflect the increasing rates on most college campuses.[1] The increase may in part be due to a greater willingness by students to admit their feelings of depression and to the increased academic, social, family, and financial pressures students feel today. But it is also due to advances in the pharmaceutical industry. The sale of antidepressant SRIs (serotonin reuptake inhibitors) has passed $10 billion. The public advertising has increased awareness, and more students with treated depression are able to get to college, where before, their depression would have made them nonfunctional. Now they are on our campuses and naturally increase the numbers seeking counseling.

Tips for Mental Health

Do not ignore symptoms of depression or delay treatment. The Centers for Disease Control reports that the vast majority of young adults aged eighteen and older who are diagnosed with depression do not

receive appropriate or even any treatment at all.*
Minorities in America fare even worse. A report from
the U.S. Public Health Service found that blacks,
Hispanics, Native Americans, and Asian Americans
face severe economic, cultural, linguistic, and physical barriers for treatment of mental illness, difficulties
that prevent thousands from being properly treated.†

This is a dangerous situation, especially given the
fact that depression raises the risk of suicide and contributes directly to binge drinking, over- and undereating, and alcohol abuse, which are all often
attempts at self-medication.

_____

*Centers for Disease Control, National Center for Chronic Disease and
Health Promotion, "Youth Risk Surveillance: National College Health
Risk Survey" (Atlanta, Ga.: Centers for Disease Control, 1995).

†"Report: Minorities Lack Proper Mental Health Care," *CNN.com/
Health*, Aug. 27, 2001. [http://www.cnn.com/2001/HEALTH/08/26/
mental.health/].

The Symptoms of Depression

Major depression shows itself in a combination of symptoms that
interfere with normal life functioning. They may appear once,
twice, or many times over a lifetime. According to the *Diagnostic
and Statistical Manual of Mental Disorders*, depression exists when
five or more of the following symptoms (including one or both of
the first two symptoms) are present over a two-week period:[2]

- Depressed mood most of the day

- Markedly diminished interest or pleasure in all or
  almost all activities

- Significant weight loss when not dieting, weight gain, or decrease or increase in appetite

- Insomnia or increased sleeping

- Restlessness or slowing down of body movements

- Fatigue or loss of energy

- Feelings of worthlessness or excessive or inappropriate guilt

- Diminished ability to think or concentrate, or indecisiveness

- Recurrent thoughts of death (not just fear of dying), recurrent thoughts of suicide, or a suicide attempt

Dysthymia and Bipolar Disorder

In addition to major depression, there are two other types of depression: dysthymia and bipolar disorder.

Dysthymia involves long-term chronic depressive symptoms that are less severe but still keep a person from being fully functional and enjoying life. I saw a classic picture of dysthymia when I was traveling with my family to Florida over a winter vacation. I bumped into a colleague in the airport who was going on the same flight with his parents and children. Everyone seemed quite excited except his dad, who had a sour look on his face. He was a person who had never sought any treatment but was known as someone who always saw "the glass is half empty." He loved his children and grandchildren, but all he could think about was his certainty that the flight would be delayed and we would miss our connection. The plane left on time, and he commented that there was sure to be turbulence and the kids would be uncomfortable. After a perfectly smooth flight and transfer, he said he was sure it would be raining and the kids would get stir crazy in the hotel. As we landed in beautiful sunshine and a warm breeze, he shook his head and said, "Now the kids are going to get sunburned!"

Often people with dysthymia are enveloped in a cloud of negativity and there is a complete loss of perspective. Small problems become magnified, and the worrying never ends.

Bipolar disorder (previously called manic-depressive psychosis) is a psychiatric illness in which a person has abnormal moods reflecting two opposite poles: depression and mania, a state of abnormally elevated energy. Students experiencing a manic episode may have periods of poor judgment, impulsiveness, reckless behavior, and sexual indiscretions. This is often followed by a period of depression and withdrawal. Bipolar disease is a complicated problem to treat because there are various forms, some of which are characterized by cycling moods with more frequent depressive periods, while another type can have frequent wide mood swings, with very psychotic, out-of-control behavior, occurring in rapid cycles.

We are probably seeing more bipolar illness on campus because of the popularity of antidepressants. It is fairly common to see a college student who comes in with depression and no evidence of manic behaviors (pressured, rapid speech, impulsive behaviors, euphoric mood, days of very little sleep, and grandiosity). So an antidepressant is appropriately started to treat the depressive symptoms. Unfortunately, antidepressants can trigger a first manic episode in someone who is bipolar. This is why it is so important to monitor students closely after starting an antidepressant, but many schools lack the resources to provide this level of care.

Bipolar illness has a strong genetic component, so if the illness runs in your family, your child should know this and report it to college physicians and mental health counselors in order to get proper treatment. Bipolar illness is very treatable but requires a lot of time, resources, and sometimes a complicated, expensive regime of medication.

The Hard Facts

A study by psychologists at Kansas State University examined trends among students seeking psychological help in three time periods from 1988 to 2001.[*] Among the findings are the following:

- The percentages of counseling clients seen with depression and of those seen with suicidal thoughts almost doubled from the first to the third time period.

- Four times as many students sought counseling after a sexual assault in the third period of time.

- Problems with substance abuse and eating disorders held steady, each at around 6 percent.

- Situational problems, where some immediate event triggered the students' troubles, jumped from about 22 percent to 58 percent.

- Students with A and B averages were more likely to seek counseling than those with C averages or below.

- In an average year, about 27 percent of those seen at the counseling centers were seniors, 23 percent juniors, 18 percent sophomores, and 16 percent freshmen. About 15 percent were graduate students.

---

[*]K. Patterson, "College Students Report More Stress, Depression, Suicidal Thoughts," *Knight Ridder/Tribune News Service*, Feb. 12, 2003, p. K2831.

Symptoms Too Easy to Ignore

Most commonly, depression doesn't show its face until a person is in his or her early or mid-twenties, just the time when he or she is attending college. When it hits, it's not something students are familiar with. It's not like the sore knee that they know acts up occasionally, and when it does at college they know what it is and what to do about it. Depression seems to come out of the blue, and its symptoms are such that whether the students are freshmen or seniors, they and their families and friends don't associate them with mental illness. We all have occasional sleep difficulties, changes in appetite, problems with concentration. But putting the constellation together and getting proper care makes the difference between an engaging, enjoyable college experience and a miserable one that often leads to leaves of absence or other ancillary problems.

A Popular Pill

Psychology Today's special edition called "Blues Buster" offered this interesting piece of information about college kids and medication: "One index of the upswing in depression on campus is prescription patterns. The number-one prescribed drug for college students is not the birth control pill or an acne medication. It's Prozac. In second place are antianxiety agents. The number-three spot goes to all other anti-depressant SSRIs combined."[*]

[*]"What's in a Pill?" *Psychology Today*, May 2002, p. 4.

Students tend to keep the symptoms of depression to themselves, but even if they do complain, often they aren't taken seriously. If they mention that they can't sleep, they're told by well-meaning family and friends, "That's just because you've got a lot on your mind and the dorm is noisy and you're in a strange bed." If they say they don't feel much like eating, they're told, "Nobody likes cafeteria food." If they mention that they don't feel connected or as if they belong, they're told, "Everybody has trouble making new friends in a strange environment." And if they admit that they just don't feel motivated, they're told, "You just haven't found your area of interest yet," or "Maybe you're in the wrong school." Soon, life experience becomes negative and hopeless. Negative expectations become self-fulfilling prophecies: for example, if you think no one likes you and you isolate yourself, then you do become socially isolated. These predictable, automatic reactions to the symptoms of depression keep the students from recognizing their problem and delay treatment.

The stigma about depression is another factor that slows the recognition and referral process. I get extremely frustrated hearing students and families saying that the student just needs to concentrate more, work a little harder, and cut out social activities, and then things will fall into place. It's the equivalent of telling someone with diabetes that she just needs to work harder and her blood sugar will straighten itself out.

By the time the student is willing to step up and say, "No, these feelings I'm having are not normal and they're not going away," it is likely that the problem has already negatively affected his or her personal or academic life in many ways.

Web Sites for More Information About Depression

- Depression and Bipolar Support Alliance, www.dbsalliance.org

- National Foundation for Depressive Illness, www.depression.org

See Appendix B for full contact information.

SLEEP DISORDERS

Sleep problems are probably the most common physical complaint of college students—and of the rest of the general U.S. population as well. In "Understanding Insomnia: Scope, Severity, and Solutions," Gary Zammitt, who runs the sleep disorder clinic at St. Luke's Roosevelt Hospital in New York City, says that according to the most recent poll, almost 69 million Americans, or 35 percent of the adult population of the United States, experiences common symptoms of insomnia.[3] At college, the numbers are even higher. A recent study found that only 11 percent of the students surveyed were getting a good night's sleep. The rest of the sample had moderate to severe sleep complaints.[4] Keith is one of these restless sleepers:

> Keith went off to college knowing he had sleep problems. In fact, back in high school, his family physician had given him a prescription medication to help him sleep. "It wasn't a constant problem," says Keith. "But whenever I was feeling stressed, I'd be awake all night. That usually happened when I had an important test the next day, or if my baseball team was going to be playing a big game, or even if I was thinking about asking a girl to go to the movies." When Keith most needed sleep, it just wouldn't come, so the pills helped him through the occasional bad night.
>
> At college, the stress-related sleep problems continued, but because the stress was greater and more frequent, so was his insomnia. "Actually," he admits, "I was feeling so stressed so often that I rarely slept soundly without the pills. So soon my sleep problems became one of my stressors. I would go to bed worrying that I wouldn't be able to sleep and that worry kept me from sleeping, so I'd take

a sleeping pill and then worry that I was taking the pills too often."

When Keith rather quickly finished his prescribed pills, he tried doing without them. "When I knew I was running out of pills, I cut back on taking them, but then without sleep, I was always so tired and I couldn't concentrate and I noticed that I was getting sick a lot. I often had a cold, or a stomach virus, or a sore throat. I tried using alcohol to get to sleep, and it worked, but only for about four hours; then I'd be awake again. Every day was such a struggle."

Finally, Keith went to the school's counseling center to get a new prescription. He got the pills, but he also got information, tips, and strategies to help him manage his sleep patterns better. Keith knew that he had developed a tolerance to the pills because they no longer worked as well as they used to, so he was looking for some other kind of help. "I didn't like taking the pills to sleep," says Keith, "and they didn't work well anymore anyway. But I didn't know what else to do. Every part of my life was affected by that awful feeling of chronic tiredness. I just dreaded going to classes and couldn't concentrate at all. After a while, I didn't even want to go out with my friends or do any kind of physical activity. I would just lie in my bed whenever I didn't have classes and try to sleep. Trying to sleep is just the worst thing in the world." (See Chapter Seven for some of the tips and strategies that worked for Keith.)

Many students, like Keith, arrive at college knowing they have sleep problems, but many others develop toxic sleep patterns after they arrive. It is a rite of passage and badge of honor to stay up all night partying on the weekend or writing a paper or studying for an exam. For many students, it is part of the college culture, and so telling our children to "get a good night's sleep" will not solve the problem. But helping them understand the cumulative effects of these habits might sway them to rethink that lifestyle.

The Stages of Sleep

This simplified version of the normal sleep cycle will explain how college students get themselves into trouble when they become sleep deprived.

There are two types of sleep: non-REM (NREM) and REM (an acronym for *rapid eye movement*) sleep. NREM sleep is divided into four stages, each lasting about ninety minutes. So depending on the amount of sleep you get every night, you can experience anywhere from four to six cycles a night.

Stage One is a transitional period between wakefulness and sleep that lasts only about three to five minutes.

Stage Two brings you to a slightly deeper sleep that lasts about thirty to forty minutes. More time is spent in Stage Two sleep than in any other stage—about 50 percent of the night's total sleep time.

Stages Three and Four are grouped together. During these two stages, brain wave activity slows down. Sleep becomes very deep as your brain emits high, wide delta waves. This sleep is valuable in restoring and revitalizing the body. Delta sleep occurs during the first three hours of the night and disappears in the later sleep cycles. In fact, only 20 to 25 percent of the night's sleep is spent in these crucial stages.

After Stage Four is complete, you ascend back through Stages Three and Two. But rather than going back into Stage One and waking, you go into a period of REM sleep. This is when dreams occur. During REM, your eyes move back and forth quickly beneath your eyelids as your mind dreams. The first REM period of the night lasts about two to ten minutes. With each sleep cycle, REM periods increase in duration.

The slow-wave sleep of Stages Two, Three, and Four is the restorative, most biologically necessary sleep stage, in which a great deal of body and cell repair and recovery takes place. It also plays a crucial role in memory retention (so important to students). Deprivation of this slow-wave period generally has a negative effect on performance.

Confusing the Biological Clock

Roseanne Armitage, a professor in the Department of Psychiatry and director of the sleep lab at the University of Michigan, gave a presentation at the first University of Michigan College Depression conference in March 2003. In a follow-up discussion, we talked about why college students are especially hard hit by sleep problems. "Our ability to fall asleep," she told me, "and to progress through the slow-wave and REM cycles is strongly influenced by our biological clock that is set by circadian factors. This is where college students get into trouble because this internal clock creates drives to maintain wakefulness and drives to maintain sleep." Light and a neurochemical, melatonin, are key factors in this cycle.

Armitage feels that students who stay up until 3:00 A.M. are at a real disadvantage because their biological clock tells them to sleep much earlier and tells them to wake at their normal morning time. If they are exhausted and don't get up at the normal time, the process of resetting the biological clock to a later time starts. When they try to get back into their normal sleep cycle after the weekend, they often find it difficult to go to sleep at a reasonable hour because they don't feel tired, since they've been awake only twelve hours instead of the normal sixteen. Going to bed at 3:00 A.M. and getting up at the normal wake-up time decreases both REM and NREM sleep.

Students who habitually go to bed in the wee morning hours eventually reset their biological clocks, causing even further sleep problems. As the sun sets and the lights go low, normally the body reacts by releasing melatonin, a hormone that helps regulate the body's cycles of sleepiness and wakefulness. When the sun rises and light reappears, the production of melatonin is suppressed. But when students stay in brightly lit rooms or sit in front of computer monitors late into the night, the release of melatonin is delayed, causing circadian rhythm disorders. Twice as many students as people in the general population report symptoms of delayed sleep syndrome in which the circadian clock shifts so that falling asleep before 2:00 or 3:00 A.M. becomes extremely difficult.[5] The syndrome is marked by difficulty falling asleep during the week, problems awakening at a planned time, and morning sleepiness that significantly impairs daily functioning.

The Warning Signs of Sleep Problems

Sleep is a general measure of how things are going. If your child complains of sleep problems such as difficulty falling asleep, early morning wakening, waking up during the night, or exceptional trouble getting out of bed in the morning but then sleeps just fine when he or she returns home (or on weekends for commuting students), this may be an early signal of emotional upset. Sleep problems often become self-fulfilling prophecies for students. They get in bed and worry that they won't be able to sleep, recognize they need sleep, and then stare at the clock, unable to relax and fall asleep.

The High Cost of Sleep Deprivation

In an article on sleep in university students, Franklin Brown and his colleagues report that the consequences of sleep disorders are vast and variable and notes that the trend toward self-imposed sleep deprivation, irregular schedules, and poor sleep quality could have far-reaching implications for college students: "Poor sleep quality can lead to significantly greater psychosocial distress. Examples include depression, anxiety, reduced physical health, general cognitive difficulties (such as poor problem solving and attention difficulties), and increased use of drugs and alcohol. Partial sleep deprivation (less than six hours of sleep per night) can lead to deficits in attention, concentration, memory, and critical thinking, along with increased depression, irritability and anxiety. Even students who regularly obtain eight hours of sleep per night, but shift their sleep schedule by more than two hours may experience attention, concentration, reasoning, and psychomotor difficulties, as well as increased irritability, anxiety, and depression."[6]

It is clear that many of the stressors and mental health problems discussed in this book are closely tied to sleep problems. In the cases of depression, for example, it is often difficult to tell which comes first: the sleep problem or the depression. Eighty percent of depressed people have sleep disorders. But John Winkelman, assistant professor of psychiatry at Harvard Medical School and director of the sleep lab at Brigham and Women's Hospital in Boston, tells me that sleep problems are a significant *cause* of depression and anxiety disorders. In fact, he notes that research has shown that sleep difficulties may be one of the major triggers for bipolar disorder, which most often initially occurs during young adulthood, and so sleep disturbance is a significant risk for students.

There is also evidence that sleep problems are related to a student's physical health. I've noticed that the students who are chronically sick with nagging colds, respiratory problems, and the like are also the ones most frequently complaining of fatigue. There are biological reasons for this. At the Van Cauter Lab at the University of Chicago, Eve Van Cauter is gathering scientific evidence showing that lack of sleep affects our bodies as well as our minds. In a recent study, Van Cauter studied the effects of limited sleep on two groups of healthy young men. The researchers curtailed the sleep of one group to four hours per night for six nights and then extended their sleep to twelve hours for the next seven nights. The second group slept seven-and-a-half to eight-and-a-half hours a night. Each person received an immunization against the flu after the fourth night. Six days later, researchers found that the "normal" sleepers had developed twice the concentration of antibodies as the sleep-deprived subjects. After three to four weeks when all subjects were well rested, the groups tested the same. Clearly, the immune system does not work as well when suffering from sleep deprivation.[7]

A Pajama Party

The challenge for mental health counselors is to get information on sleep to the students. They live in a high-pressure world where there aren't enough hours in the day to get it all done. Pulling an all-nighter is seen as a badge of honor.

To get kids to listen, the Center for Wellness and Health Communication at Harvard recently organized a program called "Why Sleep? A Pajama Party Panel." This was an attempt to educate students about the relationship between good sleep habits and overall mental health. The program offered blankets, warm milk, and cookies to pajama-clad students. In the spirit of the event, Robert Stickgold, assistant professor of psychiatry at Harvard Medical School, addressed the crowd wearing pajamas, a nightcap, and slippers.

It was a relaxed environment in one of the dorms during the evening, and the creative and fun atmosphere gave us a big turnout with good discussion. But I wonder if the message will have a lasting effect on these students who know they need more sleep but also know they need more hours in their day to meet all their responsibilities.

Sleep problems during the college years are worth taking note of. In addition to the psychological effects, there are a variety of medical sleep problems such as sleep apnea, restless leg syndrome, narcolepsy, and delayed and advanced sleep phase syndrome that also interfere with daily functioning (but are beyond the scope of this book).

Whatever the cause of sleep disorders, they affect the quality of life for our children; they influence their academic performance, and they may be the first symptoms of other physical or emotional problems.

Web Site for More Information About Sleep Disorders

- Better Sleep Council, www.bettersleep.org

- National Sleep Foundation, www.sleep foundation.org

See Appendix B for full contact information.

SUBSTANCE ABUSE

In the college setting where large groups of people are forging their way into relationships and trying to prove themselves to a bunch of strangers, some believe that alcohol and drugs offer an easy way to socialize and have fun, while at the same time masking personal fears and uncertainties. Unfortunately, as Glenn found out, this coping mechanism easily leads to abuse and addiction:

> Glenn has been there and back, and today is grateful to be alive. Glenn entered an East Coast university as a good student who liked to have a good time. "I drank a lot on weekends in high school," he remembers, "but I never thought it was a problem or that it would play a big part in my life—but it didn't turn out that way."
>
> Glenn says that he started his mental meltdown during his first freshman semester. He began drinking more frequently as he pined away for a young woman he had met on campus. "I had never had a close relationship

with someone of the opposite sex before," he admits. "I had always been nervous around girls and found that if I drank a lot at parties, then I didn't really care about picking up girls." Soon Glenn found himself avoiding parities and drinking alone in his room. "People at parties didn't drink the way I wanted to drink; they would drink and socialize and dance. I just wanted to get drunk. I was much happier doing that by myself."

Eventually, Glenn and Sheila, the girl he had fallen for, became a couple. But the drinking didn't end. It wasn't long before Glenn began inventing problems to worry about. He was convinced that Sheila was cheating on him and was laughing at him, so he drank even more to deaden his insecurities.

At the start of his sophomore year, Glenn knew he was in trouble. "I was on academic probation, I was still drinking every day, and I was miserable. But I knew I had run out of reasons for drinking. I had my girlfriend; I was majoring in history, which I really liked, and I had plenty of money from my parents. There was nothing really wrong, but I felt terrible. What I needed was psychiatric attention."

Glenn went to the college's counseling service and then moved on to private therapists in the area. Each one advised him to check in at a treatment program for his drinking problem. But he didn't buy into that solution at all and found himself at an impasse with every therapist he went to. "None of them came even close to refusing me care until I got clean, a stance I firmly believe in today," Glenn says. So although he was willing to talk about his problems, this was not helping his drinking problem.

Glenn's parents were aware of his drinking and were willing to pay for whatever help he needed, but that wasn't enough. "I'm an only child, and I had a good home environment, but my parents really didn't understand how desperate I was. My father told me that he had gone through a period of depression when he was in college and that he drank a lot back then too. So my parents thought I was just going through the same thing."

But Glenn's situation was not "just a phase." As his drinking continued, he stopped going to classes completely. He would lock himself in his room and fly into angry rages, smashing furniture and punching the walls—hard enough to break both hands on separate occasions. When the rages subsided, Glenn would distract himself from his pain by planning his death. "I ended every day thinking about how to kill myself and end it all."

Toward the end of his sophomore year, it was Glenn's roommate who finally blew the whistle to alert Glenn's parents. "My roommate came in one night around dinnertime and found me on the floor with the chair on top of me," remembers Glenn. "At first, he couldn't wake me up, and then when I did come to, I didn't even recognize him and walked out saying I was going to a bar. He must have been pretty scared to take the drastic step of calling my parents. The next morning when I woke up, my mother was sitting in a chair at my bedside. She tried to get me to eat and get organized. She helped me map out the things I needed to do to get back on track. We did talk about getting professional help, but finally I just asked her to leave and said I didn't want to see her anymore. I know my mom was miserable while I was miserable, but she didn't know what to do for me either."

Although Glenn's mother couldn't help him, he says that her presence and her concern convinced him that he could no longer pretend to be just fine. Two days later,

Glenn withdrew from college and checked himself into an inpatient detox/rehab center for alcoholism for forty days. "Although it took a while to convince me," says Glenn, "accepting that I was an alcoholic was an unbelievable relief. Finally, there was a solution to this awful pain I had been living with. The people I met in the detox center were just like me. They too had felt hopeless, and now they were enjoying life and staying sober. I wanted to do that too." Glenn spent the following year living at home with his parents, driving a taxi to make some money, and joining Alcoholics Anonymous (AA) to keep himself on track. A year later, Glenn returned to the same university a changed man.

"I'd like to emphasize," says Glenn, "that I never thought in a million years that I would belong to AA, yet now I know it is the only reason I got through, as well as the only reason that I am still sober. I hope that anyone who is in a situation like I was and thinking there is no way out might check out an AA meeting and give it a try. For me, it was a literal life saver."

I hear many stories like Glenn's that illustrate my belief that kids aren't drinking to excess on college campuses only to "party." Many abuse alcohol and drugs because they feel vulnerable and unsure of themselves, and this numbs their pain.

Alcohol Abuse

Five weeks after he started classes at the Massachusetts Institute of Technology in the fall of 1997, Scott Krueger died of alcohol poisoning during a party at his fraternity house.[8] Krueger represents all parents' worst nightmare as they send their children off to college.

Nearly 14 million people in the United States—one in every thirteen adults—abuse alcohol or are alcoholic. In general, more men than women are alcohol dependent or have alcohol problems, and alcohol problems are highest among young adults ages eighteen to twenty-nine. These facts put college-age males at greatest risk.

According to the Task Force on College Drinking prepared by the National Advisory Council of the National Institute on Alcohol Abuse and Alcoholism, the consequences of excessive and underage drinking affect virtually all college campuses, college communities, and college students, whether they choose to drink or not (see Figure 4.1).[9] These consequences include

- Death. Fourteen hundred college students between the ages of eighteen and twenty-four die each year from alcohol-related unintentional injuries, including motor vehicle crashes.

- Injury. Half a million students between the ages of eighteen and twenty-four are unintentionally injured under the influence of alcohol.

Figure 4.1. A Snapshot of High-Risk College Drinking Consequences

Category	Value
Assault by another student	600,000
Injury	500,000
Unprotected sex	400,000
Alcohol-related health problem	150,000
Arrest for alcohol-related violation	110,000
Sexual assault	70,000

Source: National Advisory Council of the National Institute on Alcohol Abuse and Alcoholism, Task Force on College Drinking, "Meeting Summary" (Apr. 3, 2002). [http://www.niaaa.nih.gov/about/min4–02-text.htm].

- Assault. More than 600,000 students between the ages of eighteen and twenty-four are assaulted by another student who has been drinking.

- Sexual abuse. More than 70,000 students between the ages of eighteen and twenty-four are victims of alcohol-related sexual assault or date rape.

- Unsafe sex. Four hundred thousand students between the ages of eighteen and twenty-four had unprotected sex, and more than 100,000 students between the ages of eighteen and twenty-four report having been too intoxicated to know if they consented to having sex.

- Academic problems. About 25 percent of college students report academic consequences of their drinking, including missing class, falling behind, doing poorly on exams or papers, and receiving lower grades overall.

- Health problems and suicide attempts. More than 150,000 students develop an alcohol-related health problem, and between 1.2 and 1.5 percent of students indicate that they tried to commit suicide within the past year due to drinking or drug use.

- Drunk driving. About 2.1 million students between the ages of eighteen and twenty-four drove under the influence of alcohol last year.

- Vandalism. About 11 percent of college student drinkers report that they have damaged property while under the influence of alcohol.

- Property damage. More than 25 percent of administrators from schools with relatively low drinking levels and over 50 percent from schools with high drinking levels say their campuses have a "moderate" or "major" problem with alcohol-related property damage.

- Police involvement. About 5 percent of four-year college students are involved with the police or campus security as a result of their drinking, and an estimated 110,000 students between the ages of eighteen and twenty-four are arrested for an alcohol-related violation such as public drunkenness or driving under the influence.

- Alcohol abuse and dependence. Thirty-one percent of college students met criteria for a diagnosis of alcohol abuse and 6 percent for a diagnosis of alcohol dependence in the past twelve months, according to questionnaire-based self-reports about their drinking.

These are staggering numbers that make all alcohol abuse counselors wonder why so many college kids get involved in high-risk drinking. New-found freedom and peer pressure certainly head the long list. In 1978, the movie *National Lampoon's Animal House* glamorized irresponsible college drinking as a rite of passage, and soon the college experience became culturally linked with drunken antics and alcohol bingeing. Since that time, college alcohol abuse has been declared a major public health problem, and alcohol prevention professionals have battled daily to undo the damage caused by this portrayal of college life.

Drug Abuse

It's no secret that drug abuse is widespread on college campuses across the country. Freely available legal drugs that are frequently abused include prescribed medications, inhalants (glues, aerosols, and solvents), and over-the-counter cough, cold, sleep, and diet medications. Illegal drugs of choice include marijuana; stimulants (cocaine and its different forms, methamphetamine, "ice"/dexroamphetamine); hallucinogens, such as LSD, PCP, or the so-called designer drug MDMA (Ecstasy); and opiates, such as heroin or methadone.

Many college kids experiment with drugs as part of their social development, but there are others who use drugs as a coping mechanism and ultimately get hooked. Those at high risk for drug abuse include those with preexisting genetic risk factors, those suffering chronic stress, those with bipolar or other mood disorders, those who feel they are socially isolated and don't belong, and those who feel overly pressured to achieve with no sense that there is a viable way out. I suspect that these risk factors affect the majority of college students.

Mind-altering substances can "medicate" the world away or at least dull the pain for a while. They give apprehensive and socially awkward kids the comfort of euphoria and bravado, and they give overwhelmed high achievers a sense of distance and space that they cannot feel in their daily grind. They also offer a way to rebel against controlling parents because drug use is among the few activities (along with sex) in which they can participate without their parents dictating every move.

In addition to those hoping to dull the pain of this developmentally difficult period of life, there are others who abuse drugs to gain an academic advantage in this highly competitive world. In a practice called pharming, students illegally use prescription drugs for purposes other than what they're prescribed for. The drugs most commonly used are Adderall and Ritalin, the small blue or orange pills typically prescribed for children and adults with attention-deficit disorder and attention-deficit hyperactivity disorder. But their effects on normal adults make it sound like a wonder drug. Specialists say they help students to focus longer and get work done quicker.

"They can be viewed as brain steroids, because in some way the drugs give students an unfair advantage," says Dr. Eric Heiligenstein, director of clinical psychiatry at the University of Wisconsin. "The productivity levels are so much higher when compared with students who do not use the medication. Students are able to accumulate more information in a shorter time frame. These drugs keep you awake longer. They minimize fatigue and help maintain a high performance level." But as is typical with all short-cuts promising to enhance performance, the drugs, chemical cousins of cocaine, have negative side effects. They can cause increased heart and respiratory rates, elevated blood pressure, sleep deprivation, dry mouth, and lack of appetite. They can cause paranoia. They can lead to withdrawal symptoms. And in rare cases, they have been linked to aggression and cardiac arrhythmia.[10]

In this highly competitive world these young adults live in, this is one more instance where they must choose between their overall health and their desire for superior performance.

Web Sites for More Information on Substance Abuse

Alcohol Abuse

- Al-Anon Family Group Headquarters, http://www.al-anon.alateen.org. Makes referrals to local Al-Anon groups, which are support groups for spouses and other significant adults in an alcoholic person's life. Also makes referrals to Alateen groups, which offer support to children of alcoholics.

- Alcoholics Anonymous (AA) World Services, http://www.aa.org. Makes referrals to local AA groups and provides informational materials on the AA program. Many cities and towns also have a local AA office listed in the telephone book.

- National Council on Alcoholism and Drug Dependence, http://www.ncadd.org. Provides telephone numbers of local affiliates (which can provide information on local treatment resources) and educational materials on alcoholism.

- National Institute on Alcohol Abuse and Alcoholism (NIAAA), http://www.niaaa.nih.gov. Makes available free publications on all aspects of alcohol abuse and alcoholism. Many are available in Spanish. Call, write, or search the NIAAA Web site for a list of publications and ordering information.

Drug Abuse

- American Council for Drug Education, www.acde.org

- Center for Substance Abuse Prevention, especially its publication "Family Guide to Keeping Youth Mentally Healthy and Drug Free," http://family.samhsa.gov

- Marijuana Anonymous, www.marijuana-anonymous.org

- Narcotics Anonymous, www.na.org

- National Clearinghouse for Alcohol and Drug Information, www.health.org

- National Families in Action, www.national families.org, which provides links by state to e-mail, Web sites, and contact information for hundreds of parenting resources to prevent drug abuse

- Phoenix House, especially its publication "Facts on Tap," www.factsontap.org

- PRIDE Surveys, www.pridesurveys.com, which provides questionnaire results, national summaries, drug information, and prevention information

See Appendix B for full contact information.

ANXIETY DISORDERS

Anxiety is a normal human emotion. We commonly feel anxious before we give a speech, or start a new job, or send our children off to college. But anxiety disorders are serious medical illnesses that according to the National Institute of Mental Health affect approximately 19 million American adults and 9.1 percent of college students.[11] Sasha is one of them:

> Sasha first showed symptoms of the anxiety disorder called obsessive compulsive disorder (OCD) at age four. Describing herself as "a checker, arranger, mental repeater, and washer," she began seeing a psychiatrist at age twelve, and then she became one of the many students who enter college with a diagnosed mental health disorder. But like so many others, she didn't tell anyone about it. "This is not something I advertise," says Sasha. "On those health forms that students fill out, I didn't mention anything about OCD or even tell my roommate."
>
> In fact, Sasha's mental health was not something her family ever openly talked about. "I think my parents partially blamed themselves for this problem and always wondered where they had gone wrong, so it was something to keep quite about. No one outside our immediate family (and that includes even my grandmother) was ever told about my OCD, and that was the feeling I brought to college with me." This fear of being "found out" can make the transition to college life even harder for someone like Sasha.
>
> "I wasn't happy at all my freshman year. I'm the kind of person who has a few really good friends, but it takes me a long time to get to know new people. Even in normal circumstances, I tend to think people are ignoring me when they're really not. In college, this feeling got so much worse. I was really lonely."

Intensifying her feelings of being out of place, the bathroom situation in Sasha's freshman dorm caused her great stress. "The bathroom was down the hall across from my room," she recalls. "I particularly disliked having to share the shower; it grossed me out that people might hang their dirty clothes where I was hanging my clean towel. So I Lysoled a lot. I also didn't like touching so many doorknobs after washing my hands, so I'd open doors with paper towels and frequently cleaned the door handle in my room. Plus, it was annoying to have to run back and forth across the hall every time I wanted to wash my hands, which could be more than thirty times a day."

After a while, Sasha noticed something else. "I felt so sad and lethargic most of the time. I had felt like this before, but this was so much more intense. My sleep was fragmented; I didn't want to go anywhere, and I could cry for several hours at a time. I'd also had such negative thoughts like 'Nobody likes me. I'm not smart. I've lost everything that was good. I want to get away from this school and my whole life.' Because I'm pretty savvy about mental health, I knew I was getting depressed." But Sasha couldn't put her finger on the reason she felt so miserable.

Although unhappy and lonely, Sasha held herself together through the first semester, worked hard, and earned good grades. But in the following spring semester, things began to unravel, and Sasha felt that she had nowhere to turn. The university was about a four-hour drive from Sasha's home, so she wasn't able to see her psychiatrist, and she didn't take the psychiatrist's advice to find a new therapist near the school. There were days when Sasha could barely drag herself to class.

Sasha's parents knew nothing about their daughter's pain until Sasha came home in March for spring break.

Feeling desperate, she scheduled a visit with her psychiatrist (whom she hadn't seen since the summer before) and left with the diagnosis of depression and a prescription. "I had never taken any medication for OCD. I was always totally against it because I felt it made me weak to turn for help to something outside myself. So when I told my parents I was on Prozac, they knew something was very wrong."

Sasha feels that the Prozac didn't help the root of the problem. "It made me numb so that I wasn't crying for hours anymore, but it didn't solve anything. I still knew everything was wrong, but now I didn't have the capacity to get riled up about it. The life problems were still there: I was still really anxious about doing well in college; I didn't have a supportive social circle; I was still obsessive compulsive, and I was lonely. My problems weren't things you could take away with a pill. So I didn't do much better when I returned to school after spring break."

Although medication is often extremely helpful for OCD and can have a dramatic effect on the symptoms, it does not work for everyone. Shortly after Sasha found that the medication was not the magic bullet she was hoping for, she developed a fear of writing, and her grades began to plummet. She just couldn't get started, and so all her papers were handed in very late, if at all. "I could get stuck for a whole day on one word—I'd go crazy trying to choose just the right word. It was horrible: my perfectionism was in overdrive, and that was turning me into a pathological procrastinator."

Sasha feels her trait of perfectionism, common in obsessive compulsives, is both her strength and her weakness. "I'd be curious to know how many other students at this very competitive university have OCD," she laughs, "because I don't think you can get here without being compulsively perfect about your school work. But then being pathologically perfect starts to work against you."

In the fall of her sophomore year, Sasha found a new therapist near her college and developed a strong group of friends. Although the OCD and depression were always there, the symptoms lessened, life was much better, and she gave up the Prozac. But in her senior year, the problems again intensified. "This was a make-or-break year for me. My major in folklore and mythology required a senior thesis, and writing was still my nemesis. So I thought for sure I'd never graduate on time. But with the help of my therapist and a behavioral therapist I started to see, somehow I began to put things in perspective. I realized that my thesis maybe wasn't going to be the best thesis ever written in the whole wide world, but it could still be damn good. I accepted that I wasn't going to wake up one day and be cured of OCD, and that I was never going to be perfect even if I tried harder. This wasn't easy to accept, but I did, and it worked for me."

Sasha recently graduated and is now living with two roommates and working in a major city. She looks back on her own college years with worries about the students she left behind who are still struggling with anxiety disorders. "Suicide," she says, "is not seen as the worst-case scenario in anxiety disorders as it is in depression. So in a sort of public health triage, depression gets treated first. But these disorders do severely affect the quality of life in social, academic, and occupational areas, so I hope that students begin to speak up about their illnesses and get the help they need and deserve."

Unlike the relatively mild, brief anxiety accompanying every-day events, anxiety disorders like Sasha's are chronic and relentless, and they can become progressively worse if not recognized and treated. Although some disorders have a genetic base, the stress of college seems to be a trigger in susceptible people, and that's why it is not uncommon for a person to experience his or her first anxiety disorder attack during the stressful college years.

The most common anxiety disorders are panic disorder, obsessive-compulsive disorder, posttraumatic stress disorder, phobias, and generalized anxiety disorder (see Table 4.1). The National Institute of Mental Health defines each as follows:[12]

- Panic disorder: Repeated episodes of intense fear that strike often and without warning. Physical symptoms include chest pain, heart palpitations, shortness of breath, dizziness, abdominal distress, feelings of unreality, and fear of dying. Panic disorder affects about 2.4 million adult Americans and is twice as common in women as in men.

- Obsessive-compulsive disorder: Repeated, unwanted thoughts or compulsive behaviors that seem impossible to stop or control. It affects about 3.3 million adult Americans. It strikes men and women in approximately equal numbers and usually first appears in childhood, adolescence, or early adulthood.

- Posttraumatic stress disorder: Persistent symptoms that occur after experiencing or witnessing a traumatic event such as rape or other criminal assault, war, child abuse, natural or human-caused disasters, or crashes. Nightmares, flashbacks, numbing of emotions, depression, feeling angry, irritable, or distracted, and being easily startled are common. (Family members of victims can also develop this disorder.) It affects about 5.2 million adult Americans, and women are more likely than men to develop this anxiety disorder. It can occur at any age, and there is some evidence that susceptibility may run in families.

- Phobias: Two major types of phobias are social phobia and specific phobia. People with social phobia have an overwhelming and disabling fear of scrutiny, embarrassment, or humiliation in social situations, which leads to avoidance of many potentially pleasurable and meaningful activities. Social phobia affects about 5.3 million adult Americans, and women and men are equally likely to develop this kind of phobia. The disorder usually begins in childhood or early adolescence, and there is some evidence that genetic factors are involved.

People with specific phobia experience extreme, disabling, and irrational fear of something that poses little or no actual danger (such as heights, open spaces, crossing bridges, flying). The fear leads to avoidance of objects or situations that can cause people to limit their lives unnecessarily. Specific phobias affect an estimated 6.3 million adult Americans and are twice as common in women as in men. Specific phobias usually first appear during childhood or adolescence and tend to persist into adulthood.

- Generalized anxiety disorder: Constant, exaggerated worrisome thoughts and tension about everyday routine life events and activities. This disorder leaves those affected almost always anticipating the worst even though there is little reason to expect it. These feelings are accompanied by physical symptoms, such as trembling, muscle tension, headache, or nausea. It affects about 4 million adult Americans and about twice as many women as men. The disorder comes on gradually and can begin across the life cycle, though the risk is highest between childhood and middle age. It is diagnosed when someone spends at least six months worrying excessively about a number of everyday problems.

Each anxiety disorder has its own distinct features, but they are all bound together by the common theme of excessive, irrational fear and dread. As you observe your child for signs of good mental health, it's important to remember that it is common for an anxiety disorder to accompany another anxiety disorder, substance abuse, eating disorders, or depression.

Table 4.1. One-Year Prevalence of Anxiety Disorders in Adults

	Percentage	Population Estimate (millions)[a]
Any anxiety disorder	13.3	19.1
Panic disorder	1.7	2.4
Obsessive-compulsive disorder	2.3	3.3
Posttraumatic stress disorder	3.6	5.2
Any phobia	8.0	11.5
Generalized anxiety disorder	2.8	4.0

[a]Based on a U.S. Census resident population estimate, as of July 1, 1998, of 143.3 million people, ages eighteen to fifty-four.

Source: National Institute of Mental Health, *Facts About Anxiety Disorders* (Bethesda, Md.: National Institute of Mental Health, Jan. 1999).

Web Sites for More Information About Anxiety Disorders

- Anxiety Disorders Association of America, www.adaa.org

- Freedom from Fear, www.freedomfromfear.com

- Obsessive Compulsive Foundation, www.ocfoundation.org

- National Center for PTSD, www.ncptsd.org

See Appendix B for full contact information.

EATING DISORDERS

From early childhood, women receive messages from society and the media that push them to use food for psychological comfort. Too often, the end result is eating disorders that, as this story of Ashley illustrates, can severely disrupt their college experience:

Ashley's struggle with depression and anorexia began in high school. "Especially in my senior year, I was really a mess," she remembers. "I was crying all the time. People in school would ask me what was wrong, and I'd say it was just the stress of taking high-level courses and applying to top schools. But I knew that wasn't it. I even failed a few classes, which never happened before. My parents didn't notice, or if they did, I guess they just figured I was in a senior slump."

Of course, Ashley brought those problems with her to college. Although she knew that the tension of being in a new environment would probably aggravate both of these mental health conditions, Ashley couldn't wait to get out on her own. "My eating problems caused a lot of fighting with my parents," she remembers. "They tried to control everything I ate and tell me exactly how much I could exercise. My mom tried to understand what I was going through because she had had her own issues with eating, but my dad was very angry about the problem, and we had a lot of arguments. I wasn't homesick at all when I got to college. In fact, the first family weekend at college was a disaster for me because my parents came to visit, and I didn't want to show them anything about my new life. I was really worried that they would keep trying to control me. I don't know how much they actually did that or how much I just worried about it happening."

Freshman year passed in a haze for Ashley. "I couldn't concentrate or focus on anything. I couldn't get up in the morning. I just wanted to sleep all the time. I started skipping classes, and I didn't want to eat. Finally, when I was really feeling desperate, I went to see a therapist at the college's mental health center. She diagnosed depression and put me on Zoloft. I know that really helps some people, but it didn't help me feel much better."

But this was a turning point. Because Ashley used her credit card to pay for her prescription, she knew her parents would find out. So she called them and for the first time told them about her struggle with depression. Ashley remembers, "They didn't seem surprised, and they didn't ask any questions. Nothing changed."

At the end of her freshman year, Ashley began to lose more weight. "I can't say exactly what triggered it, but I guess I just needed something I could have control over. Then I came home for the summer and started fighting with my parents again. They told me I had to go to a doctor that my mother picked out. She had to talk to him first and be very involved in my treatment. This made me feel like the doctor's opinion of me was already decided based on what my mother had told him. My mother didn't lie about my problem, but she did exaggerate things. My parents said that I had to be weighed by the doctor every week, and if I didn't meet a certain weight, they wouldn't pay my tuition for college in the fall. It was a horrible summer." Ashley kept her weight up and went back to school, but she says she hated that her parents had used her college education to make her do what they wanted.

In her sophomore year, things got worse. "I wasn't getting along with my roommates. They didn't like my compulsion with exercising and my eating habits. They would go out together without inviting me. They talked about me behind my back and acted so condescending when I was around. I was very unhappy, but I didn't tell anyone about it. To cope, I would leave the room every day at around 7:00 A.M. and not come back until one in the morning. I'd sleep for only about four hours a night and then get out of the room again. That way I didn't have to deal with my roommates, but it also made me feel very lonesome and depressed." These roommate issues, combined with the other anxieties of college life, made Ashley withdraw from the college community. She soon started to lose even more weight, and by the spring of her sophomore year, she hit a crisis point.

"I withdrew from college because I knew I was going to fail out," says Ashley with a little laugh. "My depression was worse, and I had no motivation to do anything. I couldn't focus, and I stopped doing my school work completely." Ashley's parents agreed with her decision as long as she supported herself. So she sublet an apartment, got two part-time jobs, and started to feel better. But soon Ashley got caught up in her eating rituals again and lost another ten pounds.

"I didn't like that my life was so controlled by these rules I set for myself," she admits. "But it was just so hard to get away from them. I'd set a certain amount of time that I had to exercise each day, and if I cut the time short, I'd feel so terrible. I'd set a rule that I couldn't eat snacks, and if I did, I'd be so angry at my own weakness and laziness. If I didn't limit my eating and increase my exercising, I just couldn't stand myself."

When Ashley went back to college for her junior year, she wasn't in good shape physically, but things were starting to look better. "I had a roommate that I liked, and I had a boyfriend. I was being more social and maintaining a healthy weight. But then I started to slide backward in the second semester around exam time. I felt like my boyfriend was taking up too much of my time and energy, and it was keeping me from focusing on my eating and exercising patterns. So we broke up. After that, I studied hard all the time, and I got stuck in a high-intensity mode that roped me back into my eating disorder behavior. I continued to lose more weight through the summer.

"During this time, I didn't see my parents very often, but when we did meet, the subject of food always came up. I'd get a lecture about how I was hurting my body, and then my father would yell at me. These conversations didn't affect me at all because I had heard the same thing a thousand times, and so nothing constructive came out of it."

Finally, in her senior year, things started to change for Ashley. "With the help of the therapist I was seeing, I was able to talk to my parents in a way that was more constructive. We worked on finding ways we could explain our feelings without shutting each other down. I told my dad how he could phrase his thoughts differently so I wouldn't react so strongly. I also got a glimpse of what they were so upset about when I had my picture taken for an ID card at the library. When I saw at myself in the picture, I thought I looked like one of those girls in documentaries about anorexia. It was the first time I hated what I saw. I also started to worry that I was getting physically weak. I was getting lightheaded, and I worried about passing out. Sometimes I'd get chest pains and worry about having a heart attack, which happens to anorectics sometimes."

The breaking point came when a primary care doctor on campus told Ashley that if she didn't weigh at least 106 pounds by Thanksgiving, she would have to leave school. "Being thin was important to me, but I didn't want my eating rituals to ruin my whole life. This ultimatum made the consequences of what I was doing much more immediate, and it took away some of my guilt about eating. I felt that I wasn't giving in or being lazy; I was choosing to stay in school.

"I had struggled with eating issues for eight years, and nothing changed for me until I decided that I wanted it to change. My father always thought that he could make me do things his way. He thought he knew how I should work on my recovery. My mother too was so involved in trying to 'help' me that it just added more pressure to my life. Once I made my own decision to change, that's when it happened."

After she handed in her senior thesis, Ashley says she finally felt relaxed and at ease. "I was ready to leave school and start my life. I think that was when I realized that I wanted to be more than just thin. Today, I get a strong sense of accomplishment from my job that has nothing to do with how thin I am. It's a great feeling."

It is too bad that Ashley could not have learned this lesson sooner. To keep eating disorders from ruining their college years, our daughters need to hear from us over and over again that their value as human beings has nothing to do with the size of their body.

Eating on Campus

I remember watching Geneen Roth, an author of books on obsessive eating, being interviewed on a television news show. She was talking very intelligently about the tragic consequences of eating disorders, but her words were soon drowned out by louder societal messages from the companies that bought advertising time on the show.

During the first commercial break, Pillsbury advertised a cake product with the message: "If you bake a cake for your family, they will love you." The next commercial break showed an advertisement for a health club with the implied message: "Work out at our club, and you'll soon look like this svelte super model." This is a perfect example of the mixed messages women receive: food is nurturing and a sign of love; you must be excessively thin in order to be attractive to others.

These are the two things people in college most crave as they struggle to fit in: to be in control and to be attractive to others. When this doesn't happen easily, some (especially females) use food to numb the pain and go on to develop an eating disorder. It is likely that this cause of eating disorders combines with a complex mix of physical, psychological, and social factors that can be overwhelming during the college years. Eating too little or too much, or bingeing and purging becomes a comfortable way of gaining control over one aspect of life, and this helps manage the emotional symptoms of distress, but at a very high price. One study published in the *American Journal of Psychiatry* found a ten-year mortality rate of 5.6 percent, with roughly half dying from direct medical effects and 27 percent from suicide. This mortality rate is twelve times higher than that of those fifteen to twenty-four years old in the general population.[13]

The three most common types of eating disorders found on college campuses and discussed in this section are anorexia nervosa, bulimia nervosa, and binge-eating disorder. These eating disorders commonly peak at the age of eighteen, the time when young women start their adult lives and start college.

The Hard Facts: A Gender Bias

Females are much more likely than males to develop eating disorders. Only an estimated 5 to 15 percent of people with anorexia or bulimia and an estimated 35 percent of those with binge-eating disorder are male.*

*National Institute of Mental Health, *Eating Disorders* (Bethesda, Md.: National Institute of Mental Health, Aug. 6, 2002). [www.nimh.nih.gov/publicat/eatingdisorder.cfm].

Anorexia Nervosa

Anorexia nervosa is an eating disorder in which people use self-imposed starvation to lose weight. The symptoms, which affect approximately 7 million women and 1 million men, are outlined in the *Diagnostic and Statistical Manual of Mental Disorders:*[14]

- The fear of being fat even when at or below normal weight

- Refusal to maintain body weight by restricting intake, leading to a weight loss of more than 15 percent of normal body weight

- A distortion of body size and shape that causes even underweight sufferers to feel fat or obese

- In women, the absence of at least three consecutive menstrual cycles

There are stereotypes of personalities and families of anorectics and bulimics that are sometimes accurate, but each person has his or her own reasons and backgrounds for developing the disorders. For some, it is 60 percent biological and genetic, while others have more external reasons (family and cultural) for developing the problems, with very little genetic or biological influence. The stereotypical picture of a young woman developing anorexia is of a revered child in a high-achieving family where appearances are very important. The girl is often a model obedient child who does well in school, is fairly compulsive in other areas of her life, and avoids conflict. Usually the family does not deal with conflict very directly.

In today's world, the majority of these stereotypical young women end up in college. But here, their ordered world often falls apart. Now there are many overwhelming decisions to be made about academic courses, relationships, sexuality, values, future careers, and on and on. An anorectic can avoid making these decisions by blocking out everything around her and focusing intently only on her body size and on what she will eat and not eat each day. Her thin body becomes concrete evidence of her willpower and self-discipline. She becomes obsessed with counting calories and weighs herself several times a day. She may create elaborate eating rituals, such as slowly, carefully, and meticulously organizing food on a plate, or dawdling over food and methodically chewing each small piece a specified number of times, or cutting the food into extremely small pieces. As she loses weight, thoughts of food and how to avoid it become the central preoccupation of her day.

Focusing on this one thing makes life much simpler. And in the uncertain and unpredictable college environment, anorexia serves an important function: it gives a young person a much-needed feeling of control over her life and helps her repress all other problems and stresses. But she also suffers the consequences of malnutrition. In the early stages, the anorectic may develop a skeleton-like appearance, anemia, dry skin, soft and fine body hair growth (called lanugo), low body temperature, and a lowered metabolism. When girls lose their menstrual cycles, they also stop depositing calcium in their bones. It is sometimes hard to tell the difference between the bone scan of a nineteen-year-old woman with anorexia and one of a sixty-five-year-old woman with osteoporosis. At this time, we don't know if this damage is reversible.

Sometimes anorexia is deadly. An anorectic may develop low blood potassium levels needed for heart function. Suddenly, without warning, she can start having an irregular heartbeat and even suffer cardiac arrest. Anorexia has a mortality rate between 7 and 15 percent, which is higher than the mortality rate of many cancers.

One of the reasons anorexia is lethal is that there isn't much warning before the situation hits crisis level. The human body is incredibly resilient, so even if the person is far below ideal weight, she can feel fine before suddenly crashing.

No Way Out

In addition to the physical consequences of anorexia, the disorder often sets up a vicious cycle that makes the initial psychological problems even worse by supplying a reason and excuse to avoid dealing with interpersonal issues. Because most social activities center on food, anorectics usually avoid social interactions, which increases their isolation and compounds their adjustment problems.

Bulimia Nervosa

Bulimia nervosa is an eating disorder in which a person has recurrent and uncontrollable episodes of binge eating followed by the urgent need to eliminate (purge) the food through some self-induced method, such as vomiting, enemas, starvation, laxatives, diuretics, or excessive exercise. Bulimia affects 2 percent of college-age people.

The *Diagnostic and Statistical Manual of Mental Disorders* lists four criteria for the diagnosis of bulimia:[15]

- Recurrent episodes of binge eating (at least two times a week for at least three months)

- A feeling of complete loss of control during the eating binges

- Persistent overconcern with body shape and size

- Regular self-induced vomiting, use of laxatives or diuretics, strict dieting or fasting, or vigorous exercise in order to prevent weight gain

Bulimics don't fit a specific stereotype but often have other impulsive behaviors as well: alcohol or drug problems, kleptomania, sexual acting out, and a significant frequency of concomitant other mental health issues such as depression and anxiety. They usually also suffer from low self-esteem and over time become very adept at getting rid of food through a variety of methods, vomiting being the most common. Some bulimics eat huge amounts of carbohydrates, and others binge on relatively small amounts of healthy food. They generally feel that once they've crossed the line and have to "get rid of" the food, they feel that they might as well continue eating since they aren't going to keep it down, and sometimes vomiting is easier with larger amounts of food in the body. There is a sense of desperation and humiliation when one is caught up in the binges, and it is not unusual for a woman to go through the trash to find leftovers to eat. Because of the shame associated with the symptoms, it often takes someone quite a while (a year or more) before seeking help. It's another one of those problems that people think, mistakenly, "I can take care of it by myself."

Bulimics are harder to spot than anorectics. They eat regular meals with their friends and family, they typically are of normal weight, and they are masters at hiding their binge-and-purge cycles. These students know the location of every bathroom on campus and know which ones are least used. Even their roommates are often unaware of the problem. I remember attending the first meeting of an eating concerns group and watching as a young woman walked into the room. She froze on the spot as her eyes widened and her jaw dropped. Sitting in the group was her roommate. Neither one knew the other was bulimic and had been vomiting several times a day all semester.

Bulimics tend to be normal weight but run the gamut of lower weight to overweight. When they purge, they are getting rid of only some of the food they have eaten, but because of the uneven absorption and metabolic imbalances, they are susceptible to a variety of medical problems. One specific area of concern is the use of ipecac, a medication used to help young children vomit after they've swallowed something toxic. Prolonged use can cause damage to heart muscle and eventually lead to serious cardiac problems. Use of laxatives also causes problems with intestinal motility, which is very uncomfortable to correct and can lead to serious medical consequences.

Bulimia can lead to an array of other medical problems. These include dehydration and dry skin, constipation from lack of body fluids, muscle spasm, kidney problems, inflammation and possible rupture of the esophagus from frequent vomiting, peptic ulcers and pancreatitis, and electrolyte imbalances. Electrolyte imbalances (which are caused by dehydration and loss of potassium and sodium from the body as a result of purging behaviors) are especially dangerous. They can lead to irregular heartbeat and possibly heart failure and death.

Those who routinely vomit also risk dental damage. Vomiting causes bleeding gums, erosion of tooth enamel, and increased cavities; silver fillings will be raised due to erosion of the teeth; and the teeth may be discolored or look dull from the acid.

Although the causes of bulimia are complex, elusive, and multifactorial, the young women who binge and purge all follow the same pattern of self-destructiveness.

Body Dysmorphic Disorder

I have been treating a female graduate student who is strikingly beautiful. Sadly, she loathes her body and cannot look in the mirror without disgust. She obsesses about every slight imperfection, such as a mole or the shape of her nose. When she walks down the hall and people glance at her, she assumes they are thinking how awful she looks. This kind of extreme distorted body image is called body dysmorphic disorder. As with bulimia, there is a great deal of shame associated with the symptoms, so it is probably underdiagnosed.

Binge-Eating Disorder

Overeating is common in college and has a more balanced gender ratio, although it is still predominantly a disorder of women. Binge-eating disorder often serves several functions. The weight gain makes the woman feel more unattractive and creates a barrier to forming intimate relationships. One woman reported that her significant weight gain after a breakup with her boyfriend was a relief; she didn't have to deal with the attention of other guys while she was feeling so vulnerable. Indeed, food is also very soothing. As one young woman told me, "Chocolate is much more reliable than guys. You always can depend on chocolate and know how it's going to make you feel."

The National Institute of Mental Health (NIMH) cites the symptoms of binge eating as follows:[16]

1. Recurrent episodes of binge eating, characterized by eating an excessive amount of food within a discrete period of time and by a sense of lack of control over eating during the episode.

2. The binge-eating episodes are associated with at least three of the following: eating much more rapidly than normal; eating until feeling uncomfortably full; eating large amounts of food when not feeling physically hungry; eating alone because of being embarrassed by how much one is eating; or feeling disgusted with oneself, depressed, or very guilty overeating.

3. Marked distress about the binge-eating behavior.

4. The binge eating occurs, on average, at least two days a week for six months.

5. The binge eating is not associated with the regular use of inappropriate compensatory behaviors, such as purging, fasting, or excessive exercise.

Like anorexia and bulimia, binge eating also has severe negative consequences. These include high blood pressure, high cholesterol levels, heart disease as a result of elevated triglyceride levels, secondary diabetes, gallbladder disease, and the health risks associated with obesity.[17]

The NIMH estimates that between 2 and 5 percent of Americans have a binge-eating disorder.[18] These people experience frequent episodes of out-of-control eating, with the same binge-eating symptoms experienced by bulimics but without the purge. Therefore, most binge eaters are overweight. Feelings of self-disgust and shame after bingeing can lead to more bingeing, creating a vicious cycle of excessive eating. The shame and guilt associated with being out of control and then with being overweight bring on bouts of depression in some susceptible women.

No Simple Cure

It would seem that the cure for all eating disorders is simple enough: for anorexia, start eating more; for bulimia, stop bingeing and purging; and for binge eating, stop eating so much. But the reason these disorders are so rampant on college campuses is that they are coping mechanisms that serve a purpose and function. They cannot be given up without leaving these young women adrift and insecure in their high-pressure environment.

Web Sites for More Information on Eating Disorders

- National Institute of Mental Health, www.nimh.nih.gov

- Harvard Eating Disorders Center, www.hedc.org

- National Association of Anorexia Nervosa, www.anad.org

- National Eating Disorders Association, www.nationaleatingdisorders.org

See Appendix B for full contact information.

SEXUALITY

We all want to fit in with our peers. During the college years, the ability to do this is often key to a healthy, happy, and productive experience. In fact, for many students, the ability to make the transition from dependent children to independent adults hinges on the kinds of relationships they form and how those relationships make them feel connected to others. To make these connections, some join athletic teams; others join fraternities and sororities; some get involved in student organizations; others get internships where they spend time with like-minded individuals. And, not surprisingly, still others seek out sexual intimacy to feel connected and to fit in and form relationships.

It's true that sexual intimacy offers an enormous sense of connection, but for college students, this method of forming relationships frequently backfires and does not offer the hoped-for sense of security. If one of the partners believes that sex implies a level of intimacy but the other sees it as a one-night form of recreation, the resulting alienation and emotional pain for both partners disrupt their efforts to find a sense of belonging.

Gender Differences

Both males and females are at risk for using sexual promiscuity to ease the internal pain of feeling disconnected in the college environment, but they use it differently.

Females, more often than males, tend to connect the act of sex with emotional commitment. Most feel more emotionally secure and have a greater sense of emotional well-being when there is a sense of intimate connection. And on the flip side, they feel a greater sense of betrayal when their intimate connection turns out to be a short-term mistake.

Males too use sex to manage some of the pressures of college life, but in different ways from their female partners. At this age, many males use sexual conquests to build their self-esteem. Each new partner boosts their sense of feeling desirable and liked, but they are not looking for a long-term commitment as a way to feel connected. They build their sense of belonging one partner at a time.

Despite these different reasons for using sex to establish a sense of connection, both males and females may cope with their fear of being alone by going from one sexual partner to another. For the moment, this relieves their feeling of loneliness. But without emotional commitment, the morning brings a rebound of loneliness.

In some extreme cases, young adults who get into the pattern of frequent sexual behavior find themselves addicted. The National Council on Sexual Addiction and Compulsivity recognizes the serious nature of this problem and offers a quick self-test to help identify patterns of sexual addiction. The test asks questions about one's obsessive thoughts, compulsive actions, and feelings of loss of control. (You can access the test at the council's Web site at www.ncsac.org.)

Internet Sex

Students, both male and female, who have difficulty making personal connections with fellow students have another option these days to create a sense of belonging. They can have on-line sexual encounters and gain the same comforting benefits, without risking face-to-face rejection. This way of exploring one's sexuality is particularly negative, however. It further isolates a person in a room with a computer, taking away the opportunity to get out and make those personal connections so necessary to mental health. It also puts this student at great risk when he or she agrees to meet the on-line partner. It is important to set up initial contacts in safe, neutral environments, as people are often not what they advertise in their personal ads.

The Consequences

Like those using alcohol, drugs, or an eating disorder to cope with daily pressures, many promiscuous young adults deny the problem and ignore the potential negative consequences. Most young collegians arrive at their schools with little or no sexual experience, but as in other areas, they want their peers to think they are sophisticated and experienced. Yet they bring with them their family and religious values and face intense guilt and shame when they find themselves jumping from partner to partner. These feelings, on top of the other pressures in college life, are fuel for stress-related problems.

Another problem with using promiscuity as a coping mechanism is due to what I call an invulnerability attitude. At this age, young adults know all about the dangers of unprotected sex with many partners: they know about STDs including HIV/AIDS, and they know about the physical, emotional, and life-altering risks of pregnancy and abortion. But they never think any of this will happen to them, especially when this group uses alcohol to take off the stress of meeting people of the opposite sex, forgetting that it also takes away their ability to make sound decisions.

The risk among college students of contracting an STD is very high. According to a 2002 Surveillance Report by the Centers for Disease Control, the cumulative number of people age fifteen to twenty-four diagnosed with HIV/AIDS is 40,896. This is in addition to the more than 4 million young adults age twenty to twenty-four infected with syphilis, gonorrhea, or chlamydia.[19] It would be naive to think that none of these infected individuals are on college campuses having unprotected sex with their classmates.

Sexually active female students with numerous partners also gamble with their future given the high number of unintended pregnancies and resulting abortions in this age group. The CDC *Abortion Surveillance 2000* lists 249,403 abortions among the twenty to twenty-four age group.[20] Faced with the emotional weight of an unintended pregnancy that could alter their career plans and shame their families, both males and females are at risk for becoming another depression-dropout statistic.

Far too many young adults learn the hard way that sexual promiscuity has long-term and serious consequences.

CUTTING

Cutting is a general term for a variety of self-injurious behaviors. If you have never been a cutter, it will be hard for you to understand why your son or daughter would want to intentionally harm himself or herself, but over 2 million people in the United States do just that. More than 70 percent of self-injurers are women, mostly between the ages of eleven and twenty-six, and they come from all races and social classes. [21] And according to my own observations, the numbers are on the rise among the college-age population. Here is the story of one young woman who is finding her way through this confusing coping mechanism:

> I started cutting during the spring semester of my sophomore year. It would happen when I was facing a lot of emotional stimulus, and it was a way of channeling my consciousness into a physical space on my body. But it was never a suicide attempt. I'm sure it had to do with the way I hated my body and my disgust of my physical self, and part of it was both a cry for help and a desire to inflict intense pain and to show others that I could handle it.
>
> I cut while I was alone in my room. I sat in a comfortable chair by my desk, dimmed the lights, and had tissues or a washcloth nearby. When I first started cutting, I used a switchblade or a butterfly knife. But by the summer, I had moved on to straight razor blades. The knives were fairly dull, and I had to apply a great deal of pressure before getting a clean cut, while the razor blades drew blood easily. I kept pretty neat about it; I used the tissues or washcloth to stop the blood while I was cutting, although you can do a lot of cutting without drawing a huge amount of blood.
>
> When I cut, I assumed the role of a surgeon and imagined my body as a distant object that needed fixing.

While I was cutting, I was always very rational and would think about anything from the work I had left to do that day to things I needed to do to improve myself. After I finished cutting and returned to the role of a patient, however, I sometimes felt disgust or fear at what I'd done. Some of this reaction was physical—I got very cold and sometimes couldn't stop my teeth from chattering. If I made only a couple of small cuts, I would feel energized and powerful afterward. But other times, when I would make a whole event of more drastic cutting, it was to help me release pain and then feel numb. I went back and forth between feeling a sense of pride and shame.

I never saw my cutting as dangerous or scary, and I didn't always try to hide it. In a perverse kind of way, I actually broadcast it to the people in my life I was having emotional issues with. It became a way of talking through my problems. When people reacted with disgust and shock, it was the most satisfying for me. Looking back on it, I see that most of my friends and family realized that the cutting was just a sign that I wanted to talk about my life but didn't know how to start the conversation. I know it's natural for a parent to react with panic, but it's better to be calm, ask questions, and decide what the next step should be. I'd rather not focus on the cutting but on what was behind it.

Throughout that spring when things were really bad for me, I cut about once a day. At other times, I cut more sporadically, ranging from one to three times a week. But then as my emotional life started to get better, I really didn't feel the need to cut. I was developing a good therapeutic relationship with my on-campus counselor. I got out of some troublesome romantic relationships, and I made a conscious effort to change some difficult friendships. I made myself reach out to friends and just be myself without worrying about how they would perceive and judge me. I also started working on managing stress better. That summer, I gave myself permission to do less without always worrying about what I could be doing to put on my transcript, although I admit that that decision sometimes made me feel more guilty and inadequate and on some days led to a downward emotional spiral.

I don't feel like I am completely through with cutting. I still keep razor blades in my room and have cut occasionally this semester. But I feel that I am developing other tools for expressing my insecurities, and the cutting is much less frequent. I see cutting as being on a continuum of body issues that began with an eating disorder that surfaced when I was thirteen, and I believe that disgust at my body and a feeling of alienation from my physical self will always be part of my experience, even when I have ceased cutting entirely. I do, however, see hope for the possibility of managing my relationship with my body better in the future, and I haven't given up on the possibility that one day my body and I will be able to peacefully cohabit.

A Secret Act

Kids involved in cutting look quite normal and fit in with their peers. They are generally good students and are actively involved in school activities. Most are ashamed of their self-inflicted injuries and are very secretive about the practice, so they often injure places that can be easily hidden by clothing, such as the arms, upper chest, and upper thighs.

Their methods of injury are varied. Cutting is the most common expression of this disorder. The person will use any sharp object—a razor, box cutter, knife, broken mirror, or even the flip top off a soda can—to cut the skin, making a shallow cut just deep enough to draw blood. Burning is also a popular method of self-injury. In this case, an item such as a lit cigarette, a piece of hot metal, a lighter, or a match is used to burn the skin. Scratching is a simpler method that involves using the fingernails to scratch at the skin until a wound is opened. Less common methods of self-mutilation are self-hitting, hair pulling, and self-biting.

Most often, the injuries are superficial, but there is always the risk of going too far. Someone who cuts too deep might accidentally hit an artery and bleed to death. And if they continually pester the injured area to prevent it from healing, they may get serious skin infections from the festering wounds.

Why?

Self-injury is a coping mechanism. It is a way to deal with life and the emotional pain it can bring. Often the first episode of self-injury is triggered by some event that causes much tension or stress (and we know there are plenty of such events during the college years). Many of those who self-injure say they do it to release pain. Fear, anxiety, anger, isolation, sadness, loneliness, or emotional pain builds up inside until they feel that they'll explode without some form of release. Self-injury serves that purpose.

Others self-injure for exactly the opposite reason: they are numb inside and feel no emotion, so they appreciate the raw pain of injury. Finally, they can feel *something*. In these cases, cutting can be a way to be temporarily distracted from real feelings.

Some who self-injure feel a strong need to punish themselves for a perceived wrong. This is frequently the case with victims of child sexual abuse who believe on some level that the abuse was their fault. Filled with self-loathing and alienation, they have an intense desire to do themselves harm.

Cutting can also be a symptom of an underlying psychiatric disorder such as depression, obsessive-compulsive disorder, Gilles de la Tourette syndrome, psychosis, borderline personality disorder, kleptomania, trichotillomania (hair pulling), eating disorder, or body dysmorphic disorder.

> ### Resources for More Information About Cutting
>
> - Self-Abuse Finally Ends (SAFE), 1-800-DONT-CUT, http://www.selfinjury.com
>
> - Dana Sullivan, "Self-Injury: Poorly Understood Problem," http://www.cnn.com/2000/HEALTH/09/05/self.mutilation.wmd/

SUICIDE

There are real people, sons and daughters, behind the startling statistics on suicides on campus:

- Michelle Gluckman, John D. Skolnik, and Stephen Bohler, New York University. All three students fell to their deaths from high university buildings in separate instances in the fall of 2003.[22]

Michelle, a sophomore from Brooklyn, New York, had shared a marijuana cigarette with two friends in a sixth-floor apartment in a private apartment building in the heart of the campus. She then lay on a bed and said, "I can't take it anymore." She cleared the way to a kitchen window and went out the window head first as her two friends tried unsuccessfully to hold her by her legs. She landed on a part of the building four floors below.

John, a twenty-year-old junior from Evanston, Illinois, jumped to his death from the upper-floor interior balconies of NYU's twelve-story Bobst Library the first week of classes in September.

Stephen, a freshman from Irvine, California, also fell from a high floor at Bobst on October 10. His mother reported that her son had had no major emotional problems, adding that the city medical examiner's office had been studying whether he was on hallucinogenic drugs at the time of his death.

- Michael Frentzel, Ferrum College, Virginia. Michael hanged himself in his dorm room in February 2000. The college had placed him on disciplinary probation after police were called during a fight with classmates and another with his girlfriend. The college's dean of student affairs had noticed he was bruised from banging his head against a wall and had self-inflicted scratches on his neck. Frentzel's family feels he was crying out for help.[23]

• Jason Altom, Harvard University. Jason drank a liquid laced with cyanide in August 1998. A graduate student in the chemistry department, Jason's suicide note began, "Professors here have too much power over the lives of their grad students." Yet no one had any idea that Jason felt unfairly treated. His was the second suicide out of this department in two years.[24]

• Elizabeth Shin, Massachusetts Institute of Technology. Elizabeth set herself on fire in her dorm room on April 14, 2000. She had been to the university's counseling center on many occasions and was given medication. Elizabeth's parents are suing MIT because they felt that her care was not coordinated and they should have been contacted with more details about her behavior. (For more on Elizabeth's case, see Chapter Five.)

Shocking Statistics

Certainly, suicide is not something you want to think about as you pack your child off to college, but it is a fact of college life. The scariest statistic that I have encountered is from American College Health Association data reporting that 9 percent of all college undergraduate students seriously think about suicide.[25]

That is a frightening piece of information; it means that in a college with ten thousand students, nine hundred of them will report thinking seriously about suicide. The good news is that actual suicide is a rare event. The bad news is that it happens, and sometimes it is unpredictable and unstoppable. It is every parent, college, and counselor's worst nightmare, but fortunately, there are things we can do to minimize the risk. And parents can help.

The statistics on college-age suicide make this a subject that can't be ignored. A significant number of college students find the pressures of college life too great to bear; feeling helpless and hopeless, they think about, attempt, or complete suicide. The facts are shocking:[26]

- Suicide is the second leading cause of death among twenty to twenty-four year olds (after accidents and homicides).

- More teenagers and young adults die from suicide than from all medical illnesses combined.

- The suicide rate peaks among young adults (ages twenty to twenty-four).

- One in twelve U.S. college students makes a suicide plan.

Who Is at Risk?

Two distinct groups of students are at risk for suicidal thoughts and attempts: those who come into the college with preexisting mental health problems and those who develop mental health problems during the college years.

Students who come to college with diagnosed mental illnesses usually keep this fact a secret. Although there are laws protecting people with any sort of disability from discrimination, the students and their families do not advertise a psychological problem in the application process and after acceptance usually keep the facts to themselves. We may suspect a problem based on the prescribed medications listed on a student's health form or the acknowledgment of certain needs on their housing applications. But for the most part, we do not know which of our incoming students have diagnosed conditions, such as depression or bipolar disorder, that put them at risk for suicide.

But we do know the numbers of these students is rising as the number of high school students suffering mental health problems increases. The Youth Risk Behavior Survey in 2001 polled 13,601 students nationally in grades 9 through 12. It found that in the twelve months before the survey, 28.3 percent of high school students acknowledged feeling so sad or hopeless almost every day for more than two consecutive weeks that they stopped doing some usual activities. Nineteen percent of students reported that they seriously considered attempting suicide, and 14.8 percent had made a specific plan to attempt suicide. And 8.8 percent had attempted suicide in the previous year.[27]

Although these numbers are startling, students with mental illnesses and learning disabilities now succeed in high school and move on to college as never before because of improvements in early diagnosis, competent therapy, and pharmacology. But when they move into the college system, they need ongoing, intensive care that not all schools are able to offer. The typical unstructured environment, erratic sleeping patterns, and academic stresses can ultimately push these students to the edge.

Then there is the group who develop mental health problems while in college. The common risk factors for attempted suicide that

The Hard Facts

The American College Health Association survey of 29,230 college students found that a significant portion of college students had been previously diagnosed with clinical depression: 11.7 percent had been diagnosed with depression, 24 percent of those were in therapy for depression, and 35 percent of those were taking medication for depression.* (The full survey results are available in Appendix A.)

---

*American College Health Association, *National College Health Assessment: Reference Group Report* (Baltimore: American College Health Association, 2002).

may begin during the college years include depression, alcohol or other drug use, and physical or sexual abuse. In fact, research has shown that more than 90 percent of people who kill themselves have depression or another diagnosable mental or substance abuse disorder.[28] Unfortunately, students often ignore these high-risk signals until they find themselves on the edge of hopelessness and despair.

Students' gender can also put them in the high-risk category. Among those age twenty to twenty-four, more than seven times as many men as women die by suicide. Women report *attempting* suicide during their lifetime about three times as often as men.[29] So a daughter is far more likely to talk about suicide or attempt suicide, but a son is more likely to use a lethal means (most commonly firearms) to go through with it.

Although it's impossible to create a foolproof profile of at-risk students, many of them feel driven to achieve more than is humanly possible; some are perfectionists who cannot bear failure; others have a history of mental illness in the family; some simply lack adequate coping skills to get them through tough times; and others have no identifiable traits at all. Whatever the cause, specific signs of potential suicide include

- Talking openly about committing suicide

- Talking indirectly about "wanting out" or "ending it all"

- Taking unnecessary or life-threatening risks

- Giving away personal possessions

Ideally, troubled students receive help long before they get to this final stage. That's why it is so important for us to pay very close attention to students like the 66.2 percent of college students who said they felt overwhelmed by all they had to do in the last year and the 46 percent who felt so depressed that it was difficult to function.[30] These are all at-risk students.

Web Sites for More Information About Suicide Prevention

- American Association of Suicidology, www.suicidology.org

- American Foundation for Suicide Prevention, www.afsp.org

- National Organization of People of Color Against Suicide, www.nopcas.com

- Suicide Prevention Advocacy Network, www.spanusa.org

- HOTLINE: 1-800-SUICIDE, which provides access to trained telephone counselors, twenty-four hours a day, seven days a week

See Appendix B for full contact information.

THE GOAL IS PREVENTION

Research estimates project that 1,088 suicides will occur on college campuses in the United States each year and that 9.5 percent of surveyed students seriously contemplated suicide.[31] These are an insurmountable number of cases for colleges to handle adequately. And this does not address the needs of the many students who are suffering from mental health problems but do not seek help from a counselor.

This is why your role in the prevention of mental health problems is so important. Because it's too easy for a student in crisis to get lost in the crowd at college and because you will not be notified of identified mental health problems without the expressed consent of your "child," who is now an adult, you will need to be aware and vigilant in order to monitor his or her health. In almost all cases, the signs and symptoms of mental health problems are there long before a crisis situation develops, and they are treatable—but they must first be identified.

In the following chapters, you will learn how colleges are handling this very serious situation and how you can help. Your awareness of the problem and your willingness to do something about it are your child's best hope for making it through the college years healthy and happy.

Part II

The Solution

For Colleges, Parents, and Students

No one will argue that the problems facing today's college students are not enormous. The statistics, the news headlines, counseling center directors, and the students themselves all make it very clear that there is a crisis on our campuses. Depression, sleep disorders, substance abuse, anxiety disorders, eating disorders, impulsive behaviors (including sexual promiscuity and self-mutilation), and even suicide are no longer rare anomalies. They are part of college life.

This isn't a casual observation. According to the 2001 National Survey of Counseling Center Directors, 85 percent of center directors reported an increase in "severe" psychological problems over the last five years.[1] A recent study at Kansas State University found that between 1989 and 2001, the number of students with documented depression doubled, and the proportion of students taking psychiatric medications rose from 10 to 25 percent. The number of suicidal students tripled.[2] This is the reality of today's college experience.

What should be done? What are colleges doing about the crisis? What more should they be doing? What can parents do? What is beyond their control? And what can students themselves do to make their college years positive, growing experiences filled with good times and cherished memories? In Part Two, I answer these questions in the hope that a proactive approach by colleges, parents, and students working together will help to turn around the upward climb of these devastating statistics.

5

What Are Colleges Doing About the Crisis? And What More Should Be Done?

Ever since Princeton University opened the first campus mental health service in 1910, there has been a growing awareness that in order to meet the educational goals of their students, colleges must tend to their emotional needs. Over the past century, however, movement toward doing something about that realization has been slow and uneven.

Today, college administrators continue to debate how much responsibility schools should be taking for the emotional health of their students. Those on one side of the debate say that colleges and universities are institutions of learning, charged with assisting students to define and meet their academic and career goals; they are not residential treatment centers for students with unstable mental health problems. The other side points out that if colleges are able to keep students emotionally healthy and in school, it allows them to maximize their academic potential and that's good for the student and financially good for the institution because it enhances retention. In the middle are those who agree it would be nice to address the psychological needs of the students but note that there is a seemingly bottomless pit of mental health resources that colleges could offer, but that their financial resources are not bottomless. Schools have found the same thing that insurance companies have found: increase the available resources, and utilization will increase. So many schools must ask, "How much is enough?"

My view is that the emotional well-being of students goes hand-in-hand with their academic development. If they're not doing well emotionally, they are not going to reach their academic potential. Therefore, colleges must put significant resources in terms of staff, facilities, and financial backing into their programs of mental health services.

You would expect that as the director of a mental health service, I of course would take this position. But I feel strongly that those who believe that the school does not have a role to play in safeguarding and enhancing the mental health of students or who complain about putting money into programs that help students with problems such as depression, substance abuse, and sleep, anxiety, and eating disorders, do not fully understand the ramifications of *not* helping these students. The mental health crisis on campus affects far more than just the mental health counselors; it affects the individual students, the student body in general, and the entire institution.

I've queried other directors of counseling centers at colleges around the country and spoken with deans, residential staff, and other administrators at a variety of institutions to get the big picture of what people are thinking about in this important area. There is surprising consistency across institutions regarding areas of concern. Throughout this chapter, I'll include some of the questions and responses posed to directors.

Survey of College Counseling Center Directors

"What are the biggest challenges you face today, and are these challenges different than they were five or ten years ago?"

The responses to this question were almost unanimous in noting the rising levels of severity and urgency of student issues. Budget problems also topped the list:

"More students are on campus with more pressing psychological concerns, and there seem to be more environmental stressors affecting them."

"We have had budget cuts, as have other departments on campus, so that we are attempting to do more with less all the time."

"Money is much tighter. More students with more chronic severe mental illnesses arriving on campus. And more demand for psychiatric services and medication."

"Dealing with more severely troubled students and the need for more prescribing resources."

"Recent budget cuts, which means diminished staff—at the same time the litigious climate and recent cases of universities being held responsible for students' behavior. This really backs us into a corner. We are more responsible but have less money to offer services."

"An extremely distressed student population that presents with more serious problems that require resources we don't have (such as long-term treatment, psychiatric care, assessment for violence potential)."

INDIVIDUAL STUDENTS BENEFIT FROM STRONG MENTAL HEALTH SERVICES

College mental health services first address the immediate needs of students with emotional or psychological problems. It would be shortsighted to ignore students with a cavalier attitude that says, "Education dollars should not pay for the emotional problems of students who can't meet the demands of higher education." Would anyone suggest that colleges do away with all health care services and that a student with the flu, a sprained ankle, sports injury, or severe asthma also be left to fend for himself or herself because the problem is not directly related to the pursuit of a higher education? Of course not. Psychological health cannot be separated from a student's physical health. Both are the responsibility of all colleges and universities that aim to educate these young people. Whether the resources come from within the college or the community depends on a number of factors, which will be discussed in this chapter.

It is a fact that the quality of mental health counseling services is directly related to the ability of many students to gain a college degree. A survey conducted by the University of Idaho Student Counseling Center found that 77 percent of students who responded reported that they were more likely to stay in school because of counseling and that their school performance would have declined without counseling. Ninety percent of the respondents reported that counseling helped them meet their goals at the university and helped reduce stress that was interfering with their schoolwork.[1] These results from Idaho mirror student responses across the country.

The increasing number of students arriving at college already diagnosed with and medicated for mental health disorders, along with the increasing demands and challenges of college life explored in previous chapters, make it absolutely necessary for all colleges to accept reasonable responsibility for the psychological well-being of their students. It is a crucial part of education to help and support students to manage stress, anxiety, and the vagaries of relationships with both peers and professors.

Survey of College Counseling Center Directors

"What are the biggest problems you face getting students into care quickly enough?"

The responses to this question show that even with the best of intentions, limited staff make it difficult for students to get quick attention:

"The wait list. We perform a triage of sorts as part of the intake process, but students still have to wait at times."

"When we determine that a particular student's service needs are beyond our scope, the referral sources supposedly available, including local full-service hospitals, are not always responsive in a timely manner."

"The insurance available for our students is woefully inadequate to cover the most pressing student needs."

"Busy schedules. Time demands on staff to attend meetings, be on committees, and so forth."

"Denial by the student, his or her family, and friends."

"For those we refer out, either for testing or because the issues are beyond the scope of our center, there are always difficulties with private-pay insurers and inadequate community resources."

"Insurance issues and financial concerns among the students who need specialized help."

THE ENTIRE STUDENT BODY BENEFITS FROM STRONG MENTAL HEALTH SERVICES

Most counseling centers on college campuses with adequate resources make an effort to reach all students with their services. They offer academic and career counseling. They sponsor informative panels, forums, and discussions on how to beat the stress of college life, how to manage time, how to stay healthy and awake, how to recognize the signs and symptoms of trouble, and how to get help.

Despite their best efforts, however, some students will experience a mental health crisis. When this happens, it affects not only the students who are struggling with emotional and psychological problems, but it also directly influences the educational experience of the other students in the school as well. And that's why a strong counseling center affects the educational experience of all students.

For example, in a recent case, one of our students was suffering from an eating disorder. Her sympathetic roommate became her nurse/parent/therapist, getting her to classes, coaxing her to eat, and distracting her from her exercise obsession. It wasn't long before we got a call from the roommate's parents demanding that their daughter be moved to another room. They felt strongly that their daughter's college experience was being very negatively affected by the needy roommate. They were right. Students have far too many of their own social and academic stresses to deal with, never mind trying to handle the distressed students around them.

In a similar way, we know that substance abuse by some students affects the entire college community. It increases the rates of sexual abuse, assault, injury, vandalism, and property damage. No one on campus is totally isolated from the actions and behaviors of others.

In extreme cases, students struggling with mental health problems are a danger to those around them. This becomes glaringly apparent when tragic events hit the headlines, as they did at Harvard in 1995 when student Trang Ho was murdered by her mentally ill roommate, Sinedu Tadesse, who then committed suicide. And recently at Louisiana Technical College, Terome Silvie was shot to death by a fellow student while sitting in an electronics class. At the University of Arizona, Robert Flores shot and killed two professors after being barred from taking a test.

Funding a mental health center does not take money away from students who do not directly use the services of the center. In many ways, the money supports and protects all students.

Survey of College Counseling Center Directors

"What are the most important things you provide to the college community outside of direct care for students?"

The responses to this question provide a picture of many services involved in consultation, crisis intervention, outreach, assessment, and training:

"The traditional counseling center may be conceptualized as an educational agency as well as a clinic. Counseling center staff often provide educational and prevention programs as well as actual college adjustment classes. Additionally, many centers train practicum students and interns."

"We teach other administrators and faculty members about mental health issues and contribute to important institutional decisions when students are having difficulty, because of emotional problems, in taking advantage of their educational opportunities."

"Consultation with faculty members about students in distress."

"Programming with students to help reduce isolation, develop skills, and build community—all as preventive antidotes to the stress factors that might otherwise cause them problems later."

"We are consultants to the community in all senses of the word. If there's an issue involving students, we are called." "We 'ground' the campus, are the lead team in all kinds of emergency management and crisis intervention. We run memorial services. We run celebrations. We are the liaison with parents."

"Education about mental health–related issues including everything from stress, to suicide prevention, eating disorder information, and alcohol interventions."

THE COLLEGE INSTITUTION BENEFITS FROM STRONG MENTAL HEALTH SERVICES

Mental health programs directly influence the reputation and educational rankings of all colleges. Most specifically, they affect an institution's retention and graduation rates, both very important to the health and vitality of a college community—and to the bottom line. These rates are touted as an indicator of student satisfaction and are considered by students and parents when choosing colleges, and they are used in the formulas that select the top-ranking colleges in the country and advertised in publications like U.S. News and World Report and The Princeton Review. Ignoring the spike in mental health problems on campuses affects retention and college reputation.

Traditionally, college administrators charged with retaining enrolled students focused on academic and social adjustment. It was thought that if students could make friends and keep their grades up, they would stay at the school and eventually graduate. Now we are realizing the importance of adding personal adjustment and mental health factors to this equation.

It is true that the first responsibility of an institution of higher learning is to educate its students, but if we adopt a "survival of the fittest" mentality and focus our energies on only the mentally strong, the college, and eventually society in general, loses out. Researchers have found that 5 percent of students prematurely end their education due to psychiatric disorders. The study authors estimated that an additional 4.29 million people in the United States would have graduated from college if they had not been experiencing psychiatric disorders.[2]

This study was done in 1995—before the spike in the mental health crisis on campus. Imagine the numbers of people today who, if given proper medical attention, could be functioning on higher intellectual levels. The colleges and society in general lose bright and creative minds—students who might have contributed to the advancement of knowledge and progress, students with potential such as mathematician John Forbes Nash Jr., an MIT professor who won the Nobel Prize in economics and whose battle with schizophrenia was so well illustrated in the movie *A Beautiful Mind*.

Many famous people have suffered from mental illness, including notables such as Stephen Hawking, Sir Winston Churchill, Claude Monet, Mozart, William Styron, Mike Wallace, and Sylvia Plath. In fact, one scientific study of the lives of almost three hundred world-famous individuals found that over 40 percent had experienced some type of depression during their lives. Famous writers are particularly prone to the problem (72 percent), but others also suffer high rates of depression (artists, 42 percent; politicians, 41 percent; intellectuals, 36 percent; composers, 35 percent; scientists, 33 percent).[3]

When students drop out of school due to untreated mental health problems, there is a ripple effect throughout the population. These people who lose the potential for higher-paying jobs can drain, rather than contribute to, society. Often their skills and promise are lost to menial jobs. We all pay this price of ignoring their needs.

It's important to offer the mental health services that will help students complete their education, but the need to improve mental health services can also be self-serving for colleges. Institutes of higher education are now realizing that if they do not adequately provide for their students' mental health and safety, they face grave financial liability.

That is the bottom-line message from a 2003 suicide case at Ferrum College in Virginia. The Frentzel family alleged in a federal lawsuit that the school had ignored signs that their son, Michael, was likely to inflict self-harm. They accepted an undisclosed financial settlement after the school admitted shared responsibility for Michael's death, the first time a college had ever done so. This case has raised the bar on the level of responsibility that colleges can be expected to take for at-risk students.

On the heels of this landmark case, the academic community is now awaiting the outcome of the Shin family suit against MIT to judge the extent of that responsibility. Their $27 million lawsuit alleges that MIT was negligent in its failure to provide adequate care for their daughter, Elizabeth, who killed herself after more than a year of treatment by campus counselors.

Even the accountants up in the bursar's office now agree that cutting too close to the bone on mental health issues is very risky business.

WHY SOME SCHOOLS DO NOT HAVE ADEQUATE MENTAL HEALTH SERVICES

Despite the benefits to individual students, the student body, and the college itself, far too many students are not getting adequate mental health care on college campuses. The reasons are varied, but as you explore the state of mental heath services at your child's school, you'll find that the most common reason for weak mental health services is money.

Higher education is a business. And like any other business, it strives to offer a quality product at a reasonable price. But in a bad economy (as we've seen lately) colleges face a double problem: their endowment is reduced, and the demand for scholarship funds increases. This puts tremendous pressure on the school to make decisions about what programs must be cut and what programs need to grow. Some obvious considerations for the school are to increase resources for programs that are bringing in revenues (students and research) and to shrink areas that don't show obvious economic advantages (student services).

So who is going to pay to support strong student services in a counseling center? The enactment of the Americans with Disabilities Act and mental health parity laws require colleges to meet the special needs of these students, but some say that only students who use the mental health center should be charged a student fee to cover their care. I disagree. We do not charge only the physically disabled students to cover the cost of installing ramps and elevators to meet the requirements of the Americans with Disabilities Act. This is no different. Whether the costs are buried in the tuition or covered by a special student fee, everyone should pay equally.

But when money is short, something's got to give. Nationwide, budget cuts are causing many departments in colleges and universities around the country to cut staff positions, mental health staff included. When this happens, services to students are affected. The two most troubling changes caused by staff reductions that I've observed in colleges in my area in eastern Massachusetts are the effect on the remaining staff and the effect on their programs.

At a time when student mental health needs are increasing at unprecedented rates, fewer staff members means more work for those remaining and less attention for the students. When the workload becomes unmanageable, staff become vulnerable to stress and burnout. Counselors who themselves are suffering psychologically are little help to the students.

Second, budget cuts have caused some colleges to make a major program shift. Time and money are frequently siphoned away from the traditional prevention and education programs directed at all students and refocused on reactive programs that address the immediate needs of students with severe psychological problems who are in crisis. Ironically, this shift that weakens prevention programs leads to more crisis situations.

Cutting the budget for mental health services in this time of increased need and demand is ethically and legally risky. Why wait for a student tragedy before suddenly providing money for the problem? Prevention is a far better investment. Unfortunately, some colleges are learning this in retrospect.

After tragic suicides at Harvard and MIT, school administrators formed committees to review their mental health services and make recommendations about how to improve them. The committees recommended a series of changes that resulted in budget increases ($838,000 at MIT and a 15 percent budget boost at Harvard) to hire more staff, conduct screening and outreach campaigns to encourage troubled students to seek counseling, improve infrastructure and support, boost social marketing, and provide more timely and accessible services.[4] These are important changes that all schools need to implement regardless of the economic climate and before a crisis hits.

Survey of College Counseling Center Directors

"What are the things on your wish list of resources you don't have that you think are needed to provide the best care for students?"

With more staff, more money, and more cooperation with community and home town mental health services, these counselors could do their jobs better:

"More staff to provide counseling and outreach."

"On-campus access to a psychiatrist. We have family docs who will prescribe for routine anxiety and depression, but have to beg for appointments in the community for more students with more complicated or urgent concerns."

"More collaboration with faculty and more cooperation from hometown therapists who forgot to refer their clients to us until there's a crisis."

"More money (naturally) to do better programming, hire top-level staff, increase our hours. More psychiatric backup for medications and coordinated clinical care with a medical facility on site."

"More concrete resources: a full-time administrative assistant to answer phones and assist in Web page maintenance. Money to pay for educational programming. A part-time nutritionist. Money to finance self-assessments to be connected to web pages or intranet for students."

RECOMMENDATIONS FOR CREATING STRONG MENTAL HEALTH SERVICE CENTERS

From an educational, financial, legal, and public relationships standpoint, it's wise for colleges and universities to recognize and respond to the increase in serious psychological problems among today's student population. Clearly, there is not a one-size-fits-all approach to the mental health crisis on college campuses. If a school has two counselors for ten thousand students, the counseling program will be far different from a school that has twenty counselors for the same ten thousand students. But I believe there are certain core competencies that should be available to meet the needs of a diverse student population regardless of the size of the school or counseling program. In centers where the following resources are lacking, it is my hope that this information will help these schools review their counseling needs to creatively develop the necessary resources.

Provide Student Education to Promote Prevention

Students arrive on campus with no knowledge of the mental health services that are available to them. And few come with the requisite knowledge to sort out symptoms of depression, anxiety, eating, or substance abuse problems from the normal travails of college life. This is why so many suffer extensively and unnecessarily, usually with significant consequences to their own academic well-being as well as consequences on others in their community. Counselors cannot sit back and wait for students in trouble to seek them out. They must proactively advertise and educate.

All students should be given information that clearly explains all available mental health services. These might include the customary brochures and flyers, but also useful items that students might keep and use, such as pencils, planners, water bottles, and bookmarks that give important college resource and contact information as well as informative Web site addresses.

We're all aware that incoming students are deluged with information, and mental health care is probably the last thing on their minds when they arrive at school enthusiastic and energized. So reminders during the year, particularly during high-stress times (during midterms, final exams, and holiday periods), are also a good idea.

We must also reach out to student groups that may not normally be exposed to helpful information and consequently be unfamiliar with the warning signs of mental problems. This includes athletes, various ethnic groups, dorm residents, and fraternity and sorority house members. It also is necessary to reach out to international students, who may be confused by the U.S. health care system and have a very different cultural orientation that makes them feel they can seek medical help only in the most dire of situations.

Schools should plan educational forums to answer questions and provide individualized information. These forums sometimes occur during various national mental health awareness weeks with emphasis on screening for depression, anxiety disorders, eating disorders, and so on. They also are staged during times of stress, such as right before exam week. And they can be offered as part of resident life activities.

This kind of social marketing, however, has its limitations. In fact, some, including Henry Wechsler, a researcher at Harvard University's School of Public Health, feel that social marketing is largely unhelpful, at least in the area of alcohol education. Despite billions of dollars spent on alcohol education, the frequency of binge drinking is largely unchanged on most campuses. This is why many schools are now developing more innovative and creative programs to prevent or at least recognize common problems.

In my experience, this innovation requires student involvement and interest, as we are continually learning at Harvard. We usually run a screening program during National Depression Screening Week. In the past, we would screen approximately fifteen students in a two-day period. In 2003, the Student Mental Health Advocacy and Awareness Group got involved in publicizing and supporting the event. They knew best where to advertise the event and destigmatized student involvement and participation. Along with free incentives (such as free stress balls, massages, and candy), there was a dramatic increase in student interest. The results were remarkable: 202 students were screened with one-on-one meetings with clinicians. It was clear that when students themselves run the show, other students are far more likely to step forward and join in.

Afterward one student sent me an e-mail in which she confirmed my feelings. She wrote:

> I think that student involvement is perhaps the most important factor to educating the college community on mental illness. Mental illness has unfortunately become one of those "safety" topics along with fire drills and wearing seatbelts that students tend to belittle. Pamphlets about depression find themselves in the same wastebasket with those prohibiting candles and microwaves. The majority of students are far more inclined to trust and believe their peers than a group of university administrators that we have never met. By involving students in campaigns for reducing stigma and educating about mental illness, the subject suddenly becomes much more real to the rest of the student community. It's not a faceless administrator telling them what's up—it's their friends, their roommates, those people who sit on the left side of the lecture hall and hang around joking before sessions. Ultimately, the only people who can get through to students with any degree of consistency are the students themselves.

Many schools do realize the positive impact that students can have on their peers. Visible students (such as athletes, student leaders, news editors, musicians, and activists) who have had firsthand experience with depression, anxiety, substance abuse, and other issues can have a big impact on their fellow students. When they share their experiences, a community of openness and honesty can develop, which tightens the bonds of relationships across the campus. Connections may be the most important thing that helps us to function, keeps us safe, and helps us avoid a sense of helplessness and hopelessness. Normalizing these experiences reduces stigma and allows other students to recognize problems and seek appropriate help. Having students talk about these experiences seems to be far more effective than having counselors say the same thing.

Survey of College Counseling Center Directors

"Have you found ways to reduce the stigma of getting students to seek care?"

All the counseling services in the world won't help our kids if they don't feel comfortable asking for them. This is what some schools are doing to reach out:

"We tell students, 'No one knows why you are coming to the counseling center.' Most of our counseling staff teach classes and students frequently make appointments to talk about their classes."

"Other professors frequently give their students assignments in which they have to interview one of our staff. Other students come here to volunteer for the Peer Education Program. So no one really knows why you are here."

"Our presentations to student groups, classes, etc., help normalize using the mental health center."

"Many of our students felt seeking counseling was a betrayal to their families. Since I've been presenting to the families during orientation, our parent-based referrals have increased markedly."

"Key faculty administrators outside the counseling center who have used counseling in their lives have openly disclosed that to students in the process of trying to facilitate a referral, and students have reported these disclosures to have encouraged them to give counseling a try."

"Our presence at the annual health fair, where we provide screenings for anxiety, depression, substance abuse, eating disorders, and vulnerability to stress, as well as educational information on a variety of topics."

Fund Adequate Staffing

When asked, all college administrators of course say they want to reach out to educate students about mental health and prevent emotional breakdowns. But they also know that good preventive mental health programs have a downside. When schools do a good job of social marketing, they often face the "no good deed goes unpunished" paradox. If we do good outreach, more students will come to our services, waiting times will be lengthened, and as the staff becomes clinically stretched, the need for an increased budget becomes unavoidable.

According to my own informal survey of college counseling center directors, lack of adequate staffing is the number one complaint. This finding is supported by the 2002 National Survey of Counseling Center Directors compiled by Robert Gallagher at the University of Pittsburgh. Gallagher found that the average ratio of full-time mental health professionals to students is 1 to 1,574. The mean number of psychiatric hours per week per 1,000 students is 2.6 (up from 1.3 in 2001).[5] (I point out that these are self-reported data from counseling center directors, and schools have different ways of gathering these data and widely varying caseloads.)

High student demand at counseling centers is a concrete sign of a strong preventative education and outreach program. But without an ample supply of funds, it is also a sure way to raise the number of student complaints. I'm aware of a large institution with a high commitment to the emotional well-being of students that has more than double the average ratio of staffing and a twelve-fold higher ratio of prescribers. Yet students at this school are currently complaining (quite loudly in the school newspaper) that services are inadequate. We are finding more and more cases like this where even schools with far above-average staffing numbers are unable to meet rising demands of their students. This is not an area where schools can put their head in the sand.

From their initial contact with a counseling center, staffing affects a student's attitude toward mental health care and likelihood of follow through. Making that first call or first visit is very difficult and often comes only when the student is in a crisis situation. How is that first contact handled? Does the student in crisis get a voice mail with a message: *Press 1 if you're depressed. Go to the local emergency room if you feel unsafe*? Does the student get a harried secretary who is doing three other things at the same time? Is the student told to call back next week when a counselor will be free to talk? When students get poor, delayed, and inconsistent service, they quickly give up and spread the word that going for counseling is a waste of time.

In contrast, the University of Massachusetts has a system that is a good example of how a counseling staff can prioritize student problems to make sure that a student in crisis is never neglected, regardless of daily staff schedules. Chief of counseling Harry Rockland-Miller has set up a triage system in which all students new to the counseling center have same-day access to a senior clinician. If seventy new students call in a week, those seventy students will get fifteen-minute telephone appointments. During these calls, the clinicians gauge the level of urgency, prioritize the students' needs, and try to match the student with appropriate resources. Those in true crisis are seen immediately. Those with less urgent needs are scheduled a day or two later. And those with moderate problems (like sleep difficulties or academic adjustment problems) are given an appointment at a later date. This is the kind of program all colleges must strive to achieve.

Increased student demand also makes it harder to track students through the system. Some counselors are so busy seeing students that they can't create adequate access. They don't have data and resources to predict the fluctuating demand. We all know that the number of students seeking care skyrockets around the holidays in the winter and in the spring. This is fairly predictable. But the service needs to know how many new students use the counseling services each and every week and how much care they can reasonably provide. Is it two sessions? Eight sessions? Or twelve sessions? How many on weekends and holidays? A counseling center can't provide adequate staffing at the right times if the counselors don't know how many students will be arriving and when they are likely to be there.

Counselors also need to keep track of each student accessing care. Because many counselors work part time, a student may be receiving counseling or medication from a number of clinicians, who need to coordinate their recommendations and care. How often is a student coming for counseling? Is there a pattern to a student's periods of crisis? Which students are receiving care off-campus as well? What medications has this student been prescribed by other clinicians? Which students have been hospitalized and released? This kind of coordination is time-consuming because careful notes must be taken, transcribed, and often entered into a computer database after every meeting.

When clinicians are overworked and harried, this kind of tedious paperwork is easily slighted. This lack of tracking and integration is one of the complaints alleged by the parents of Elizabeth Shin in their lawsuit against MIT. Elizabeth had been to the counseling center on five of the last ten days of her life. She allegedly saw a different clinician each time, and the question has been raised as to who was in charge of integrating an organized plan for her care. All colleges must address this question.

Emphasize Community Outreach

The truth is, even as college administrators recognize the need for adequate staffing at their counseling centers, campus counselors will never be able to reach all students in need. Paul Joffe at the University of Illinois made a careful review of the nineteen students who had committed suicide between 1977 and 1984. Sixty-three percent had been known to be suicidal by a previous attempt, but only one had been seen by a psychologist or social worker (and 68 percent had been seen by a psychiatrist, who was primarily available for medication management and not ongoing treatment).[6] In a 1990 meta analysis of four studies looking at suicides, Schwartz and Whitaker reported that only thirty-six of ninety-nine students had had professional contact before they died.[7]

In response to this finding, the University of Illinois task force on suicide has taken the approach that suicidal behavior is not just a cry for help but also a statement of hopelessness and despair that must be quickly addressed. The university now has a policy requiring students who make a suicide attempt to come to at least four counseling sessions. If they fail to do so, the school puts them on leave. The school believes that it is a privilege to be in college, and students who don't follow the rules cannot stay. This has been very successful in reducing the suicide rate on campus.

This example shows that to reduce the numbers of completed suicides, we must do a better job of identifying and reaching out to students in psychological pain. But mental health counselors cannot successfully do this alone. I strongly believe that all faculty, staff, coaches, clergy, student advisers, resident hall advisers, and administrators should be aware of the signs and symptoms of trouble and should play a role in prevention, providing support, and directing students in need to appropriate resources.

To engage the entire college community in a mental health campaign, counseling center staff must conduct outreach programs to educate that community about mental health problems in the college population and provide them with information on how to recognize troubled students, approach them, and refer them to appropriate services.

The outreach must be persistent and ongoing. All members of the college community, especially those who interact with students (including academic advisers, graduate assistants, resident assistants, dining hall staff, and faculty), should be given current information through educational workshops, written materials, e-mails, and Internet site referrals. All new employees might be given information as part of their orientation to impress on them their role in identifying and supporting troubled students.

A strong outreach program that reaches the entire college community, from students to the college president, has the added benefit of helping to reduce the stigma associated with mental illness. When those working directly with students on a daily basis learn to identify signs and symptoms of mental health issues and feel empowered to approach a student in obvious psychological pain, we will be better able to get out the important message that mental health issues are not a sign of personal weakness, but rather common problems among college students that can be treated and managed.

Community outreach takes time and puts demands on the mental health staff, but it's a necessary function of the counseling service.

Give Follow-up Care

Let's say that a student comes to the college counseling center suffering symptoms of depression. She meets with a counselor, who refers her to the resident psychiatrist for medication. The doctor writes her a prescription, and she returns to her dorm room with pills in hand. Then what happens?

A recent study found that 41 percent of college counseling centers did not have formal follow-up procedures in place.[8] This lack of follow-up is dangerous in a world where the number one prescribed medication for college students is Prozac,[9] and total antidepressant sales are now over $10 billion a year.

The treatment of psychological disorders with medication is an inexact science. It often follows a trial-and-error pattern until the right type and dosage is found. Giving students a prescription and then sending them off without prompt follow-up is quite risky. This risk is compounded by the fact that students with undiagnosed bipolar disorder may find that the prescribed antidepressant actually triggers a manic episode. Somebody has to be keeping track of that. (See Appendix B for more information on medications.)

Ensure Off-Campus Resources and Coordination of Care

A college mental health center cannot adequately handle all long-term or crisis situations. For this reason, counselors must build working relationships with community mental health providers to ensure appropriate off-site referrals. This can be a complex matter.

Available off-campus resources vary enormously from school to school depending on the location, the insurance coverage, and the relationships within the community. If there is a local medical school and outpatient mental health clinic, there is often a synergy to provide psychotherapy opportunities for advanced trainees in exchange for sliding-scale or low fees. Some community mental health centers have good affordable resources for students; others do not.

Insurance coverage for students plays a major role in the use of community resources. Sometimes the school insurance policy covers care at local medical facilities. Other times, the care must be covered by the student's family policy, which is extremely variable and may not cover services outside the provider's home area.

When using off-campus resources, it is also important for the outside care providers to understand the rhythms and expectations of the college institution. This directly affects the coordination of care. For example, if the student is having emotional problems in residence, is there a mechanism for the residential dean to speak with the off-campus therapist? What is the "need-to-know" information? "Need to know" is an important legal and administrative concept about communication between college personnel, mental health providers, and families. The guidelines for medical confidentiality are clear and strict. Confidentiality can be broken only if a student is deemed to be in "imminent danger to himself or others." If students feel their confidence is going to be broken, they will be reluctant to speak with clinicians. In a situation where there is concern about a student in residence who is seeing an off-campus provider, the outside provider has a "need to know" that the student is in trouble. If the outside provider feels the student may be in imminent danger, then the family or the head of residence has a "need to know" that the student is unstable or at risk. The information shared would be the concern about the student, not confidential details about diagnosis or content of therapy sessions. It is always best for students to initiate this contact or at least be told of the concerns by the appropriate parties.

This situation also raises questions about contracts. Residential staff need to know a student is safe living in the dorm. If the student presents one picture to the off-campus therapist and a much more alarming one to the resident adviser, how does communication occur? The situation is complicated further if psychotherapy is happening in one place and medication is being prescribed in another. Time must be allotted for coordination of care.

Frequent, ongoing, and clear communication between on-campus administrators and off-campus care providers is vital to the safe care of college students, but is too often overlooked in the complex and crowded health care system. Student cases are much more easily managed internally, adding one more strong reason to have adequate counseling services on campus.

Improving Counseling Services

There are many ways to improve mental health services to students. Here are a few that most counselors agree on:

- Put the counseling center in an area with other common services (like the student government office or the career counseling center) so students don't feel marked going there.

- Improve visibility and information.

- Provide anonymous screening on Web sites.

- Offer more immediate and accessible appointments.

- Provide telephone consultations.

- Offer evening and drop-in appointments.

- Consider using peer counselors as a link to the community and provide them with regular supervision and education.

- Reach out to parents to normalize the problems.

INNOVATIVE IDEAS

There are many wonderful programs across the country in large and small, public and private schools that are striving to meet the mental health crisis on college campuses. A small sampling of a few good ideas include the following:

- The University of Maryland offers for-credit courses to freshmen aimed at helping them deal with stress and time management, and similar other issues. They have found that 86 percent of the students who took the course returned for their sophomore year, compared with 69 percent of a comparable group who did not take the course. Such courses are now offered by about two-thirds of the nation's schools.[10]

- The University of Rochester has a unique way to counter freshman academic stress and encourage intellectual curiosity. Rochester now omits first-year grades from transcripts. The university also assigns volunteer faculty members to groups of twenty to forty students to demystify the faculty. The professors meet with the students informally and take fun outings to get to know each other.[11]

- The University of South Carolina, the University of Nevada-Reno, and Texas A&M offer in-depth seminars on the transition to college that help students get to know one professor really well.[12]

- MIT is putting together support teams of physicians, other health care professionals, and experienced counselors to spend time in the dorms socializing with the students and keeping an eye on them.[13] MIT also has a comprehensive alcohol screening and education program for incoming students.

- At Johns Hopkins, every student who visits the counseling center answers a battery of questions designed to identify those who should be placed on the center's "suicide tracking" list. In a recent year, 170 of the center's 756 clients were on the list. The Hopkins staff, which includes seven psychologists and three consulting psychiatrists, meets once a week to review the students' status.[14]

- In 2002 the American Foundation for Suicide Prevention (AFSP) launched a College Screen Project with second-semester freshmen at Emory University in Atlanta, Georgia. The project is scheduled to expand to the entire student body and eventually be open to universities across the country. In this program, a screening instrument, the Student Health Questionnaire, identifies students at risk for suicide and is accessible to them on-line through a secure Web site. Students are asked about symptoms of depression, suicidal ideation and attempts, anxiety, alcohol and drug abuse, eating disorders, and physical symptoms. A counselor reviews each questionnaire and, based on the responses to specific questions, sends an individually tailored assessment back to the student's log-in ID. Students whose responses suggest psychological difficulties are invited to come in for a face-to-face evaluation. The AFSP and college counselors are hoping that students will react favorably to this kind of initial anonymous dialogue.[15] (For more information about this program visit, www.afsp.org, or call 888–333-AFSP.)

All colleges must continue to examine their programs and look for better ways to serve their students. The Jed Foundation, a non-profit organization devoted to suicide prevention, has partnered with several colleges and universities to study college mental health programs. This is the first intercollegiate study to determine which kinds of programs make a measurable difference in reducing stigma and helping students get into care. More of this kind of shared effort among schools is needed to pool knowledge, experiences, insights, and resources.

THE WEB GENERATION

This generation of students is computer savvy and far more comfortable seeking information by logging on-line than by walking into a counseling center and asking for a printed pamphlet. For this reason, many colleges are finding an alternative way to address the students' needs by going to where they are: on-line. A few of the more popular sites include:

- Ulifeline.com. The Jed Foundation is the nation's first non-profit group dedicated solely to reducing suicide on college campuses. Founded by Phillip and Donna Satow, whose son Jed killed himself when he was a sophomore at the University of Arizona, the group seeks to expand the mental health safety net by offering on-line services for students. They have created this free, anonymous Web site customized to link students to their college counseling centers and a library of mental health information.

- Campusblues.com. This site, sponsored by a for-profit company, is designed specifically to help students find appropriate mental health services on or near their campuses.

- Outsidetheclassroom.com. This subscription site offers prevention-based health education with particular focus on high-risk drinking on college campuses.

In addition to sites created specifically for students, many colleges encourage their students to visit these popular sites for information on mental health:

- National Mental Health Association, www.nmha.org. This site offers information specifically for college students, with fact sheets on adjustment to life changes, anxiety disorders and depression, eating disorders and depression, alcohol and drug abuse and depression, and suicide and depression.
- National Institute of Mental Health, www.nimh.nih.gov. This site offers sound information on symptoms, diagnosis, and treatment of all mental health problems.
- WebMD, webmd.com. Students can search a term (such as *depression*, *anorexia*, or *anxiety disorders*) to find links to valuable and comprehensive information and resources.
- Mental Help Net, www.mentalhelp.net. This site is a comprehensive source of on-line mental health information, news, and resources.

Preventing Campus Suicide

The Jed Foundation and the National Mental Health Association offer the following checklist for universities to help safeguard against student suicides:[*]

- Is a screening program in place? Are on-site mental health services available?

- Is transitional support available for families of incoming students who already have been diagnosed as having a mental illness?

- Have faculty, staff, coaches, clergy, and student or resident advisers received training to identify suicidal behaviors?

- Are students educated to identify their own at-risk behaviors and those of their fellow students?

- Are campus health care providers trained to handle suicidal clients? If not, is training available?

- Have working relationships been established with community mental health providers to ensure appropriate off-site referrals?

- Is a crisis management plan in place if a suicide or other traumatic event occurs on campus?

-----

*The Jed Foundation, "Preventing Campus Suicide," http://www. jedfoundation.org, 2004. Reprinted with permission.

There is no question that it is very difficult to sort out developmental and existential concerns from serious mental illness. And even when we do, it is impossible to prevent mental health problems completely. Yet if a college community makes a commitment to the growth and development of its students, risks can be minimized and students can better make their way through this time of stress and transition and come out on the other end in one solid piece.

In the next chapter, you will learn how you, the parents of this new generation of college students, can help the counselors at your child's school protect and nurture optimum mental health.

6

What Can Parents Do?

Your role as a parent at this crucial developmental point is a complicated one. It is a time to let go with confidence and allow your children to try on new identities and interests. They need the opportunity to make mistakes and learn from them. At the same time, you are still their parent, and they need your guidance and wisdom to recognize problems and address them. You walk a fine line to balance these two tensions.

The goal is to balance these opposing needs to help your child navigate through the sometimes stormy college years and help him or her avoid an academic and personal shipwreck. There is a compelling reason for making this effort: your child's educational experience depends on it.

As this chapter explains, you'll find that you can best support your child's college experience by being aware of the stresses your child faces, trying a new way of communicating, encouraging problem-solving skills, knowing the warning signs of trouble, identifying a college's mental health resources, and creating an action plan to handle a potential crisis.

BE AWARE

What do you think is the biggest challenge facing your child today? Is it problems with sexual intimacy? Drug or alcohol use among peers? Choosing a major? Getting along with roommates? Before you answer this question, ask yourself if you have yet asked your child this question. The best way to find out what is on a person's mind is to ask. It is helpful to read this book and learn about the pressures on college students, but to use that information to help your child grow healthy and strong through the young adult years, you have to take time to find out your child's personal needs, challenges, fears, hopes, and expectations.

College is a time when we are asking our young adult children to think for themselves and develop emotionally and academically. Yet a big mistake we (parents, counselors, and administrators) make is trying to help, guide, and reach conclusions about them without the most important constituent at the table: the student. When we poll parents at student-parent orientation meetings, we find an enormous discrepancy between what parents think their students are concerned about and what students actually report. If you look at the factors that students themselves say impede academic success, they are not the difficulty of classes, or poor scheduling, or bad professors; they are almost always health and emotional factors.

When asked in the National College Health Assessment in 2002 to name factors that affected their academic performance (received an incomplete, dropped a course, received a lower grade in class, on an exam, or on an important project), 31 percent said *stress*, 21 percent said *sleep difficulties*, 20 percent said *concern for friend or family member*, 15 percent said *relationship problems*, 14 percent said *depression/anxiety*, and 10 percent said *alcohol use*.[1] Quite clearly, college difficulties are not solely caused by the challenging academic curriculum of higher education. Once you are tuned into that fact, you are in a far better position to be aware and prevent emotional and psychological problems from interfering with your child's education.

Student Thoughts

"I told my parents I needed to see a therapist when I came home over the summer. They found a good doctor, and I started going regularly. They never asked me anything about it. They're very hands off. When I asked them years later why they never asked any questions, they said they didn't want to interfere in my personal business and they figured that if I wanted them to know something, I'd tell them. Looking back now, I wish they had just talked to me even to say, 'If you want to tell us anything, we're here to listen.' I would have liked this kind of opening."

TRY A NEW WAY OF COMMUNICATING

Once our children have moved on into young adulthood, there are not many things we can physically do to keep them mentally healthy. We can't tuck them into bed insisting that they get a full eight hours of sleep each night and then prepare a nutritious, well-balanced breakfast in the morning. We can't call their professors to explain circumstances that may have made them unprepared for a test. We can't arrange play dates so they can make new friends. And we can't sign them up for extracurricular activities so they have a balanced schedule of work and play. So . . . what can we do?

The parental factor that most directly affects the mental health of a college student is communication. This may surprise you because I'm sure it seems as if your college-age children haven't listened to anything you've said for the last few years and it doesn't look promising that they will start again any time soon. But don't give up. College health surveys report that 72.5 percent of students say that they get most of their health information from their parents.[2] They do listen, especially if you take time to think about the way you communicate.

Consider that the goal of communication with young adults changes when they are in college. Instead of communicating solely to tell your child what to do, now it's helpful to use your conversations to strengthen your connections. In his book *Worry*, Dr. Ned Hallowell explains why connections are so important to emotional health:

> It is made up of the sum of all our connections: connections to our immediate family and extended family; connections to our past and our traditions; connections to our friends, neighbors, and colleagues; connections to institutions, organizations and country; connections to information and ideas and connections to whatever is transcendent, whether we call it Nature or God or some other name. This entity, the sum of all our meaningful connections, I call connectedness, and it is, in my opinion, the key to emotional health and the surest protection we have against the psychological ravages of worry.[3]

I often see students who are overcome with worry because they have lost some key element of connection in their lives: relationships ending badly; disappointment at not getting a role in a play; coming out to one's family and feeling rejected; a realization that a life goal (becoming a doctor, musician, lawyer, or something else) is not really what one wants to do. But I've also seen how those with a strong connection to their families are better able to get past difficult periods and move on.

This is especially apparent when we consider what can happen to students whose family culture is less open to dialogue and conversation. I was recently told about a student from Pakistan who had been talking frequently about jumping from his tenth-story dorm room. When he told a friend at lunch that he "knew how much aspirin you need to take to kill yourself" and then left the room saying he had to stop at the pharmacy, a series of events were triggered. His frightened friend told a professor. The professor had been to a workshop about recognizing students in distress (a communitywide effort to educate faculty and staff). He recognized this as a serious problem and called me for advice. Because we already knew the student and were very worried, I contacted his therapist, and we agreed to call the police to take him to the emergency room for an evaluation. It turned out that he wasn't "imminently" planning to kill himself.

The student was furious with me and the police. "Do you have any idea," he yelled, "what it's like in my culture to be hospitalized for a mental illness?" He felt he had shamed his family name and was horrified that his parents would find out. He experienced this as "being rudely dragged off to jail." How different life would be for this young man if he had the kind of family connection that would allow him to talk to his parents about the stress he was under.

Here are some communication tips that might help you strengthen your connection and keep your kids talking to you.

Model Strong Communication Skills

One of the big challenges your child will face is how to work out emotional differences with roommates and other peers. The way he does this depends largely on how you do this in your family confrontations. If you can't address things directly with your family members, or if everyone has to bury personal feelings in these discussions, your child will have the same patterns with peers, which increases the risk of developing anxiety, depression, or relationship problems.

That's why it is very important to model the communication skills that you want your child to learn—and it's not too late. Through the conversations you initiate, show that it is okay to talk about sensitive and emotional subjects. Show that it is okay to disagree and be upset, but that you can come back and continue the discussion at a later time without damaging or destroying the relationship.

Another way to model the kind of conversation you want your children to have with you is to talk about your own family history. Often parents decide not to burden their children with information about their own depression or other life challenges, and so the kids go off not knowing that depression is a part of their family history. Yet if one or both parents are depressed, there is a much higher incidence of depression in their children.

Be honest about mental health. Tell your kids if Mom or Dad or Aunt Sally or cousin Karem has gone to therapy or been on medication for psychological problems. Talk about friends who suffered from phobias such as fear of heights or bugs. Talk with empathy and understanding about the value of professional psychological help. These casual conversations help reduce the stigma of talking to you about emotional and psychological issues and seeking your help if needed.

College-age kids today are more sophisticated about mental health than any generation before them, but they still connect many psychological issues with shame and embarrassment. This became glaringly apparent to me when I formed my first eating disorder group at a college. Although I knew, based on the college's own research, that at least 4 percent of the students had eating disorders, no one showed up at the meetings for the first year and a half of our existence. Finally, I decided to change the name from "eating disorders group" to "eating concerns group" to make it sound less stigmatizing. Twenty women came to the next meeting—with "concerns," not "disorders." This simple word change and its dramatic results illustrates the importance of normalizing mental health issues by talking openly and frankly about problems in your family, among your friends, and in the world in general.

Similarly, we should be honest with our children about the history of our own lives that we bring into these interactions. If we were the victims of unwanted sexual advances in college or had a pattern of drinking too much, this may be the reason we are overly cautious when we see these patterns in our children. Being aware of the triggers for your own strong reactions and sharing some portion of them with your children helps them to understand the basis for your reactions, and it models the kind of open communication that is crucial at this time. Most people find that sharing personal and even painful experiences elicits a deeper level of sharing by others. If you are open about your own experiences and insecurities, your child may be more likely to share his own.

Listen, Listen, Listen

Most of us have developed the habit of conversing defensively. This means that we do not hear what our children are saying because we're too busy thinking about the flaws in their arguments and planning our response. Just as we stop listening, our children will also stop listening after the third or fourth word of our response because they are busy planning *their* response. I have had countless meetings with families where we could talk 'til the cows come home, and it is quite evident to me that everyone's views are divergent and are going to stay that way.

The best remedy for this ineffective pattern of communication is to learn to be an active listener. Four-time Emmy Award–winning television anchorman Steve Adubato explains in his book *Speak from the Heart* the importance of active listening, which I believe could dramatically improve communication between parents and their young adult children. In a recent conversation, Steve told me:

> The key to being a good listener is patience. It's hard to hold back and let another person make a point. But with effort, we can all learn to focus on what the speaker is saying rather than jumping ahead and anticipating what we think is going to be said. Turn yourself down and wait— don't interrupt, don't finish the other person's sentences,

and don't push ahead in the direction you want the conversation to go. And then when the other person is finished, rather than throwing out a defensive block, you might ask for clarification by saying, "What makes you say that?" Or you might decide to avoid an argument by saying something simple like, "I never thought about it that way." Such responses don't mean you agree with the other person or that you will do what this person suggests; they simply acknowledge that you have heard what the person said. This is a powerful communication tool.

Here are a few active listening tips adapted from Adubato's book that will help you keep the lines of communication open:[*]

- Count to two before responding to a statement.

- Don't jump ahead and finish another's thought.

- Give people the respect of letting them finish their own sentences.

- Listen in the moment and do not let your mind wander away.

- Listen with empathy when someone has a problem, and do not interrupt or jump in with a quick solution.

- Use nonverbal listening techniques, such as establishing good eye contact, leaning in just a bit, nodding occasionally, and smiling at the appropriate time.

- Use verbal prompts, such as, "Tell me more" and "That's interesting."

---

*Adapted with permission of The Free Press, a division of Simon & Schuster Adult Publishing Group, from *Speak from the Heart: Be Yourself and Get Results* by Steve Adubato, Ph.D., with Theresa Foy DiGeronimo. Copyright © 2002 by Steve Adubato. All rights reserved.

This advice supports my feelings that come from an old Alcoholics Anonymous expression that says, "Take the cotton out of your ears and stick it in your mouth." As your child approaches adulthood, it's time to do more listening and less talking.

Student Thoughts

"Things that seem obvious still should be said. Things such as: 'We love you.' 'We're proud of you.' 'We're glad you're our daughter.' I needed to hear those things when I was in college. But instead I heard, 'We expect you to get good grades.' 'We know you're capable of doing better.' 'I'm not paying this kind of money so you can party all night.'"

Talk About Important Issues Without Lecturing, Dictating, Judging, or Criticizing

Even when we listen with care, we like to believe that as parents, we know what is best for our children. That's why when your children were younger, you could solve most of their problems by telling them what to do. If they were tired during the day, you told them to go to bed earlier that night. If they got poor grades at school, you told them to give up TV and study harder.

But now, the truth is that sometimes we don't know what's best, so it's time to avoid controlling words like *must* and *ought* that shift the dynamics of the conversation back to a parent–young child exchange. It is extremely important to have balanced, open conversations with your child that build a mature relationship and guide (not push) her toward choices that promote strong mental health.

If there is tension in your family because your plans for your child are clashing with your child's plans, your job isn't to make him see that you're right and he's wrong. Your job is to have a conversation that offers your point of view as something to think about. You may feel that the amount of the paycheck is the most important thing to consider. Or you may feel that the opportunity for advancement within a particular field is vital. There's nothing right or wrong about these beliefs; they are simply your point of view. You can help your child understand your views by presenting them in ways that are not judgmental, critical, or dictatorial. If you do this, you'll be able to play a vital support role by listening, asking thoughtful questions, and steering your child in the direction where he is most likely to find his own answers.

Here's a typical scenario of conflicting dreams and how the parent and child might approach it.

Let's say that Frank, John Student's father, is a successful lawyer, and law has been a satisfying career for him. His own father had a difficult and financially shaky life as a musician. So when John shows a strong interest in music, Frank recalls his own childhood; he discourages John's music studies and strongly advises his son to keep focusing on prelaw. Depending on the way this message is conveyed, this advice can be helpful or an invitation for disaster.

Keeping in mind that part of the journey of being a college student is to try on identities and ideas, if Frank pushes too hard, it will probably lead John in the opposite direction. But if Frank lets John know his personal experience with this and urges John to keep in mind the potential instability of his chosen lifestyle, John has the benefit of the information yet the freedom to make his own choices. John might make mistakes and poor decisions along the way, at least from his dad's perspective, but we all make mistakes and usually learn from them. Because we're no longer in charge, we have to learn how to strike a balance between supporting the things we believe in strongly while keeping an open mind and open ears to the needs and ideas of our children. That is how we can help them to grow.

The goal here is to help John develop a process and philosophy of life that is *his* but also to accept the responsibility of the consequences of those choices. If you can predict where things might lead or explain what your concerns are—without lecturing, dictating, judging, or criticizing—your children may be more open to considering your ideas.

Or they might not. Newscaster Diane Sawyer spoke at the Wellesley College graduation several years ago and talked about how important the "detours" in her life were, times when she wasn't focused on a predetermined life plan. Sometimes young adults need to make their own mistakes and learn from them. No amount of demanding or begging will change that.

QUICK TIPS FOR GOOD COMMUNICATION

Here are some communication tips you can use to help support your child's mental health:

* *Keep open communication going on a regular basis.* If your child is free with the e-mails or text messages on her cell phone and loves to keep in close touch, that's great for both of you. But if your child chooses to try on independence by cutting off daily communication, make an effort to set up a regular contact time. You might suggest that every Sunday, for example, you will call to say hello.

Creating a communication routine is good for you because you won't feel intrusive when you call, and it's good for your child because if he were to stay out of touch for weeks on end and then need to talk about a problem, it would be too difficult to break the silence and admit he needs your advice.

* *Let your child know that she does not have to protect you from her problems.* You might assume she knows this, but it's something you should say out loud. You might say something like this: "I know you expect to do well in your classes and make many good friends, but I want you to know that if you should ever want to talk about a problem or if you should feel unhappy or sad, I'm here to listen and support you. You don't ever have to hide your feelings from me. Okay?"

This is the kind of message that students tell me means a lot to them, but I've noticed that they are quick to forget those words of support when trouble hits. So say it once, send them off, and then remember to say it again and again as they move through their college years.

• *Agree to disagree.* When you find yourself going in circles with your child around the same point over and over, it may be time to accept the fact that you may always have different perspectives on the subject. In this case, you might try a new communication approach that does not focus on who's right and who's wrong. You might say, "Since we probably aren't ever going to agree about this, can we agree to disagree and find some middle ground?"

Sometimes that acknowledgment and suggestion alone will remove some of the emotional intensity. In black-and-white situations like deciding on a course of study, or whether to transfer to another school, or take a junior year abroad, or live at home, in a dorm, or an off-campus apartment, the goal is to think of some solution where you both can feel listened to and respected. For example, if your concern is about academic performance because of a living situation, can you agree to a trial period with some expected results and consequences if the results aren't met? This kind of solution gives you both a part of what you want.

• *Take a time-out.* If emotions get out of hand while talking to your child, you might say, "We're probably too upset to talk about this right now. Let's take a break and come back to this discussion later." Then set a specific time to come back to the discussion, and be sure that you do. If you don't follow up, you give the opposite message: you are going to sweep this under the rug or don't take it seriously.

ENCOURAGE PROBLEM-SOLVING SKILLS

No matter how much we educate ourselves about mental health issues and no matter how much we work on our communication skills, our children are still likely to hit the occasional trouble spot during their college years. Life is like that. When this happens, how will they respond? How will you respond?

Like all of us, your young adult children are more likely to feel overwhelmed by daily challenges when they feel powerless. But their ability to feel empowered and to take charge of difficult situations has a lot to do with how *you* react to their problems. Stop and think for a minute: What would be your first plan of action if your child called home right now and told you that she can't study or sleep because her roommate is partying and keeping her up?

You are a loving parent, so of course you want to get involved and help your child with this problem. You might call a college administrator to complain. You might want to talk directly to the roommate. You might call the resident adviser and insist on a room change. But none of these actions is best for your child. If you initiate the calls, contacts, or complaints, your child loses a very important opportunity to do this herself.

As you're about to offer a solution, stop yourself. First, try to get the facts about exactly what is going on, and then help your child brainstorm her own solutions. Teach her to weigh the pros and cons of each option, and then decide for herself what to do—all the while trying your best to keep your answer to the problem to yourself.

This is easier to do when the problem is a typical one like a noisy roommate, but far more difficult when the issues are more extreme (lifestyle differences such as attitudes about sexuality, sleep patterns, or divergent religious views and emotional stresses such as eating disorders, depression, or alcohol or drug issues). Yet the same guideline applies. These issues can be a distraction from academic focus and cause worry or even alarm on the part of your child. But these are issues your children are going to face throughout their lives. They will run into people who aren't reasonable or who have emotional problems in the workplace, living next door, or in the family of their spouse or significant other. Part of being in college is to learn about different philosophies and lifestyles and to learn how to problem-solve when life presents tough problems.

It is important to recognize these situations as opportunities for learning about how to deal with unexpected events and life relationships. If you jump in to solve problems for your child, once again, an opportunity is lost.

I am not saying that you should stay out of a dangerous situation such as a roommate who is selling cocaine out of your child's dorm room. What I am suggesting is that you help your child think about how to approach this problem and get him to weigh the pros and cons of possible solutions. Let him come up with options:

"Maybe I could tell my roommate that if he doesn't stop selling drugs, I will have to report him to the resident adviser."

"I could change rooms, but if I do that, what will I tell the housing office to justify this?"

"Or maybe I should call the police."

Then ask him to evaluate the consequences of each one and decide which is best. This gives your child the chance to problem-solve and find a solution that will work for him rather than relying on your solution.

It isn't easy to hand over the decision-making power. The tendency to become Mr. or Ms. Fixit is strong because it tends to bring you into the more familiar parent-child pattern of relating. It is important to be aware of the need for changing parameters in the relationships and to try to be helpful but avoid going back to old patterns of relating. When problems pop up, remind yourself that they offer your adult child opportunities to practice mature decision-making skills. If your child actively moves to solve his or her problems but is ignored or stonewalled by administrators, it is then time to ask if your son or daughter would like you to step in. Even in college, it sometimes takes a phone call or visit from parents to make things happen.

KNOW THE WARNING SIGNS

You know your child better than anyone else on earth. So even after he heads off to college, you should still keep alert to signs of change, upset, and distress. If you notice symptoms of the following problems (which are more fully discussed in Chapter Four) or simply sense that something is wrong, don't wait—but don't panic either. Start a dialogue with your child that will open the door to support and help.

Symptoms of Depression

Major depression shows itself in a combination of symptoms that interfere with normal life functioning. Clinicians believe that depression should be considered when five or more of the following symptoms (including one or both of the first two symptoms) are present over a two-week period:[4]

- Depressed mood most of the day

- Markedly diminished interest or pleasure in all or almost all activities

- Significant weight loss when not dieting, weight gain, or decrease or increase in appetite

- Insomnia or increased sleeping

- Restlessness or slowing down of body movements

- Fatigue or loss of energy

- Feelings of worthlessness or excessive or inappropriate guilt

- Diminished ability to think or concentrate, or indecisiveness

- Recurrent thoughts of death (not just fear of dying), recurrent thoughts of suicide, or a suicide attempt

Symptoms of Sleep Disorder

Sleep problems may be an early signal of emotional upset. Talk to your children about their sleep habits and listen for these tell-tale symptoms:

- Difficulty falling asleep

- Early morning wakening

- Waking up during the night

- Exceptional trouble getting out of bed in the morning

Symptoms of Substance Abuse

The National Institute on Alcohol Abuse and Alcoholism tells parents to watch for these signs of alcohol abuse.[5] They are also signs of other forms of drug abuse:

- Lower grades

- Never available or reluctant to talk with you

- Unwilling to talk about activities with friends

- Trouble with campus authorities

- Serious mood changes

Symptoms of Generalized Anxiety Disorder

There is a difference between normal feelings of concern about college academics and social activities and the kind of worry that accompanies a generalized anxiety disorder. When your child talks to you about college life, listen for these signs that she may need help:[6]

- Constant, exaggerated worrisome thoughts and tension about everyday routine life events and activities, lasting at least six months

- Almost always anticipating the worst even though there is little reason to expect it

- Worrisome thoughts accompanied by physical symptoms, such as fatigue, trembling, muscle tension, headache, or nausea

Symptoms of Eating Disorders: Anorexia

Signs of anorexia are as much in the obvious appearance of weight loss as in what your child says about her eating habits. Watch and listen for these behaviors and attitudes:[7]

- The fear of being fat even when at or below normal weight

- Refusal to maintain body weight by restricting intake, leading to a weight loss of more than 15 percent of normal body weight

- A distortion of body size and shape that causes even underweight sufferers to feel fat or obese

- In women, the absence of at least three consecutive menstrual cycles

Symptoms of Eating Disorders: Bulimia

Signs of bulimia are tough to monitor from a distance. Still, keep these symptoms in mind when you talk to your child about eating habits:[8]

- Recurrent episodes of binge eating (at least two times a week for at least three months)

- A feeling of complete loss of control during the eating binges

- Persistent overconcern with body shape and size

- Regular engaging in self-induced vomiting, use of laxatives or diuretics, strict dieting or fasting, or vigorous exercise in order to prevent weight gain

Symptoms of Suicidal Thinking

Talking about suicide and other specific changes in behaviors are often outright warning signs. Pay attention to these signs of potential suicide, and take them seriously:

- Talking openly about committing suicide, or talking indirectly about "wanting out" or "ending it all"

- Expressing a sense of hopelessness

- Withdrawing from friends and social activities

- Taking unnecessary or life-threatening risks

- Giving away personal possessions

- Losing interest in personal appearance

- Increasing use of alcohol or drugs

- Having attempted suicide in the past, however half-heartedly

BE PROACTIVE WITH THE COLLEGE

There is approximately a one in two chance that your child is going to have trouble with depression or alcohol problems at college. While many students get a handle on both of these problems over time, one would think with a 50 percent likelihood of trouble that families would be paying closer attention to the available emotional and medical resources at the college of their choice.

Sadly, this isn't the case. But you can change that. You can protect your child (even from a distance) by paying attention to the quality of the mental health resources offered by your child's school. When parents start asking more questions and demanding parity for mental health programs, schools will come to realize that safety and emotional well-being are important considerations for increasingly informed consumers and will provide appropriate resources to address these issues.

Certainly a school with inadequate chemistry labs or athletic facilities will upgrade its resources to remain competitive; however, most schools don't think of their health and wellness programs as primary selling points. But as parents and students become more educated consumers, I believe they should. For most parents, a primary concern is that their child gets a solid education in a setting where he or she will grow and prosper academically and emotionally. With the increased awareness of the pervasiveness of common stress and mental health problems, parents should and will be asking about support resources. Schools that don't provide a supportive, safe environment will face more scrutiny by families. I believe that a good measure of a quality school is the wisdom to recognize that emotional and academic development go hand in hand.

Be Honest

To help the school give your child the best care possible, you must be honest about your child's mental health history. It is a common, but mistaken, idea that not mentioning previous mental health problems on college health forms affords an incoming student a "fresh start." Coming to college is a fresh start, but the burden of having these problems and keeping them secret ironically often makes them worse. The student feels more isolated and gets the sense that she is different and must hide her problems.

Let the college know if your child has had psychological difficulties or needs any special services. This is an ideal opportunity to be proactive. You might say, "Our daughter has had panic attacks in the past, and we'd like to know what resources you have to help her if this happens again." She will not be singled out due to this information, and she will not suffer any academic consequences or discrimination. But she will know that there are people at the college who can help her, and she will be given the information she needs to manage her own mental health.

College is not a fresh start from mental health issues. They come with the student and need to be acknowledged and cared for, especially since the stress of college can make them worse, not better.

You can also be proactive and work with the school's counselors if you notice symptoms of a mental health problem (like those discussed in Chapter Four and listed previously in this chapter) after your child is enrolled in school. Although your child is an adult and you cannot make the counselors contact your child, you can call and explain your reasons for worry and ask about available support services. This may irritate your child, but if you explain that you're a thousand miles away and are worried, he will most likely come to see that the call was made out of love. You can then pass on the information you obtained and encourage your child to follow up at the counseling center.

Getting parental permission to admit and treat mental health problems is psychologically very important for many students. They don't want to admit they aren't strong and independent, but if those who love them give the message that seeking help is not a sign of weakness but rather a sign of maturity, they are far more likely to take care of their emotional self.

Know Confidentiality Rules

You may be paying your child's tuition bills and medical insurance costs. You may stay involved in your child's life and be proactive about his or her health and education. But it's very possible that you will be left in the dark if your child seeks mental health services at school.

When eighteen year olds got the right to vote in 1972, new federal privacy regulations made students the guardians of their own academic, health, and disciplinary records too. This has had positive and negative repercussions. An article in the *New York Times Magazine* noted that across the country, state courts have found that colleges are not obliged to protect adult students from their own stupidity. As an example, the article states: "In Colorado, courts concluded that it wasn't a university's duty to keep trampolines off frat-house lawns to prevent drunk students from falling off them. In Louisiana, the courts found that a university had no special obligation to prevent students from sledding downhill on garbage-can lids and crashing into light poles."[9] These rules made many states and college administrators assume that the common law doctrine of in loco parentis (legally standing in the place of the parents) was dead.

But uncertainty remains. If the student is responsible for himself or herself, does the school have an obligation to tell the student's family about physical or mental problems? Of course, college counselors want to have contact with families to provide a better support network for students, but at the same time we recognize this would have a chilling effect on students' willingness to seek care if they can't depend on confidentiality. At this time, the rules of medical confidentiality are quite stringent and clear: unless students are in imminent danger of hurting themselves or others or are completely unable to care for themselves, doctors and psychologists cannot share clinical information with anyone, parents or college officials, without permission from the students, assuming they are over age eighteen.

Still, college counselors are often caught between a rock and a hard place as we await the outcome of the yet-undecided Shin case, which may change the existing privacy and confidentiality rules. The Shins' $27 million lawsuit alleges that MIT was negligent for not telling them that their daughter, Elizabeth, was suicidal. If they win their case, the rules of confidentiality could change.

But at this time, do not assume that you will be told if your child is given a prescription medication for depression, or if your child is regularly seeing a therapist to address an eating disorder, or is seeking psychiatric consultation for any other reason. This is why it is so vitally important that you develop a strong system of communication with your child so that he will be able to tell you himself if he needs help.

> ### Student Thoughts
>
> "What do I wish my parents had done? I would have liked them to reiterate that they thought I was fabulous and would still have thought I was fabulous even if I did poorly in college; that the reason they thought I was fabulous was not related to the fact that I was smart or accomplished; that I was not to blame for any emotional problems that I was having; and that they would help me and be supportive of me getting the best possible care. That's what I wish."

CHECKLISTS OF QUESTIONS

In this information age of increasingly educated consumers, parents can speak with their checkbooks and choose schools that provide the best balance for the psychological needs of their children. Use your consumer power to choose schools that give parity to mental health issues and continue to push for adequate mental health resources in the school you select.

When your child is applying to college, make an effort to attend the college open houses offered to prospective students, and look for signs that mental health is an issue the school takes seriously. Is there a booth set up by the counseling center where you can talk to someone? Among the many handouts offered, is there information about counseling services, student health services, and student issues such as time management and stress management?

As you continue to investigate each school, use this list of questions to help you evaluate the resources and activities that help ease the stress of the college years:

- What kind of freshman orientation does the school have?

- Is there a structured way in which students can meet peers?

- How do students choose roommates? How are roommate disputes handled?

- Are there social activities for students on the weekends, or does the campus empty out?

- What tutoring resources are available if a student is having learning difficulties in a particular subject?

- How do students get academic advisement for choosing courses and a major?

- Does the school provide resources for student wellness: workshops for dealing with stress, or recognizing depression, or handling eating concerns?

- Does the school's Web site have links for information about mental health?

If your son or daughter is in recovery from a drug or alcohol problem, you should ask questions about how prospective schools support students in this situation. At Rutgers University in New Jersey, nearly two dozen students in recovery live together and help one another stay sober. Augsburg College in Minnesota, Dana College in Nebraska, and Texas Tech University all have organized support programs in place. The University of Texas at Austin has a Center for Students in Recovery, which offers a support system along with a three-credit academic course titled "Complete Recovery 101." You can get more information about programs like these through the Association of Recovery Schools at www.recoveryschools.org.

Once your child has zeroed in on a school (or is down to the final cut), it's time to make direct inquiries. To start, call the school's main number and ask for the school counseling service. Tell the person who answers the phone that you have a number of questions about the school's counseling program and would like to be connected with a person who can answer them.

This simple phone call will give you some insight into the workings of the counseling center. If you get voice mail, or the runaround, or an uninformed person, you'll know that this is the kind of response your child will get if he or she ever needs these services.

If your child has a diagnosed mental health disorder, it is very important for you to evaluate the college's counseling services. If you do this when looking for a college, this information will help you and your child choose a place that will give proper support and services. If your child is already in college and has a diagnosed disorder, these are questions you should ask so that you will know what services your child can and cannot count on. If you know the school has limited counseling services, for example, you'll understand that you need to find a psychiatrist in the surrounding town or make arrangements to bring your child home on a regular basis for follow up with her home-town physician. The goal is to be prepared. As some say, it is best to plan for the worst and hope for the best.

When you do talk to someone from the school's counseling center, these are some questions you might ask:

- What are the counseling resources? Is there a separate fee for using them?

- Are there limits on the number of counseling sessions per student?

- Is there a psychiatrist available to prescribe medication if necessary?

- What is the staff-to-student ratio for counselors? (The national average is 1 per 1,574.)

- How long is the waiting list in November and March (when typically counseling centers are busiest)?

- Does the school have an infirmary where students who need brief or extended care can stay when hospitalization isn't required?

- Who should a student call if there is an emergency in the dormitory?

- Can my child's medication be monitored, and is there a separate cost for that?

- In what circumstances would a student be referred to a health provider or hospital outside the college community?

- What local facilities does the college refer students to?

- What kinds of mental health services outside the college community will the school insurance cover? (Be sure to check with your own provider also. Your child may need to come home to see a participating provider.)

- Have the faculty, staff, and residential staff been trained to identify and properly refer students struggling with mental health issues?

- How does a student contact the counseling service center to make an appointment?

- What are your guidelines on confidentiality? Under what circumstances would I be contacted?

If your child has no history of mental health problems, you might feel awkward asking these questions, both when searching for a college and once your child has landed in a chosen school. Unfortunately, there is still a stigma attached to mental health disorders, and I know that parents worry that if they ask me about our counseling services, I will assume their child has psychological problems and this will send up a red flag marking their child as a high-risk student. They also worry that this misinformation will somehow get back to professors, coaches, or friends and label the child as a potential "whacko."

I understand why they feel this way, and I know that it keeps many parents from getting the information they should have. There are two things to keep in mind if you have these concerns. First, there are very strict confidentiality laws that prohibit every licensed mental health counselor from talking to *anyone* about a particular student. They cannot call professors, resident directors, or coaches and tell them to watch out for Johnny because he may be having some emotional problems. Without the student's written permission, all information is confidential. Second, if this does not ease your concern, remember that you do not have to identify yourself to get information. You can call as "Mrs. Smith" and ask these very general questions.

It is vital to have this information at hand in the event of a crisis. When your child calls in a panic with no idea where to turn or what to do, you'll be glad you've gathered this information in advance and know who to turn to.

Be Prepared

Keep these emergency phone numbers with you, and give a copy to your child to keep in his or her wallet:

- College health care center
- College counseling center
- College resident director

- College dean of freshmen students (or for an upperclassman, the dean of students)

- Campus police

- Local city police

- After-hours emergency contact

CRISIS ACTION PLAN

The phone rings. It's your child, and she needs emergency help right now. What do you do?

The first thing to do is to tell her, "I'm so glad you called me. I want to be here for you and help you figure out how to get the help you need." With that calm, supportive base established, follow these steps:

1. *Get the facts.* Ask, "What exactly is the problem?" "What are the specific symptoms, behaviors, actions, drug or alcohol abuse, or self-medications that are going on right now?" "When did it start?" "Whom have you spoken to so far about this among friends, professors, or counselors?" "How are you feeling right now?"

2. *Acknowledge your limitations.* If your child is at a school far from home, you are not in a strong position to give hands-on help. After listening to the problem, you might say, for example, "I've read about the symptoms of depression, and it sounds like you have about six of the possible nine symptoms. I don't know if you're depressed, but I think you should go talk to a professional who can help you sort things out."

3. *Decide who to contact.* If your child is sounding suicidal and you fear for his safety, assess the level of danger. If you feel it is an authentic, immediate crisis, call the local police in the college community so your child can be transported to the hospital.

If it is a serious crisis but you feel it can be handled by counselors on campus, make arrangements to get an immediate evaluation through emergency channels. In this case, you have to assume that your child cannot make mature or responsible decisions, and it's appropriate for you to take charge while telling your child exactly what you are going to do. Due to confidentiality laws, when you call for help, you may come up against someone who says he or she can't talk to you because your child is an adult. If this happens, remember that although health care providers cannot talk to you, you can certainly talk to them. Get the name of the person resisting your request, and ask for a supervisor. Explain the emergency nature of your call, and aggressively go up the ladder all the way to the counseling director or head of campus security if necessary, until you get someone who will arrange for an immediate evaluation or transport to a nearby hospital. Then ask for a return call to keep you informed about your child's status. Although you may not be able to get a medical status report, you can certainly expect to be told if your child is in a safe place.

If the problem is less urgent but still serious and you feel your child needs immediate attention, encourage him to call for emergency help (or if he is too distressed, ask him if he would like you to call). Contact the resident director of your child's dormitory (in most schools, this person lives in the dormitory, is on call twenty-four hours a day, and is trained to respond to emergencies) or if the call comes during office hours, call the school's counseling center. If your child lives off-campus, he must call 911, or you can call the local city police number.

4. *Arrange a meeting with a mental health care counselor for an assessment.* If you get the crisis telephone call in the middle of the night or on the weekend when the campus health center is closed, arrange for transfer to an off-campus emergency facility. This is why it is so important to have contact phone numbers on hand before an emergency; it is likely that the panic call will come when the

main college switchboard is closed and you cannot easily find the people you need.

If your child calls you on a weekday or can wait until the morning, have him call the school's counseling center and ask for an appointment to see a counselor. He will have to explain the urgency of his needs if he wants an immediate appointment.

5. *Arrange for a return call.* Get your child to promise to call you back when he or she is safe and in the care of a responsible adult.

6. *Ask your child to give the counselor permission to speak to you.* Because your child is a legal adult, his medical records are confidential. A counselor cannot talk to you about your child's problem unless your child gives written permission.

7. *Identify the contact person.* Once you've determined that your child is safe and in good hands, find out who will be coordinating care and will be your liaison at the school. If your child is moved to off-campus care (a hospital or local psychiatrist), identify who you can contact for information (with the permission of your child).

8. *Monitor follow-up.* Make certain that your child's case is not dropped once the emergency passes. He should get follow-up care appointments. There should also be follow-up between all health care providers both on and off campus.

Create a time line to make decisions. Don't rush to remove your child from school or run to his side. You might decide with your child, for example, to wait five days to see how the situation evolves and then see what he wants to do next.

9. *Decide as a group what steps to take next.* Ask for a conference call with you, your child, and the counselor as soon as possible. Talk together to determine the next steps, and find out what you can do to help. Discuss if it is appropriate for you to come to the school or for your child to come home.

10. *Keep in touch* at least once daily to give support, without sounding panicked yourself.

RECOGNIZE YOUR LIMITS

Although strong and open parent-child communication and proactive involvement with the college are absolutely necessary to help young adults avoid mental health problems, you will always walk that fine line during your child's college years between guiding a young adult who needs your help and stepping back to let him or her grow in independence. It's not always easy to do as one former student recently reminded me.

Kaylee had battled an eating disorder during her college years and now, with a satisfying job, is in recovery. Looking back on her situation, she says: "Parents need to understand that unless their son or daughter wants to change, wants to recover, nothing they say will make it happen. No matter how much you talk, argue, plead, or yell at them, it won't work. My sister recently began to have an emotional problem, and when I would try to talk to her about it, that's when I realized how frustrating it had been for my parents. It opened my eyes to what they had been through and I realized it was tough."

Yes, good parenting can be very tough.

As you work to give your children the information they need to stay psychologically strong during these difficult years, show them the next chapter. It is written for college students and gives them specific tips to manage stress so they will stand proudly on graduation day with both diploma and good mental health in hand.

7

For Students Only

There's a lot of good to be said about going to college. Besides the obvious opportunities for advanced education and the boost in your career potential, college gives you a fresh start with infinite possibilities. You have a whole new world to explore and enjoy. And you finally get a major dose of long-awaited freedom.

But the truth is that sometimes the college years can be really tough. You've left behind your established relationships, elements of self-confidence, and high school identity. And now you're expected to stand alone and be responsible, fun, cheerful, independent, smart, and studious.

Some college students manage these expectations just fine and get through school with a minimal amount of stress. But more and more students are finding the pressure and expectations difficult to handle, and many of those students deal with the uncertainty and stress with self-destructive coping mechanisms that compound their problems.

The most painful thing I experience as a clinician is witnessing the amount of suffering that students endure before seeking help. They often suffer alone, which compounds the problem. They don't want to burden parents or friends, and ironically that selfless desire increases their isolation, which worsens the problem. They haven't learned yet that sharing stress invites others to share their own stresses, solidifies connections, and provides opportunities for new perspectives and solutions.

I don't think I can explain this state of pain and confusion better than Kara did in the following article that she wrote to her college newspaper when she was in her first year of graduate school as a business student. (With permission, I've changed names to protect the privacy of the individuals involved.)

Being Depressed at UBS

I almost took my life three times during my first year at University Business School. And I was just as normal as you when I started here. I was really excited to come to UBS. The first month or two were filled with new friends, and great challenges. But then one day I noticed that I wasn't feeling like myself anymore. I didn't think much of it at the time, and it was no big deal.

Then it happened again. Soon I started to feel sad all of the time. I kept asking myself if I was really enjoying school here. Was everyone happy besides me? Why wasn't I having any fun?

Maybe it was because the weather had started to turn cold and gloomy.

Perhaps I was overwhelmed by the zillions of recruiters calling me, when I was already confused about "what I wanted to do with the rest of my life." Maybe I was starting to get sick of seeing the same 80 people every single day, and that annoying guy in the corner who pointed his finger whenever he raised his hand. Whatever it was that began it all . . . everything else was just piling up and making it even worse.

I began to find myself crying myself to sleep. I didn't want to go out anymore. I stopped exercising, which only made me feel worse, both physically and emotionally. I started questioning everything I would say in class. I couldn't focus on what the professor was saying. I felt like every case I read was longer than *War and Peace*.

I started hating myself for ever applying to UBS. And then one day I just didn't get out of bed. I stayed in bed all day and just cried and cried.

Then a strange calmness came over me. "Everything would be all right if I just killed myself," I thought. "Then it would all go away." So I made my way to the bridge and stood there for nearly an hour. But I couldn't jump off.

The next three weeks were the worst weeks of my life. I would spend class periods thinking of how to kill myself, and how that was the real answer to all of my problems. I skipped class just because I didn't want to get out of bed. I went to the bridge two more times. I wasn't scared anymore. I was ready to die and I didn't care.

A friend saved me, without even realizing it. She thought I looked sad and suggested that I go see Dr. Patricia Miller, Director of MBA Program Support Services. That was the beginning of my road back to recovery.

Dr. Miller realized that I was severely depressed and she got me some help. I went and saw Dr. Nicholas Johnson, a psychiatrist at UBS. I didn't want to go at first. I was a UBS student, and I wasn't about to go see a shrink. God forbid if anyone ever found out. I was supposed to be strong—a winner. Winners don't go see psychiatrists or admit that they're depressed. I felt like a complete failure for going to see Dr. Johnson.

But he helped me realize that I wasn't. Every year the staff of the Mental Health Services Department sees about 140 UBS students. That's about 1 out of every 11 people. That's 7 people in your section alone. Not to mention the fact that there are many UBS students who go see outside providers without ever going through University Health Services.

I began to re-focus my life. Although I didn't feel comfortable telling any of my friends that I was struggling, I did tell my parents. They, along with Dr. Miller, would call or email me every day to cheer me up and encourage me. I began forcing myself to exercise no matter how bad I felt. I sought out tutoring from some second years. And I began taking anti-depressants. That was a very difficult hurdle to overcome. I thought that surely I must be a loser if I was so depressed that I had to use medication to get better. I was scared of the side effects and of the possibility that people might find out. But once again Dr. Johnson calmed my fears.

Although I don't know the exact numbers, I do know that you walk by someone every day that's using Zoloft or Prozac. You don't even know it. And do you know why? Because the medicines work; and no one can tell the difference. Not everyone has to take medicine, but if you do, it's nothing to be ashamed of or scared of. It simply means that you need a boost to get your positive brain waves going again.

Combining the medicine with daily exercise made all of the difference in the world. Within a month, I felt happy again from time to time. Within 2 months, I felt happy most of the time. Within 3 months, I was me again.

Why did I write this article you ask? Because I want you to know that it's okay to be depressed but it's not okay to stay depressed. That may sound stupid or simple to you if you feel fine. But it was exactly what I needed to hear when I wanted to end my life. I also want to remind you that it's okay to ask for help.

And I pray that you do. You ask questions in class all the time. Why should you feel any embarrassment about asking for help when the answers provided are a million times more important than any ones you'll ever hear in class?

I chose not to submit my name because this is a very private experience. However, it's not an unusual experience. It's all around you. Please take the time to look out for your friends and notice when they seem down.

But most of all, take care of yourself. UBS is an amazing place full of phenomenal people and fantastic experiences. The staff and faculty here want to help you make sure that you can benefit from every aspect of the UBS experience. You can only do this if you are healthy and happy.

Remember that I started out feeling fine too. Get help before you sink as low as I did. Your life and UBS are too precious to miss out on.

It took courage for Kara to write this article, but the results have been worth it. Every year the student newspaper runs this piece during National Depression Screening Week, and after it is printed, a number of students always come into the counseling center saying, "I have all the same symptoms that were in that letter but didn't put it all together."

I'd like this chapter to help you put it all together. Earlier in this book, I addressed my comments to parents and college counselors and administrators. But the key message is for *you* because only you know what the pressure feels like. And in the end, only you can really make a difference in the way you experience your college years.

I'm offering the following advice and tips to help you do three things: prevent, recognize, and deal with mental health problems so that they interfere as little as possible with these years and help you develop the tools you'll need to have a more fulfilling adult life.

A Good Book

For more information on college life, I recommend a wonderful book by Richard Light, *Making the Most of College*.* In this book, Light surveys students about their most important experiences in college and expands in great detail on several of the areas I briefly mention in this chapter.

———
*R. Light, *Making the Most of College* (Cambridge, Mass.: Harvard University Press, 2001).

TAKE CARE OF YOURSELF

I'm going to sound like your mother here, but it really is important to take care of yourself by exercising, eating, and sleeping reasonable amounts on a daily basis. I estimate that 50 percent of the students who come to the Harvard counseling center are struggling because they have neglected one or all of these basics.

Exercise Often

Some students are very active physically. These are the ones who belong to collegiate or intramural athletic teams, or like to work out to keep themselves in shape. But others (in fact, most) find that they spend the majority of the day sitting in classes, and then sitting in front of their computers, and then sitting to read textbooks, and then sitting in the cafeteria, and then sitting in front of the TV.

If this describes your day, take a look at this list of just some of the things exercise could be doing for you if you changed a few daily habits:

> *Exercise can alleviate tension and elevate mood.* Sustained movement at target heart rate causes your body to produce greater amounts of the beta-endorphins, which counter stress and depression and help you to sleep.

Exercise can improve alertness. A thirty-minute round of aerobic exercise has been shown to improve short-term memory and increase mental performance.

Exercise can give you increased energy. Energy levels increase as the muscles become better able to use oxygen, the heart's pumping capacity improves, and the resting pulse slows. This allows the heart to pump the same amount of blood with fewer beats.

Exercise can stimulate the immune system. This will help you ward off the bacterial and viral germs that congregate in the cramped quarters of college classes and dormitories.

Exercise keeps off excess weight. Just eight to twelve minutes of aerobic activity can decrease appetite, boost the metabolic rate so you continue to burn calories at a higher rate for up to two days, and build lean tissue, which occupies less space than the replaced fat.

I know you're busy, but you don't have to spend an hour in the fitness center or the gym every day to keep yourself healthy. Just make a conscious effort to find ways to keep moving:

- Take a longer route to walk to your classes.

- Always use the stairs instead of the elevator.

- Park your car, if you have one, far from the building.

- Find small, easy ways to get your heart pumping a couple of times a week, even if it's simply to run in place for ten minutes while you're watching a TV show in your room.

If you do these things, it won't take long at all to feel the difference in your overall physical and mental health.

Eat Well to Stay Strong

Everybody knows about the "freshman 15." But to keep yourself healthy, you need to understand where that extra weight comes from and why poor eating habits can interfere with a good college experience. (I told you I was going to sound like your mother here.)

Think about it. What did you eat today that actually had nutrients in it that will give your body strength, stamina, and good health? The students I see who complain of being overweight, run-down, sluggish, or exhausted usually admit that their meals consist mostly of high-calorie junk. Pizza, hamburgers, french fries, and ice cream are the main diet for many students.

Whether you live on campus or are running in and out of your home as you commute to school, Mom and Dad aren't organizing well-balanced, nutritious meals for you anymore. You're in charge of what you eat, so be sure (at least occasionally) to choose wisely:

- Drink lots of water.

- Add a salad to every dinner meal and go light on the salad dressing.

- Substitute a piece of fruit for a high-calorie dessert at least once a day.

- Substitute whole wheat bread for white bread.

- Have a bowl of fortified cereal instead of a bagel or doughnut.

- Put a vegetable on your plate as you walk through the cafeteria line.

- Don't bring high-calorie junk snacks like potato chips and nachos into your dorm room.

Small changes like these add up to big benefits by the end of the week.

While many college students suffer nutritional deficiencies due to lack of time and effort, another segment of the college community struggles with eating problems with much more severe and complex roots. Here is a quick summary of information about eating disorders, a very common, but very treatable, issue that many young women and some young men face.

The three most common types of eating disorders found on college campuses are anorexia nervosa, bulimia nervosa, and binge-eating disorder. Those suffering these disorders need to be especially aware of their physical and mental health and reach out for help.

Here are some of the reasons that these three eating disorders should not be ignored:

- Anorexia nervosa is an eating disorder, affecting 7 million women and 1 million men, in which people use self-imposed starvation to lose weight.[1] Anorexia has a mortality rate between 7 and 15 percent, which is higher than the mortality rate of many cancers.
- Bulimia nervosa is an eating disorder, affecting 2 to 5 percent of college-age people, in which a person has recurrent and uncontrollable episodes of binge eating followed by the urgent need to eliminate (purge) the food through some self-induced method such as vomiting, enemas, starvation, laxatives, diuretics, or excessive exercise. Bulimia can lead to an array of medical problems, including dehydration and dry skin, constipation from lack of body fluids, muscle spasm, kidney problems, inflammation and possible rupture of the esophagus from frequent vomiting, peptic ulcers and pancreatitis, and electrolyte imbalances (which can lead to irregular heartbeats and possibly heart failure and death). There is also extensive and expensive damage to the teeth, and it takes the average person over a year to seek treatment from the onset of symptoms. Don't wait! The longer you have the disorder, the harder it is to treat and undo the harm.
- Binge-eating disorder is a common phenomenon in college and has a more balanced gender ratio, although it is still predominantly

a disorder of women. In some cases, the weight gain brought on by bingeing makes the person feel unattractive, allowing him or her to avoid forming intimate relationships. Like anorexia and bulimia, binge eating also has severe negative consequences: high blood pressure, high cholesterol levels, heart disease as a result of elevated triglyceride levels, secondary diabetes, gallbladder disease, and the health risks associated with obesity.

These eating disorders commonly peak at the age of eighteen, just the time when young people enter their adult lives and start college.

Quick Tip: Prevent Binge Eating

The strongest predictor of binge eating at night is undereating in the morning. Be sure to start out your day with breakfast that contains some protein and isn't loaded with sugar. You can do this simply by spreading peanut butter on your toast rather than margarine, choosing scrambled eggs rather than pancakes, and adding an occasional yogurt.

Sleep Well

Sleep is a general measure of how things are going. If you have sleep problems such as difficulty falling asleep, early morning wakening, waking up during the night, or exceptional trouble getting out of bed in the morning but then sleep just fine when you return home (or on weekends if you're a commuting student), this may be an early signal of emotional upset or even the cause.

Poor sleep quality is known to lead to many mental health problems. These include depression, anxiety, reduced physical health, poor problem solving and attention difficulties, and increased use of drugs and alcohol.

Partial sleep deprivation (less than six hours of sleep per night) can lead to deficits in attention, concentration, memory, and critical thinking, along with increased depression, irritability, and anxiety.

Even students who regularly obtain eight hours of sleep per night, but shift their sleep schedule by more than two hours (by sleeping late on the weekends, for example), may experience attention, concentration, reasoning, and psychomotor difficulties, as well as increased irritability, anxiety, and depression.

There's no doubt that sleep is vital to good mental health and can directly affect your academic GPA. It's a myth that the best students stay up all night studying. It has been scientifically proven that it's the student who gets a good night's sleep, not the student who studies through the night, who does better academically.

One of these studies was done at Harvard. Dr. Robert Stickgold taught a group of undergraduates to look for a particular visual target on a computer screen and then to push a button as soon as they saw it. At first, the students were slow to recognize and react to the image, but after an hour of training, they were quick and accurate.

Then Stickgold divided the group into two. Half of the students were allowed less than six hours of sleep, and the other half got more than six hours of sleep. The results were remarkable. The sleep-deprived students showed no improvement in the task the following day. But the students who got a good night's sleep were far quicker and more accurate than they had been the day before. After several nights of good sleep, they got even better at the task.

The study concluded that sleep allows information that has been gathered during the day to flow from a short-term memory bank into a long-term one. The process preserves information for future reference. In the later stages of sleep, the brain runs through the data it has stored in the previous hours. This reinforces and strengthens connections that make up memory. Without more than at least four hours of sleep, the process can't happen.

Although occasionally you may have to pull an all-nighter to get required work done, when it comes to studying for a big test, you'll do far better if you study and then get to sleep. Here are some tips to help you:

- Stay away from caffeine, nicotine, and alcohol in the late afternoon and evening. That cigarette or can of cola will make it difficult to drift off to sleep. And although alcohol may make it easier to fall asleep, it will interrupt your sleep and awaken you later in the night.

- Don't nap during the day if you're having trouble falling asleep at night. A nap can confuse your biological clock.

- Exercise regularly but not right before bedtime. Give yourself at least three hours between a workout and sleep time.

- Give your brain the signal to sleep by establishing a nighttime ritual. Leave time to relax and unwind with the lights turned low. Stay back from the TV and computer screen because their light can confuse the day-night rhythms of the body.

- If you can't fall asleep after thirty minutes, don't toss and turn worrying about not sleeping. This can become a self-fulfilling prophecy. Instead, get up and do some kind of relaxing activity like listening to music or reading. Try to clear your mind and not worry about not sleeping. When you start to feel tired, get back to bed.

Quick Tip: Speak Up to Save Your GPA

If you miss classes while you're struggling with emotional issues, the problem gets compounded by the fear of lowering your GPA. In this case, the mental health counselors on your campus can help you. I often write notes for students to give to their professors asking for appropriate considerations, such as extending the deadline on a paper or offering a test at a later date. This letter does not give specific reasons and will not break the bond of confidentiality by saying something like: "Kristen is suffering from depression and therefore needs additional time to hand in her term paper." Rather, the letter simply shares information the professor needs to know: "Kristen has a medical problem that has been interfering with her ability to do her class assignments. Please make appropriate accommodations and allow Kristen to make up any missed work." Speak up and let the health care counselors know what you need.

STAY CONNECTED

You're on your own. Your parents won't be contacting your professors to check on your grades. If you live at school, they won't be calling the dean of housing to make sure you're in bed at a certain hour. And you don't need their permission to stay out late. This is a life passage when you separate yourself from your parents. Feels good, huh?

This separation is good, natural, and normal, but don't cut off all contact with home. Having the connection with your family while you make new connections in the college community is very important to your sense of comfort and security. How you feel about taking risks, accepting challenges, and trying new things is tightly bound to how secure you feel at your base. For many students, the family is the base, and it's good to know that they're there when you need to go back for a dose of security.

However, when you lose that connection (because perhaps you haven't contacted them in over a month), it can be very hard to then pick up the phone and admit that you're struggling with a problem. When you lose that intimate connection and the thrill of taking that independent step in college begins to wear off, it can be a very lonely feeling.

At least until you have strong connections among your college peers and professors, keep the connection with your family alive. Send them e-mail and pick up the phone when they call. It's a little dose of insurance in case the day comes when you're out there alone and you need to hear a kind, familiar voice.

If that day does come, your first impulse may be to hide your troubles from your parents, a kind of protective reaction because you don't want to worry or disappoint them. That sounds admirable, but it's not. Keep in mind when you're struggling with a problem that your parents are usually much more aware of what's going on than you might think. There's probably no one else on the planet who cares more about you, and that's why when they sense that you're unhappy or scared, they'll bug you with questions like, "What's the matter? Are you okay? Is there anything wrong?"

You have to make your own decisions about when to talk to your parents and how much to tell them about your life. But when making that decision, remember that being an independent adult doesn't mean going it alone. Part of being mature is learning when to share problems and concerns and when to ask for help. Even if your parents can't understand exactly what you're going through, their love goes a long way; what they don't get, they'll usually try to understand and work with you to get through it.

At the same time, take stock of your relationships with peers. We all need connections with others to feel wanted and secure. These connections are so important that feeling engaged with other students and professors is a key for academic and emotional well-being.

If you find yourself feeling left out or alone, do something about it. Every college community has programs and activities for everybody from activists to artists, from computer techs to feminists, from atheists to fundamentalists. Find a group that shares your interests and passions. Reach out, talk to people, go to meetings, take a risk. You spend only twelve to eighteen hours a week in the classroom; that leaves a vast amount of time for nonacademic experiences with peers and friends. Take advantage of the college environment to make connections that will make you feel important and valued. We all need that.

Not True!

Each of the following quotations is a myth that too many college students believe. When you're talking to yourself, stop short and evaluate what's really going on if you hear yourself saying any of these. They are sure signs that you're headed for trouble:

"I don't need to sleep."

"Alcohol isn't dangerous. It helps relax me in social situations and unwind after a hard week of work."

"I can't believe I screwed up that test. I'll never amount to anything. This is going to ruin my life."

"This person is the love of my life. I couldn't live without him [her]. He [she] would never hurt me or let me down."

"My parents have no idea what I'm going through. They would be so disappointed if I told them."

"They must have picked up the wrong folder when they admitted me. I don't belong here."

ORGANIZE AND EVALUATE YOUR TIME

You have so many people pulling on you from all directions that sometimes it feels as if you can't get everything done, meet everybody's expectations, and keep yourself sane. When the going gets really tough, you might figure that you have only two choices: go nuts or give up. Fortunately, time management skills give you another option.

Good time management requires that you block out time periods during the day to get things done. Use a daily planner or Palm Pilot to set up a doable schedule in specific blocks of time. Each day, block out your class time; then schedule in time for things like studying, laundry, and homework. Schedule in the stuff that has to get done, and give it a particular time of day. This way you won't be trying to squeeze all the things on your "must-do" list into the last hours before bedtime.

When you're blocking out time periods in your day, don't forget to give yourself time for exercising, eating, socializing, and sleeping. If your day zips by and as you fall into bed you realize that you didn't sit down to eat a meal or talk to a friend, you've got to plan better for the next day. If you start cheating yourself out of time for *you,* you'll soon find yourself worn out and open to loneliness and depression.

Look at your day and create a balanced time schedule. *Balance* is a key word here. To do your best at college, you need to find a way to balance the need to do your academic work, create and nurture relationships, and take care of your own physical and mental health needs—*not* too much play or too much work. There is a time and place for everything if you think ahead and map it out.

At the end of the week, look back and take inventory. How did you do? Did you meet your academic goals? Did you make time for fun extracurriculars? Did you leave time to relax and recuperate? Did you spend time with friends? If you had a magic wand and could change the past week, what would you do differently? With this information in mind, decide what you can try to do next week that might improve your experience.

Don't let life just happen to you. The people who have the most successful college years, both academically and socially, are the ones who consciously take control of their lives. They plan, evaluate, take inventory, and make the effort to create an experience that meets all their needs and keeps things in balance.

Quick Tip: Think Locally

When you're making up your daily schedule, think locally, not globally. Instead of thinking that you have to write your fifteen-page history paper this week, think, "I have to write five paragraphs today between two and three o'clock." Breaking down your work into manageable sections will keep you from feeling overwhelmed.

REACH OUT

Many graduates look back on their college years and say that their most valuable experiences involved getting to know people of different cultures and backgrounds. Keep an open mind while you're in school, and don't get stuck in your own small world. You may never again find yourself in such a diverse environment, so take advantage of the situation and find out what makes other people tick.

A diverse environment gives you the opportunity to take your family beliefs and values and hold them up against those of others. How do your classmates feel about religion? Sexual mores? Politics? Gathering information and mixing it up with your own does not betray the connection with your family. It is part of growing and maturing.

Accepting and enjoying people who look and act differently from you is also a great stress reducer. It helps you feel more connected to your college community, and it will raise your comfort level when you find yourself in a class or circumstance with a bunch of "strange" people around you. Reach out and enjoy the situation.

Breaking Free

Naturally, different students respond differently to mental health problems. However, I've noticed that students from diverse minority backgrounds often don't get the health care services they need before reaching college. In fact, a new report from the U.S. surgeon general, Dr. David Satcher, has found that minorities in the United States suffer a disproportionate burden of mental illness for several reasons. He says that they often have less access to services than other Americans, they receive lower-quality care, and they are less likely to seek help when they are in distress. The report noted that while serious mental disorders like depression, schizophrenia, panic disorder, bipolar disease, and substance abuse occur in all races, ethnicities, and socioeconomic classes, minorities tend to be overrepresented among those most vulnerable and in need of mental health treatment.[*]

If you come from a family that sees mental health problems as a personal weakness or from a family that doesn't believe in seeking treatment for emotional pain or cannot afford to, now is the time to break free of these things that have kept you from taking care of your mental health. The services offered in your college community are there to help you. There is no shame or family disgrace in taking this step. It is an intelligent and mature person who can recognize a problem and ask for appropriate help to find a solution regardless of race, nationality, or ethnicity.

---

[*]U.S. Department of Health and Human Services, *Mental Health: Culture, Race, and Ethnicity: A Supplement to Mental Health: A Report of the Surgeon General* (Washington, D.C.: U.S. Government Printing Office, Aug. 26, 2001). [http://www.surgeongeneral.gov/library/mentalhealth/cre/exec summary-1.html].

BE INFORMED

Ignorance is a major factor in the increase in mental health problems on college campuses. Too many students don't recognize the
signs and symptoms of trouble, and those who do feel ashamed or
embarrassed, and so they keep the problem to themselves. If we are
to make even the slightest reduction in the numbers of students
struggling with emotional and psychological problems, each one of
you needs to start paying attention to yourself, your needs, and your
feelings.

What? Me Worry?

You can start to get to know yourself by keeping track of the way you
worry. Dr. Ned Hallowell talks about anxiety and stress in a very read-
able and useful book called *Worry*. He notes that we all worry about
things to one degree or another, and the key is to focus on "productive" versus "toxic" worry.[2]

Let's say you're worried about an upcoming exam. If you handle
that worry by scheduling time to study, reviewing your notes, and
preparing for the exam, you are practicing productive worry. But if
you spend the time before the exam obsessing about how hopeless
your life will be when you fail the exam, you are stuck in a state of
toxic worry.

You can use productive more often than toxic worry if you follow these steps when you have a problem:

1. Be aware of the circumstance that is causing you to worry.

2. Recognize the patterns you fall into when you're worried
   (obsess? eat more? sleep less? give up?).

3. Challenge the negative patterns, and actively do something
   to take you a step closer to resolving the problem.

4. Reach out. Support from friends and teachers can get you
   through bad situations.

The key is to be aware of how you are feeling and what you're doing to cope. Face your fears; it's the only way to defeat them. Denial is the enemy of growth.

Know the Symptoms

Everybody feels unhappy and down sometimes. It's part of life. But a willingness to accept these feelings as "normal" even when they persist for weeks at a time may keep you from recognizing the symptoms of excessive stress, anxiety, or depression.

Over and over again, I see students who have trouble concentrating, aren't sleeping well, are losing motivation and confidence, and withdrawing socially, who say they just need to focus and apply themselves more. They don't see the danger signs or choose to ignore them, fearing that depression or an anxiety disorder is a personal weakness or character flaw. Rather than face the issues and seek help, they end up in denial, trying to convince themselves how they ought to feel rather than accepting what they actually feel. They become victimized by depression, sleep disorders, substance abuse, anxiety disorders, eating disorders, various self-destructive "coping styles" such as chronic procrastination, preoccupation or obsession around relationships or sexuality, cutting or other self-mutilating behaviors, and in the most extreme cases overt suicide attempts.

Don't let this happen to you. Know the signs of mental health problems and be willing to seek help when you need it. These are the primary symptoms of stress, anxiety, and depression to watch out for:

- Sleep changes (early morning wakening, waking through the night, or trouble getting out of bed in the morning can all be early warning signs of depression)

- Increase or decrease in appetite

- Loss of motivation

- Social withdrawal

- Loss of concentration

- Feelings of hopelessness or loss of self-esteem

- Loss of interest in activities that are usually pleasurable

- Intense worry without foundation for concern

- Small problems that feel overwhelming

- Physical symptoms of anxiety: rapid heart rate, upset stomach, feelings of panic, headaches, sweaty palms

Any of these symptoms by themselves may be passing signs of stress, but if they cluster and become more persistent, they should be cause for concern.

Be Proactive

To keep yourself out of the dark, be proactive about getting information on mental health:

- When your school offers workshops or seminars on topics such as substance abuse, sexual assault, depression, and eating disorders, go to them—not necessarily because you are directly affected right now, but because it's smart to have this information just in case.

- Read the mental health materials that are handed out all over campus. Contrary to popular belief, these flyers are not really wastebasket liners. They have been put together to inform, encourage, and support all students so you can have the best possible college experience, both academically and socially.

- Know where the counseling services are offered on your campus. Get familiar with the building and the setup. Take a look around and gather some of the printed material offered. If you should need the help of a counselor in the future, you will feel more comfortable asking for it if you have previously been in the center.

If you don't feel comfortable attending workshops or visiting the counseling center, you can also get lots of information on-line at sites created specifically for college students who like the anonymity of the computer. There are many top-quality sites listed in Appendix B you should check out. Here are an additional few that are for students only:

• Ulifeline.com, www.ulifeline.com. The Jed Foundation is the nation's first nonprofit group dedicated solely to reducing suicide on college campuses. Founded by Phillip and Donna Satow, whose son Jed killed himself when he was a sophomore at the University of Arizona, the group seeks to expand the mental health safety net by offering on-line services for students. They have created this free, anonymous Web site customized to link students to their college counseling centers and a library of mental health information.

• Campusblues.com, www.campusblues.com. This site is sponsored by a for-profit company. It is designed specifically to provide on-line education and to help students find appropriate mental health services on or near their campuses.

• Outsidetheclassroom.com, www.outsidetheclassroom.com. This subscription site offers prevention-based health education with particular focus on high-risk drinking on college campuses.

• National Mental Health Association, www.nmha.org. This site offers information specifically for college students, with fact sheets on adjustment to life's changes, anxiety disorders and depression, eating disorders and depression, alcohol and drug abuse and depression, and suicide and depression.

• MyStudentBody, www.mystudentbody.com. This site offers personalized and confidential health information through interactive tools, flash animation peer stories, and informational pieces.

• Active Minds on Campus, www.activemindsoncampus.org. This site is a student-run mental health awareness, education, and advocacy organization designed for the college campus. The group aims to remove the stigma that surrounds mental illness and create a comfortable environment for open discussion of mental health issues.

- Facts on Tap, www.factsontap.org. This site has interesting links to subjects such as drugs, alcohol and your body, alcohol and sex, commuter students, children of alcoholics, and dealing with a friend's drinking.

Quick Tip: Do Something About It

Feeling distracted? Unable to focus? Studying hard but getting nowhere? Don't wait for these problems to fix themselves. Your school has tutoring and counseling services that are there to help you if you ask. I think that most students are aware of less than half of the resources they could be using in all areas, including academic, social, and physical and mental health services.

Check with the dean of your college, go on-line to your college site, or ask your resident adviser. Do something to help yourself!

DON'T SUFFER LONG— DON'T SUFFER ALONE

I've been helping college students deal with the pressures of young adulthood for twenty-five years. And yet I confess that when I was in college, I did not take the advice that I now give to you. I still regret it. I clearly remember some of the mistakes I made along the way and wish I had the wisdom in my youth to seek help that would have avoided a lot more mistakes, pain, and lost opportunities.

I remember thinking that I was comfortable, confident, and autonomous when I left for college. I had been a strong high school student, a three-sport athlete, and socially very engaged and confident. When I arrived at college, among a group of very bright, accomplished other students, I felt insecure but never admitted this to myself or anyone else. I felt the best way to prove that I could manage was to be sure I didn't need anyone. I drank a lot on many weekends, like many other college students, to bolster my confidence in social situations, but it didn't really work and probably interfered with forming deeper relationships with peers. I threw myself into literature and reading and isolated myself, trying to prove that I was autonomous and didn't need anything from other people.

If you had asked me at the time, I would never have described myself as depressed and would not have seen my drinking and isolation as "coping mechanisms." I frequently pulled all-nighters to study for exams and finish papers, having no idea of the negative effects of sleep deprivation. And I admit that the thought of seeking counseling never entered my mind.

It took me years to learn that the patterns and behaviors practiced in college don't disappear when you graduate. You must address them to develop as a person. I now know that there is no need to suffer long or suffer alone.

Keep that thought in mind. When you start to feel unhappy or anxious, it is a normal reaction to withdraw from friends. You probably figure that they don't want to be around someone who's unhappy or struggling, and you don't want them to worry about you. But once you're isolated, you might find out that you feel worse. Then you might think that the feeling will pass; it's just a mood, after all. But it doesn't pass.

Now you've created a vicious cycle. You've withdrawn from your friends, but then you feel worse, and feeling worse makes you less willing to socialize, which makes you feel even lonelier, and the bad feelings just go around and around. Still, you think that eventually you'll get these awful feelings under control. But another day goes by, and then another, and another, and still you can't shake it.

If you suffer any of the symptoms of depression and anxiety listed earlier for more than two weeks, it's going to be very hard, if not impossible, to get over this tough spot without the help of others.

We all need each other to feel connected, engaged, and mentally healthy.

The result of reaching out to others when times get tough opens the way to a secure and happy future beyond college. You don't have to take my word for this. Take a look at this e-mail that I received from Kara when I wrote to ask for permission to publish the personal letter about depression she wrote four years ago that opened this chapter:

> I wish you the best of luck with the book. And I am delighted to hear that my article has helped so many over the years. I am so grateful for the time that you spent helping me, as well as the countless others. I have learned how to recognize "bad" days, and they never get past "so-so" days anymore. It's wonderful! My spouse and I have been very open about the topic and we have discovered similarities in our pasts—likely due to both being so driven and ambitious. This has helped us grow and also achieve a new focus in life—energy with underlying strength and assuredness. I have enjoyed every moment of it, including the stressful days.
>
> I can never thank you enough for encouraging me to follow the full path of treatment and for giving it time. It has made the world of difference.

If you should ever feel alone and hopeless, remember Kara. There is treatment, there is a life of joy beyond college, and there is hope.

THE BOTTOM LINE

Above all else, I'd like you to remember these five things:

- Self-care is not the same as being selfish.

- Be honest with yourself about what you're feeling.

- Eat, sleep, and exercise.

- Stay connected to others.

- Think of proactive ways to address problems.

Good grades and impressive jobs don't mean anything if you feel miserable all the time. There are people—family, friends, peers, and counselors—who can help you, so reach out when you need to.

Appendix A:
The 2002 American College Health Association Survey Results

	Never			1–10 Times			11 or More Times		
	Male	Female	Total	Male	Female	Total	Male	Female	Total
Within the last school year, how many times have you:									
Felt things were hopeless	44.0%	30.0%	35.3%	47.0%	60.0%	54.6%	9.0%	11.0%	10.1%
Felt overwhelmed by all you had to do	11.0	3.0	6.3	67.0	65.0	66.2	21.0	31.0	27.4
Felt exhausted (not from physical activity)	14.0	5.0	8.7	65.0	67.0	66.0	21.0	28.0	25.3
Felt very sad	27.0	13.0	18.0	62.0	71.0	67.4	11.0	16.0	14.6
Felt so depressed that it was difficult to function	60.0	52.0	55.3	33.0	42.0	37.6	6.0	8.0	7.1
Seriously considered attempting suicide	91.0	90.0	90.1	8.0	9.0	9.0	0	0	0.2
Attempted suicide	99.0	99.0	98.4	1.0	1.0	1.4	0	0	0.2

	Yes	Male	Female
Have you ever been diagnosed with depression?	11.7%	7.0%	14.0%
If yes to the above,			
Have you been diagnosed within the last school year?	36.9%	34.0%	37.0%
Are you currently in therapy for depression?	24.0%	21.0%	25.0%
Are you currently taking medication for depression?	35.0%	28.0%	38.0%

Note: N = 29,230.

Source: Reprinted from American College Health Association. *National College Health Assessment: Reference Group Executive Summary Spring 2002.* Baltimore, Md.: American College Health Association, 2003.

Appendix B:
Everything You Need to Know
About Medications

The last thing parents want to think about is giving their children psychotropic medication for a mental health problem. But if a clinician recommends medication to help your child better cope with the challenges of the college years, you should know the facts before you accept or reject the idea.

I understand that getting these facts can be difficult because people tend to have strong feelings on this subject that color the truth. On one hand, activist groups imply that if you take Ritalin or an antidepressant, you'll become a drug addict or suicidal. Some say it's a sign of character defect or worse. On the other hand, some of the drug manufacturers present antidepressants as wonder drugs and as a panacea for everything from self-esteem and social problems to academic concerns. Then there are those who believe that "natural" treatments such as St. John's Wort for depression are more benign and "better."

My hope in this appendix is to educate you so you can avoid this kind of polarized thinking. Before your child begins any medication, you should assess the potential risks and costs of taking medication and weigh those facts against the potential benefits.

Deciding on medication is a personal and philosophical choice. The information I offer in this section is meant as a guide to help you better understand the uses, risks, and benefits of medication. But it is not meant to be a comprehensive description of medication or to cover all of the risks and potential side effects. You must work closely with a physician to manage those concerns.

This information is meant only as a starting point in understanding and considering the use of medication for a variety of problems. The facts and numbers alone say that this is something we should be alert to. Chickering Insurance, one of the largest insurers of student health plans, reviewed over one million line items of insurance claims in the twelve-month period ending March 31, 2001, and found the following:

- 14.5 percent of clinical contacts outside of the students' health centers and counseling centers were for psychological illnesses.

- Of the claims for prescriptions paid for the calendar year 2000, the most frequently prescribed class of drugs were selective serotonin reuptake inhibitor (SSRI) antidepressants at 11.3 percent of the total number of prescriptions paid.

- The U.S. sales of the SSRIs class of antidepressants has risen 800 percent since 1990.[1]

Despite the fact that there is often a long lag of several years between onset and diagnosis of depression and bipolar disorder, more and more young adults are now being promptly diagnosed. A survey of 900,000 youths found that the use of psychotropic medications increased 200 to 300 percent from 1987 through 1996.[2] The most common types of medication used in college settings are antidepressants, antianxiety medication, and sleep aids. I am going to divide these types into the following categories (even though some are misnomers, which I will clarify later):

1. Antidepressants

2. Antianxiety medications

3. Hypnotics and sleep medications

4. Mood stabilizers

5. Stimulants

6. Antipsychotics

7. Herbal alternatives

ANTIDEPRESSANTS

Antidepressants are the most common psychoactive medications used in the college population and in the general population. They have been used effectively for a long time, but until the arrival of Prozac in 1987, they weren't nearly as popular because of the risks and side effects of the older antidepressants, called tricyclics. These include drugs such as Norpramin (desipramine), Elavil (amitriptilene), Sinequan (doxepin), and Tofranil (imipramine).

The mechanism of action of antidepressants is still not completely understood, but there is general agreement that they affect levels and functioning of the neurotransmitters serotonin and norepinephrine in the brain. The tricyclics usually had a dual action, some more specialized to one or the other neurotransmitter, and they were also effective for depression.

But they were never popular because they frequently caused side effects, including weight gain, which is the "kiss of death" for any medication that a college student is willing to consider. From a clinician's standpoint, they were also problematic because they could have effects on cardiac conduction, could be quite lethal when taken in overdose, and had a variety of other unpleasant side effects such as dry mouth, lethargy, night sweats, constipation, urinary hesitancy, jitteriness, and sexual side effects.

When Prozac arrived on the scene in 1987, it caused an explosion in antidepressant use. This drug, which was a selective serotonin reuptake inhibitor (SSRI), appeared to have almost no side effects, and people who had been chronically depressed sometimes had remarkable turnarounds. There was also an initial decrease in appetite, which led many people to my office requesting the medication, not because they were depressed, but because they heard it was an effective diet pill. Others claimed that these drugs made people "better than normal," and their popularity soared.

A steady stream of SSRIs came to market: Zoloft (sertraline), Paxil (paroxetine), Celexa (citalopram), Luvox (fluvoxamine), and Effexor (venlafaxine), a dual uptake inhibitor (also affected norepinephrine reuptake at higher doses as well as serotonin).

Side Effects

Like most new medications, the positive news came first and problems appeared later. One major side effect of all of these medications is sexual dysfunction: decrease in libido, difficulty maintaining erections, and difficulty having orgasms.

It was thought that the prevalence of sexual dysfunction was about 2 percent during the clinical trials, but it turns out that the side effect probably occurs around 50 percent of the time. The initial low incidence was due to the fact that no one asked about sexual function and patients were reluctant to raise the question.

There are strategies to manage and somewhat control this side effect, so it isn't a reason to reject the idea of taking the medication. However, as you might imagine, this is a very worrisome side effect for students, some of whom are embarking on their first sexual experiences. It is beyond the scope of this book to fully discuss treatments, but suffice it to say this is usually a very manageable side effect.

There are other usually transient side effects that include nausea (if medication is taken on an empty stomach), jitteriness, occasional headaches, and other infrequent, benign side effects that are usually self-limited.

There has been a great deal of alarmist news and concern in the media about antidepressant use. One area of risk occurs when bipolar disorder symptoms are triggered with an antidepressant trial. The college years are the peak age of onset for bipolar disorder, and the first episode may present with depressive symptoms; the prescribed antidepressant can then trigger a manic episode. (That's why it is important to get a careful family history of bipolar disorder and, if it exists, to monitor a medication trial very closely, as the risks of developing bipolar disorder are then higher.)

Another side effect is akathesia, or "restlessness." People usually experience this in their legs and feel that they can't sit still. This can lead to increased anxiety and agitation and may be one reason they feel more desperate.

Recently, in England, these medications have been banned for use by children under the age of eighteen because of higher suicide rates. The use of SSRI antidepressants is currently under review in this country. On February 2, 2004, the *Boston Globe* reported that in 2002 there were almost eleven million prescriptions dispensed in the United States to patients under age eighteen. According to the article, FDA files show 110 reports of suicide amongst youths taking these medications since they were released in 1987.[3]

My experience mirrors these findings. I have personally seen these medications save and turn around the lives of many adolescents, and in the final analysis the benefits seem to outweigh the risks when the medication is prescribed appropriately and closely monitored. We have to wait for the final scientific analysis, but there is pressure to take these drugs off the market because the voices of those families with tragic outcomes are louder than those of the large number of people who have been helped. I hope that careful scientific analysis of the data will give us an unbiased answer.

Should Your Child Use?

Now, let's get to the key question for you: When you are considering an antidepressant trial with your child, what are the things to weigh and how do you decide whether or not to try the medication? As with most decisions in life, it is important to weigh the risks and potential benefits.

How do you know if someone has a "biologic" depression that will respond to medication? Or if that person would respond better to psychotherapy? There are no simple answers to these questions. There is a lot of current research looking at chemical changes in the body, and I think most of us hope that someday there will be a blood test to tell us whether someone is clinically depressed and which neurotransmitter is abnormal, guiding us to medication choice. But we aren't there yet.

There is also bias on the part of providers toward or against prescribing medication for depression based on training and background. If you're a hammer, everything looks like a nail. Some prescribers have a very biologic orientation and recommend medication as part of most treatments. If your school of choice has limited prescribing ability or the counseling staff has a developmental background and approach, they believe that most things are developmental and psychotherapy is the solution. As usual, the truth lies somewhere in between. Most prescribers ask about "vegetative" signs of depression, and if several symptoms are persistent over at least two to four weeks, depending on severity, medication and psychotherapy combined might be the answer.

Some of these signs include

- Changes in sleep patterns: insomnia, waking through the night, early morning waking or lethargy in the morning

- Changes in appetite: either increases or decreases

- Concentration problems

- Decreased energy

- Loss of interest in usual activities that used to be enjoyable

- Social withdrawal

- Loss of self-esteem

- Feelings of hopelessness or despair

- Irritability: little day-to-day frustrations getting to you that didn't before

- Seeing the negative side of everything: "The glass is always half empty"

- No external reasons (such as losses, disappointments, and so on) for these symptoms

- Significant family history of depression or alcoholism

There is no hard and fast rule here, and many of us trained in psychotherapy and prescribing feel that a trial of psychotherapy is usually the first course of treatment. But because medications take three to six weeks to work, if students are way behind academically, feeling overwhelmed, and have a significant number of symptoms, sometimes medication and psychotherapy are started simultaneously, especially when speed of response is paramount.

I have seen many students over the years who were resistant in principle to medication and had a number of other issues that we worked on in psychotherapy. They eventually decided to try medication because their symptoms persisted, and it was not unusual that after a month or two, the student would say, "You know this medication has made a huge difference for me, and although I enjoy talking with you about these other issues, I feel like myself again. I'd rather be out with friends and come to see you when needed for refills." I'm not implying that psychotherapy isn't valuable, but biology is sometimes 70 to 80 percent of the problem.

Which Ones and How Long?

How do you decide which antidepressant to use? The standard of care today is to start with an SSRI as the first-line medication. These types of antidepressant medications are very effective, usually have minimal side effects, and are very safe to use. The choices of one SSRI over another probably are most driven by safety, provider experience, cost factors (some are now available in generic forms), and prior experience or symptoms of the student. They are all probably equally effective. It is not unusual for primary care doctors to prescribe antidepressants, but when that is the case, it is important that the person is followed regularly and the dosing is optimum. For example, if one has a lot of obsessive symptoms or binge eating urges, higher doses of medication are often needed to address those symptoms.

The other question that is frequently asked is: How long do I stay on these medications? The answer varies depending on benefits and side effects. In general, for a first episode of depression, it is recommended that people stay on medication for nine to twelve months. The reason for this is that the relapse rate is much lower if people stop after nine months.

When a person stops the medication, it is important to stop gradually. It is all too common that students forget their medication when they leave on break or vacation, and either have some discomfort withdrawing (sometimes it is irritability, sometimes flu-like symptoms or lethargy), or feel fine off the medication and decide they don't need it anymore. Unfortunately, the recurrence of symptoms often occurs one to three months after stopping the medication, so they don't notice any problems immediately.

There are several other antidepressants on the market that can be quite effective and have some different benefits and side effects. These include Wellbutrin (buproprion), Remeron (mirtazapine), Serzone (nefazodone), Desyryl (trazodone), and Luvox (fluvoxamine). The older tricyclics and another category of medication called Monoamine oxidase (MAO) inhibitors are also used. They each have their benefits and their place. Wellbutrin, for example, does not cause sexual side effects and may have some benefit for attention problems. Serzone, Remeron, and Desyryl can be sedating and help with sleep, which is a benefit or problem, depending on symptoms. One other medication worth mentioning in this category is Lamictal (lamotrigine), an anticonvulsant that shows promise in the treatment of bipolar depression, where the other antidepressants may pose the risk of causing mania. Lamictal has some rare but serious side effects and requires close monitoring.

Key Points About Antidepressants

- For some people, depression is largely biologic, and medication makes a huge difference. Your child isn't signing up for the rest of his or her life, just a three to six week trial. If it works, usually nine to twelve months is the length of time to use them.

- Antidepressants in general are very safe. There are unusual and rare side effects, but millions of people have been using antidepressants, and there appear to be no long-term deleterious effects.

- When you or your child has questions or concerns about effects or side effects, ask the prescriber. There aren't any "dumb" questions.

- Don't stop medication abruptly. Tell your child that if he or she should forgot to bring the medication home on break or such, a temporary supply can often be obtained with a phone call to the prescriber or pharmacy.

ANTIANXIETY MEDICATIONS

The function of antianxiety medications is to reduce the feeling of anxiety, which in some cases can become extreme in the form of a panic attack, which can be quite incapacitating.

The antianxiety medications include the very popular class of medications called benzodiazepines, which include drugs such as

Valium (diazepam), Librium (chlordiazepoxide), Xanax (alprazo-lam), Ativan (lorazepam), and Serax (oxazepam); many of the anti-depressants described above; and other agents such as Buspar (buspirone), Beta blockers (inderal, atenolol), and a variety of anti-convulsant medications and atypical neuroleptics.

Key Points About Antianxiety Medications

- The SSRIs are probably the first choice for the long-term treatment of significant anxiety for the same reasons as described in the previous section. They do take several weeks to be effective.

- The advantage of the benzodiazepines is that they usually work almost immediately and are very effective and relatively safe.

- The disadvantage of benzodiazepines is that they can cause sedation and can become addictive, as people develop a tolerance to them over time. They can also affect cognitive function.

- Benzodiazepines are popular drugs of abuse, so they require close monitoring and are usually con-traindicated in someone with a substance abuse problem.

- There is a place for the other medications mentioned above and they also have advantages and disadvantages in certain situations that are beyond the scope of this book.

HYPNOTICS AND SLEEP MEDICATIONS

Because sleep problems are the primary presenting complaint of many students, there is often a request for a "quick fix" with medi-cation. Sleep medications can be effective and safe when used for up to a couple of weeks, but learning good sleep hygiene (as ex-plained in Chapter Seven) is the best longer-term approach to this problem.

A careful diagnosis to determine the cause of a sleep problem is the most important consideration. Many sleep problems are sec-ondary to stress or other problems and treating the underlying con-dition is the best solution.

There are several types of medications used to help with sleep:

Antihistamines, which are found in many cold preparations, can be purchased over the counter, and are very popular and min-imally effective. Benadryl (diphenhydramine) is one of the most common.

Barbiturates are an older, less-safe class of medications no longer in frequent use.

Benzodiazepines (as described in the anxiety section) such as Restoril (temazepam) and Dalmane (flurazepam) are very pop-ular for short-term use with the same caveats about tolerance and addictive potential.

Ambien (zolpidem) and *Sonata* (zaleplon) are newer medications that have become very popular and seem to be effective. Their long-term addictive potential is unclear at this time.

Some of the antidepressants, particularly Desyrl (trazodone), seem to be effective sleep medications, but can have more side effects.

Key Points About Hypnotics and Sleep Medications

- Long-term use can cause one to develop tolerance and make the medication less effective.

- Some people experience "rebound" or difficulty sleep-ing when they stop taking a sleep medication.

- Some of the preparations are shorter acting (two hours) versus longer acting (eight hours), so it's important to choose a preparation that matches the symptoms. For example, if the problem is falling asleep, a shorter-acting preparation may be the more appropriate choice, whereas if the problem is waking intermittently through the night, a longer-acting preparation is probably a better choice.

- Sleep medications often interact with other drugs, so the prescribing doctor must know about any other medication your child is taking.

- Sleep medications can affect cognitive function and memory.

MOOD STABILIZERS

There are a number of medications called "mood stabilizers" that are generally used to treat mania or bipolar disease. It is particularly important to diagnose and treat this disorder because it appears that there can be longer-term damage and increased likelihood of relapse if left untreated. Sometimes it is necessary to stay on these medications indefinitely.

Lithium carbonate is the most commonly used mood stabilizer and for several decades has been used as an effective treatment for mania. However, it does have a number of troublesome side effects, including weight gain, frequent urination, headaches, and nausea, and over time it can cause some chronic damage to the kidneys. One unique research finding about Lithium is that it is one of the only medications that is associated with a reduced incidence of suicide, so it bears consideration in cases of severe disorders.

Depakoat (Valproic acid) and Tegretol (carbamazepine) are other commonly used mood stabilizers. Along with Lithium, all require blood level monitoring to ensure safe use.

There is a whole generation of new medications which are being studied, most of which are used as anticonvulsants. These include

Topamax (topiramate), Lamictal (lamotrigene), Trileptal (oxcarbazine), and Neurontin (gabapentin), which are being investigated for a variety of uses from mood stabilization to anxiety and sleep and weight management.

Key Points About Mood Stabilizers

- There is a high risk of relapse if the medication is stopped prematurely.

- Many of these medications require regular testing of blood levels.

- Some of the newer uses being explored for several of the mood-stabilizing medications described above include decreased appetite, reduced anxiety, improved sleep, and pain management.

STIMULANTS

Stimulant medications can be very helpful and effective in treating learning problems. This is important for you to know because, although it is thought that attention deficit problems usually begin in childhood, the condition is often not diagnosed until later in life. It is not uncommon for learning disabilities to show themselves during the college years when the academic requirements are tougher. There is also evidence that these problems can persist into adulthood.

Stimulants such as Ritalin (methylphenidate) and amphetamines (such as Dexedrine) are popular and effective for this use. There are a variety of newer, longer-acting preparations of these medications, and newer drugs are in the research pipeline.

A new drug, Strattera (atemoxetine), which has recently been released, is not a stimulant but has been proven to be effective in the treatment of attentional problems. It has the advantage of not being addictive nor having the abuse potential of many of the drugs in this class. There is anecdotal evidence that some of the antidepressants can also be effective with attention problems, but they are not "first line" drugs.

There is a push to find alternative medications for learning disabilities due to the potential for abuse and serious side effects of the most commonly prescribed stimulant, Ritalin (methylphenidate). Some families are passionately against the use of this drug, and they picket outside of psychiatric conventions at every opportunity. The controversy has now spread to the college campus, where Ritalin (or "vitamin R," "R ball," and "cramming drug" as it is sometimes called) is fast becoming a major substance abuse problem.

Some students have found that this stimulant improves their academic capabilities by allowing them to stay awake for many hours in a row while they study, and it helps them maintain abnormally high levels of concentration. Other students use Ritalin so they can consume more alcohol or mix it with other drugs to party longer without falling asleep. In fact, of 2,250 undergraduates who completed an Internet survey, 3 percent reported illicit methylphenidate use in the past year associated with weekend partying.[4]

To achieve these results, some students take Ritalin tablets whole, but others gain stronger stimulation by crushing tablets and snorting them. Still others grind the tablets, mix them with water, "cook" them, and inject the mix intravenously.

In addition to this misuse of a potent and potentially addictive drug, there are serious side effects that also need to be considered. Nervousness, insomnia, irritability, hypertension, rapid heart rate, and GI problems are occasional side effects, particularly if the dosage of medication is not monitored closely. When the medication is abused in high doses or concentrations there are risks of paranoia and psychosis. And some people have significant depression upon withdrawal of medication.

These are legitimate concerns over the use of stimulants. However, the scientific evidence is that the medications are relatively safe if used thoughtfully and monitored closely.

Key Points About Stimulants

- Although attention problems are usually present from an early age, sometimes they don't surface until college.

- Stimulants are often prescribed to treat learning disabilities.

- Stimulants have the potential for abuse, addiction, and serious side effects.

- Stimulant medications are safe if used with close supervision.

ANTIPSYCHOTIC MEDICATIONS

Antipsychotic medications have been around since the mid-1950s. They are antagonists of the neurotransmitter dopamine and have effects on other neurotransmitters as well. The first antipsychotic was Thorazine (Chlorpromazine), which was originally developed as a surgical anesthetic, but a newer class, now called "atypical" antipsychotics, has recently been developed.

The term *antipsychotic* is an unfortunate misnomer because it implies that these medications are useful only for psychosis. But there is growing evidence that they can be very helpful as an adjunct for treatment-resistant depression as well as severe anxiety. They are effective in treating a variety of symptoms such as depression and lethargy that older medications were not very effective for.

There have been several new medications released in the past several years that include Risperdal (respiridone), Clozaril (clozapine), Seroquel (quetiapine), Zyprexa (olanzepine), Geodon (ziprasidone), and Abilify (aripiprazole).

Unlike the antidepressants, these medications have more complicated side effects and risks associated with them. For example, they can affect cognitive functioning and sleep, making their use even more challenging in a college setting, where students require maximum concentration. However, they do play an important role in treating more severe mental health problems.

Key Points About Antipsychotic Medications

- These are very potent medications with a variety of side effects that must be closely monitored, including effects on blood pressure, blood sugar, and cholesterol levels; immune system effects; muscle spasms; and tardive dyskinesia (potentially irreversible movement disorders).

- Despite the side effects, these medications can have powerful, positive effects on more serious mental health problems. They will probably play an increasing role in treatment-resistant depression.

HERBAL ALTERNATIVES

A number of herbal preparations are widely used for a variety of ailments. But you should be cautious when considering this choice. Most of these "natural products" have no oversight or monitoring of their actual contents.

There has been a lot of research conducted on a few popular herbs used to treat mental health problems: St. John's Wort, for depression; omega 3 fatty acids, for depression and bipolar disorder; ginkgo biloba for some mild cognitive effects; and melatonin and valerian, for sleep problems.

St. John's Wort, in particular, has been studied for its effect on depression. The results of most studies show that it is helpful in very mild forms of depression, but is probably no more effective than regular exercise. A study reported in the *Boston Globe* on January 10, 2000, independently tested a variety of St. John's Wort preparations and found wide variance in content and quality.[5]

This would never happen with prescription medications, but it does with herbal supplements because in 1994 Congress passed the Dietary Supplement Health and Education Act, which allows FDA intervention only if there is clear evidence that a product is harmful. So I don't find the argument that "natural is better" to be very compelling.

My advice on the use of herbs is that if you are going to try supplements, report it to your doctor and try to use products from reputable, established companies.

Key Points About Herbal Alternatives

- Herbals do get metabolized by some of the same pathways as medications, and because they aren't well studied, unforeseen and harmful drug interactions are a risk.

- There is no compelling evidence that herbals, by themselves, are effective for moderate to severe mental health problems.

This has been a brief summary of the common classes of psychotropic medications and herbal supplements. It is by no means exhaustive, but provides some basic information. I feel it is very important to be an "open-minded," informed consumer when it comes to making decisions about medications because many students are resistant to the idea of medication, seeing it as a character flaw or weakness, and believe the "herbal" or "natural" treatments are somehow safer and healthier. I also see too many students who downplay the seriousness of their symptoms or parents who have rigid views about the evils of medication, keeping the student from getting the necessary care. They need help to see their options more clearly.

The fact that antidepressants alone are a more than ten billion dollar industry isn't only because of good marketing. If your child had thyroid disease or diabetes, you wouldn't tell him or her to focus and work harder, you'd provide appropriate medical care. Psychological conditions are no different, and I hope that this information will be useful if you need to make this decision.

Appendix C:
Checklists for Colleges and Counseling Centers

As student mental health continues to be scrutinized in the media, it is very important for colleges and counseling centers to review all aspects of their programming. This is not meant to be a comprehensive list, but the following information gives you a good look at the issues that must receive priority attention.

COLLEGE CHECKLIST FOR COUNSELING REVIEW

✓ What is the expected scope of service inside the counseling center, and what are the resources outside? You can anticipate that somewhere between 10 and 25 percent of students ought to use the counseling service and that antidepressant medication will be one of the highest pharmacy costs. These medications are necessary and unaffordable for many students, so consideration about availability must be discussed. It is a challenge to have reasonable coverage and keep the benefit affordable. Considerations should include

A. Programs for outreach and education to students, faculty, and staff

B. The amount of therapy to be provided inside and what insurance resources are available outside

C. The amount of medication coverage and monitoring

✓ Are there consistent assessments across providers and centers (if more than one)? Who oversees mental health care for the community? Is there a central reporting structure?

✓ How do academic counseling, support, and disability assessment get addressed with respect to counseling?

✓ How can you best ensure oversight and integration of mental health care across the campus? I would make a strong recommendation for a structure or coordinating board that would involve the counseling service, student health service (if separate), and representatives from the dean's office, the residence office, the chancellor or provost, and perhaps students. Among larger schools, this would present an opportunity for schools to learn from one another and share expertise. When a crisis occurs in one setting, lessons learned can be carried over to others. Having the provost or chancellor represented provides leverage and support for education or outreach programs. This also affords the opportunity for integrated efforts in such areas as disaster planning or dealing with serious campuswide issues such as alcohol abuse and depression.

✓ What is the make-up of your institution, and are the various constituencies (international students, different cultures of individuals and programs) served by the counseling service? Does the center reflect the cultural diversity and sensitivity of the community in its staffing? Can it meet the clinical demand along with providing the other essential services described above?

✓ Are time and resources provided for education and outreach to the community? Does the counseling service play an active role in the community? Educational programs to recognize common mental health problems and manage stress should be an integral part of every school's curriculum. Stress is an important part of college life and will affect about 50 percent of students. Stress management is part of a well-rounded college education designed to maximize the short- and long-term potential of students.

COUNSELING SERVICE CHECKLIST

✓ What is the make-up of your staff and how does it fit with the demographics and needs of the student population? Do you have prescribers and clinicians with sensitivity to the diversity of your student body?

✓ What data do you track and how do you manage the triage function, sorting out who needs to be seen today versus sometime soon? Harvard has implemented a triage program borrowed from the University of Massachusetts in Amherst. We have brief phone intakes available every day with senior clinicians to determine if someone needs to be seen immediately, whether that student needs to see a prescriber, someone with eating disorder expertise, and so on. This process has had a major, positive influence on both students and staff.

✓ Do you have a good scheduling system to manage your resources? Our system automatically sends out e-mail reminders of appointments forty-eight hours in advance. We have dropped our no-show rate from 15 percent down to 7 percent, which translates into about seventeen hundred additional available visits for students. Knowing seasonal demand and having adequate staff is crucial. Central scheduling and referral must be present in all but the smallest counseling services. Scheduling must be done centrally to address the ebb and flow of community needs. If individual clinicians keep their schedules independently, they will not be able to see the big picture needs of the community.

✓ What is your scope of service? Providing a consultative, educational function for the college community maximizes your effectiveness and value to the college. This would often include

A. Training and ongoing consultation for residential staff

B. Programs to destigmatize mental health problems on campus

C. Active participation in work groups dealing with alcohol and other common campus health problems

D. Support for administrative faculty and staff to help recognize problems, make referrals, and address complex emotional problems seen in the classroom setting

E. Focus on wellness activities: stress management skills, sleep hygiene, tolerance, and celebration of diversity

✓ How are decisions made regarding resource utilization? It is probably pretty consistent that 10 to 25 percent of students will access services with appropriate outreach. We know that a small percentage of those will have serious resource-demanding mental illnesses, some will come in once or twice for brief help with a crisis, and some will come in to work on developmental or personal problems. Decisions must be made on how best to allocate available resources to serve the needs of the community.

✓ What roles do students play in your service? Do you sponsor peer-counseling groups, student health advisory groups, or residential supports or education? Hearing from your primary consumers is very important.

✓ What are the standards of care for psychotherapy for your discipline in your community? Your documentation should meet or exceed these standards. There should be standardized assessment questions during initial evaluations so that students are receiving consistent care across clinicians and disciplines. Visits must be documented with clear mental status assessment if you are providing psychotherapy.

✓ What efforts are in place for quality improvement? Are there regular satisfaction surveys and metrics to measure available access and follow-up times?

✓ Is regular staff training available to develop new skills and expand skills in common problem areas such as alcohol, eating disorders, or sleep problems?

✓ What is the center's role with academic or disciplinary problems? Is there mandated assessment or treatment?

✓ What is the interface with the disability officer and resources for testing?

✓ Do you have a group program? Although often difficult to start, groups are very cost- and clinically effective programs for many problems. Students find them extremely helpful once they cross the threshold to join a group.

✓ Do you have contact and outreach to international students and students from different cultures who may feel isolated or have difficulty accepting or accessing mental health care?

✓ Do you have a robust Web site that describes services and provides on-line screenings and health information? Do clinicians communicate with clients via e-mail? Many students on many campuses do much of their communicating over the Web.

✓ What information comes to the school from pre-registration medical forms? Are there mental health questions on those forms? Is any prescreening done? What screening programs take place during the year?

✓ Do you serve special populations, such as athletic teams, graduate students, multicultural groups, and fraternities? What are the unique needs of these groups?

✓ What kind of educational programming and discussion groups do you provide for students? These might focus on topics such as academic support, stress management, and sleep hygiene to name a few.

✓ How do you track referrals and follow-up? You should have a central tracking system that might include an electronic bulletin board, voice mail, or other method for keeping staff up-to-date on worrisome, high-risk students. It is very important to track referrals and follow up. We have just started sending a satisfaction survey to referred students to see what their experience is.

✓ What is your crisis management and referral process? This is last, but not least. There should be clear systems of communication when students have off-hours crises. There should also be a plan in place for students who may not require hospitalization but are also not appropriate for a dormitory setting. Many college infirmaries have closed down because they are expensive to run, but there should be contingency plans for situations like this and good working relationships with local emergency rooms, including careful handoffs. When students are hospitalized, there should be a clear reentry process. And when students take a medical leave (a good policy to have), it is important to screen students to determine their readiness to return to school.

Appendix D: Resources

CHAPTER ONE

American College Health Association
P.O. Box 28937
Baltimore, MD 21240
(410) 859–1500; www.acha.org

National Institute of Mental Health
Office of Communications
6001 Executive Boulevard, Room 8184, MSC 9663
Bethesda, MD 20892–9663
(301) 443–4513 or (866) 615–NIMH (6464), toll free;
  www.nimh.nih.gov

Parents, Family and Friends of Lesbians and Gays
1726 M Street, NW, W. 400
Washington, DC 20036
(202) 467–8180; www.pflag.org

CHAPTER TWO

Institute of International Education
1400 K Street, NW
Washington, DC 20005
(202) 898–0600; www.iie.org

National Association for Equal Opportunity in Higher Education
8701 Georgia Avenue, Suite 200
Silver Spring, MD 20910
(301) 650–2440; www.nafeo.org

United Negro College Fund
8260 Willow Oaks Corporate Drive
Fairfax, VA 22031
(800) 331–2244; www.uncf.org

CHAPTER THREE

Association of Independent Consumer Credit
    Counseling Agencies
PMB 626
11350 Random Hills Rd., Suite 800
Fairfax, VA 22030
(800) 450–1794; www.aiccca.org

Federal Student Aid, "The Student Guide to
    Funding Your Education"
www.studentaid.ed.gov

National Center for Post Traumatic Stress Disorder
(802) 296–6300; www.ncptsd.org

National Center for Victims of Crime
2000 M Street, NW, Suite 480
Washington, DC 20036
(202) 467–8700; www.ncvc.org

National Foundation for Credit Counseling
801 Roeder Rd., Suite 900
Silver Spring, MD 20910
(800) 388–2227; www.nfcc.org

Student Gateway to the U.S. Government
Reliable links to information on planning for your
   education and paying for it.
www.students.gov

CHAPTER FOUR

Depression

Depression and Bipolar Support Alliance
730 North Franklin Street, Suite 501
Chicago, IL 60610–7224
(800) 826–3632 or (312) 642–0049; www.dbsalliance.org

National Foundation for Depressive Illness
P.O. Box 2257
New York, NY 10116
(800) 239–1265; www.depression.org

Alcohol Abuse

Al-Anon Family Group Headquarters
1600 Corporate Landing Parkway
Virginia Beach, VA 23454–5617
www.al-anon.alateen.org

Alcoholics Anonymous World Services
475 Riverside Drive, 11th Floor
New York, NY 10115
(212) 870–3400; www.aa.org

National Council on Alcoholism and Drug Dependence
20 Exchange Place, Suite 2902
New York, NY 10005
(800) 622–2255; www.ncadd.org

National Institute on Alcohol Abuse and Alcoholism
6000 Executive Boulevard, Suite 409
Bethesda, MD 20892–7003
(301) 443–3860; www.niaaa.nih.gov

Drug Abuse

American Council for Drug Education
204 Monroe Street, Suite 110
Rockville, MD 20850
(301) 294–0600; www.acde.org

Marijuana Anonymous, World Services
P.O. Box 2912
Van Nuys, CA 91404
(800) 766–6779; www.marijuana-anonymous.org

Narcotics Anonymous
P.O. Box 999
Van Nuys, CA 91409
(818) 773–9999; www.na.org

National Clearinghouse for Alcohol and
  Drug Information
P.O. Box 2345
Rockville, MD 20852
(301) 468–2600; www.health.org

PRIDE (National Parents' Resource Institute
  for Drug Education)
166 St. Charles St.
Bowling Green, KY 42101
(800) 279–6301; www.pridesurveys.com

Anxiety Disorders

Anxiety Disorders Association of America
8730 Georgia Avenue, Suite 600
Silver Spring, MD 20910
(240) 485–1001; www.adaa.org

Freedom from Fear
308 Seaview Avenue
Staten Island, NY 10305
(718) 351–1717; www.freedomfromfear.com

Obsessive-Compulsive Foundation
337 Notch Hill Road
North Branford, CT 06471
(203) 315–2190; info@ocfoundation.org; www.ocfoundation.org

Eating Disorders

Harvard Eating Disorders Center
WACC 725
15 Parkman Street
Boston, MA 02114
(617) 236–7766; info@hedc.org; www.hedc.org

National Association of Anorexia Nervosa and Associated Disorders
Box 7
Highland Park, IL 60035
(847) 831–3438; www.anad.org

National Eating Disorders Association
603 Stewart Street, Suite 803
Seattle, WA 98101
(206) 382–3587; www.nationaleatingdisorders.org

National Institute of Mental Health
6001 Executive Boulevard
Bethesda, MD 20892
(866) 615–6464; www.nimh.nih.gov

Sex Addiction

National Council on Sexual Addiction and Compulsivity
P.O. Box 725544
Atlanta, GA 31139
(770) 541–9912; www.ncsac.org

Sleep Disorders

Better Sleep Council
501 Wythe Street
Alexandria, VA 22314–1917
www.bettersleep.org

National Sleep Foundation
1522 K Street, N.W., Suite 500
Washington, DC 20005
(202) 347–3471; nsf@sleepfoundation.org; www.sleepfoundation.org

Suicide

American Association of Suicidology
4201 Connecticut Avenue, NW, Suite 408
Washington, DC 20008
(202) 237–2280; www.suicidology.org

American Foundation for Suicide Prevention
120 Wall Street, 22nd Floor
New York, New York 10005
(888) 333–AFSP or (212) 363–3500; inquiry@afsp.org; www.afsp.org

National Organization of People of Color Against Suicide
47145 Sargent Road, NE
Washington, DC 20017
(202) 549–6039; nopcas@onebox.com; www.nopcas.com

Suicide Prevention Advocacy Network
1025 Vermont Avenue, NW, Suite 1200
Washington, DC 20005
(202) 449–3600; www.spanusa.org

CHAPTER SIX

Association of Recovery Schools
17 Lyle Lane
Nashville, TN 37210
(615) 248–8206; www.recoveryschools.org

RECOMMENDED READING

Depression

D. Burns, *The Feeling Good Handbook* (New York: Plume, 1999).

Bipolar Disorder

K. R. Jamison, *Touched with Fire: Manic Depressive Illness and the Artistic Temperament* (New York: Free Press, 1996).
K. R. Jamison, *An Unquiet Mind: A Memoir of Moods and Madness* (New York: Vintage Books, 1997).
K. R. Jamison, *Night Falls Fast: Understanding Suicide* (New York: Vintage Books, 2000).

Anxiety

E. Hallowell, *Worry* (New York: Ballantine Books, 1998).

Medication

W. Appleton, *Prozac and the New Antidepressants: What You Need to Know About Prozac, Zoloft, Paxil, Luvox, Wellbutrin, Effexor, Serzone, Vestra, Celexa, St. John's Wort, and Others* (New York: Plume, 2000).

P. Kramer, *Listening to Prozac* (New York: Penguin, 1997).

A. Stoll, *The Omega-3 Connection: The Groundbreaking Antidepression Diet and Brain Program* (New York: Free Press, 2002).

Eating Disorders

S. Reindl, *Sensing the Self: Women's Recovery from Bulimia* (Cambridge, Mass.: Harvard University Press, 2002).

M. Siegel, *Surviving an Eating Disorder: Strategies for Family and Friends* (New York: Perennial, 1997).

Obsessive Compulsive Disorder

R. Wilson and E. B. Foa, *Stop Obsessing! How to Overcome Your Obsessions and Compulsions* (New York: Bantam, 2001).

The College Experience

Y. Jenkins (ed.), *Diversity in College Settings: Directives for Helping Professionals* (New York: Routledge, 1998).

R. J. Light, *Making the Most of College: Students Speak Their Minds* (Cambridge, Mass.: Harvard University Press, 2001).

Notes

CHAPTER ONE

1. G. Vaillant, *Aging Well* (New York: Little, Brown, 2003).

2. P. Recer, "Social Hurt Can Register in Brain Like Physical Pain," *Record*, Hackensack, N.J., Oct. 10, 2003, p. A-11.

3. American College Health Association, *National College Health Assessment: Reference Group Report* (Baltimore, Md.: American College Health Association, 2002).

4. C. Bohmer and A. Parrot, *Sexual Assault on Campus* (San Francisco: New Lexington Press, 1993).

5. L. Fraser, "Body Love, Body Hate," *Glamour* (Oct. 1998): 201.

6. E. S. Hetrick and A. D. Martin, "Developmental Issues and Their Resolution for Gay and Lesbian Adolescents." *Journal of Homosexuality*, 1987.

7. J. B. Miller, *Toward a New Psychology of Women* (Boston: Beacon Press, 1976).

8. American College Health Association, *National College Health Assessment: Reference Group Executive Summary Spring 2002* (Baltimore, Md.: American College Health Association, 2003).

CHAPTER TWO

1. H. Wechsler and others, "Trends in College Binge Drinking During a Period of Increased Prevention Efforts: Findings from Four Harvard School of Public Health College Alcohol Study Surveys, 1993–2001," *American College Health* 50 (2002): 203–217.

2. I. Allen, "Therapeutic Considerations for African American Students at Predominantly White Institutions," in Y. Jenkins (ed.), *Diversity in College Settings: Directives for Helping Professionals* (New York: Routledge, 1998), p. 37.

3. R. J. Herrnstein, *The Bell Curve* (Carmichael, Calif.: Touchstone, 1996).

4. S. Fordham and J. Ogbu, "Black Students' School Successes: Coping with the 'Burden of Acting White,'" *Urban Review* 18 (1986): 177.

5. P. Van Slambrouck, "Asian Students Struggle with High Rate of Success," *Christian Science Monitor*, Mar. 18, 1999, p. 29.

CHAPTER THREE

1. Nellie Mae, "Sticker Shock: Why College Costs So Much" (2003). [http://www.nelliemae.com/library/college_costs.html].

2. J. Sahadi, "College Costs Take Another Leap," *CNN/Money*, Oct. 21, 2003. [www.money.cnn.com/2003/10/20/pf/college/q_costs/index.htm].

3. Sahadi, "College Costs Take Another Leap."

4. Sahadi, "College Costs Take Another Leap."

5. CBSNEWS.com. "Beware of Student Credit Cards," Sept. 3, 2003. [http://www.cbsnews.com/stories/2003/09/02 /earlyshow/contributers].

6. CBSNEWS.com. "Beware of Student Credit Cards," Sept. 3, 2003. [http://www.cbsnews.com/stories/2003/09/02 /earlyshow/contributers].

7. S. Baum and M. O'Malley, "College Credit: How Borrowers Perceive their Education Debt," *Research and Information*, Feb. 6, 2002. [http://www.nelliemae.com/library/research_10.html].

8. National Center for Education Statistics, "Projections of Education Statistics to 2009," Washington, D.C., 2000.

9. National Association of Colleges and Employers, "New College Grads Earning Less." *NACE Press Room*, June 25, 2003. [http://www.naceweb.org/press/display.asp?year=2003&prid=176]; National Association of Colleges and Employers, "Year-End Report Shows Lower Salaries for Class of 2003." *NACE Press Room*, Sept. 8, 2003. [http://www.naceweb.org/press/display.asp?year= 2003&prid=178].

10. CBSNEWS.com. "Beware of Student Credit Cards," Sept. 3, 2003. [http://www.cbsnews.com/stories/2003/09/02 /earlyshow/ contributers].

11. "College Shooting Spree," WBALChannel.com, Oct. 21, 2003. [www.thewbalchannel.com/print/2568623/detail.html].

12. "Fraternity Brawl Results in Critical Injuries," Oct. 14, 2003. CNN.com. [www.cnn.usnews.printhins.clickability.com].

13. T. Withers, "Graduate Nabbed in Case Western Shooting," Philly Burbs.com, May 11, 2003. [www.phillyburbs.com/pb-dyn/ articleprint.cfm].

14. "Student Slain in College Shooting," CBSNEWS.com, Apr. 7, 2003. [http://www.cbsnews.com/stories/2003/04/07/national].

15. "Three Professors Killed at University of Arizona," CNN.com, Oct. 28, 2002. [http://cnn.usnews.printthis.clickability.com].

16. "Catawba College Shooting." *Salisbury Post*, Salisbury, N.C., Jan. 28, 2002. [www.salisburypost.com/2002jan/012802ed.htm].

17. "Two Die in Community College Shooting," Click10.com, Jan. 18, 2002. [www.click10.com/print/1196320/detail.html].

18. B. Fisher and J. J. Sloan, "Unraveling the Fear of Victimization Among College Women," *Justice Quarterly* 20 (2003): 633.

19. U.S. Department of Health and Human Services, "College Takes Toll on Mental Health," 2003. [healthfinder.gov/news/newsstory.asp].

20. P. Tjaden and N. Thoennes, "Prevalence, Incidence, and Consequences of Violence Against Women: Findings from the National Violence Against Women Survey," in *National Institute of Justice Centers for Disease Control and Prevention Research in Brief* (Nov. 1998), pp. 1–16.

21. National Center for Victims of Crime, "Sexual Assault," 1998. [www.ncvc.org].

22. C. Bohmer and A. Parrot, *Sexual Assault on Campus* (San Francisco: New Lexington Press, 1993).

23. National Center for Victims of Crime, "Sexual Assault."

24. National Center for Victims of Crime, "Sexual Assault."

CHAPTER FOUR

1. K. Patterson, "College Students Report More Stress, Depression, Suicidal Thoughts," *Knight Ridder/Tribune News Service*, Feb. 12, 2003, p. K2831.

2. American Psychiatric Association, *Diagnostic and Statistical Manual of Mental Disorders*, 4th ed. (Washington, D.C.: American Psychiatric Association, 2000).

3. G. Zammitt, "Understanding Insomnia: Scope, Severity, and Solutions" (Califon, N.J.: SynerMed Communications, May 2003).

4. W. C. Buboltz, F. C. Brown, and B. Soper, "Sleep Habits and Patterns of College Students," *Journal of American College Health* 50:3 (2002): 131–135.

5. F. Brown, B. Soper, and W. Buboltz, "Prevalence of Delayed Sleep Phase Syndrome in University Students," *College Student Journal* (Sept. 2001): 1–5. [http://www.findarticles.com/cf_0/m0FCR/3_35/80744660/p5/article.jhtml?term].

6. F. Brown, W. Buboltz Jr., and B. Soper, "Relationship of Sleep Hygiene Awareness, Sleep Hygiene Practices, and Sleep Quality in University Students," *Behavioral Medicine* (Spring 2002):

1. [http://www.findarticles.com/cf_dls/m0GDQ/1_28/92724721/ p7/article.jhtml?term=(1/6)].

7. K. Spiegel, J. F. Sheridan, and E. Van Cauter, "Effect of Sleep Deprivation on Response to Immunization," *Journal of the American Medical Association* 288:12 (2002): 1471–1472.

8. D. Sontag, "A Suicide at M.I.T.," *New York Times Magazine*, Apr. 28, 2002, pp. 57–61, 94, 139.

9. National Advisory Council of the National Institute on Alcohol Abuse and Alcoholism, Task Force on College Drinking, "Meeting Summary," Apr. 3, 2002. [http://www.niaaa.nih.gov/about/ min4–02-text.htm].

10. M. Khan, "Researching Two New Campus Drugs," *Boston Globe*, July 13, 2003, p. A5.

11. American College Health Association, *National College Health Assessment: Reference Group Report* (Baltimore, Md.: American College Health Association, 2002). National Institute of Mental Health, *Anxiety Disorders Research at the National Institute of Mental Health* (Bethesda, Md.: National Institute of Mental Health, Dec. 7, 2000). [www.nimh.nih.gov/publicat/anxresfact.cfm].

12. National Institute of Mental Health, *Anxiety Disorders Research at the National Institute of Mental Health*. National Institute of Mental Health, *Facts About Anxiety Disorders* (Bethesda, Md.: National Institute of Mental Health, Apr. 30, 2003). [www.nimh.nih.gov/ anxiety/adfacts.cfm].

13. P. F. Sullivan, "Mortality in Anorexia Nervosa," *American Journal of Psychiatry* 152 (July 1995): 1073–1074.

14. American Psychiatric Association, *Diagnostic and Statistical Manual of Mental Disorders*.

15. American Psychiatric Association, *Diagnostic and Statistical Manual of Mental Disorders*.

16. National Institute of Mental Health, *Eating Disorders*.

17. National Eating Disorders Association, "Health Consequences of Eating Disorders" (Seattle, Wash.: National Eating Disorders

Association, 2002). [http://www.nationaleatingdisorders.org/p.asp?
WebPage_ID=320&Profile_ID=41143].

18. National Institute of Mental Health, *Eating Disorders*.

19. Centers for Disease Control, *2002 Sexually Transmitted Disease Sur-
    veillance Report* (Atlanta, Ga.: Centers for Disease Control, 2002).
    See "Table 34 Primary and Secondary Syphilis" [http://
    www.cdc.gov/std/stats/tables/table34.htm]; "Table 11 Chlamydia:
    Reported Cases and Rates" [http://www.cdc.gov/std/stats/tables/
    table11.htm]; "Table 22A. Gonorrhea: Reported Cases by Age, Sex,
    and Race" [http://www.cdc.gov/std/stats/tables/table22A.htm]; and
    "Cases of HIV Infections and AIDS in the United States 2002"
    [www.cdc.gov/hiv/stats/hasr1402/table1.htm].

20. L. Elam-Evans and others, "Abortion Surveillance—United States,
    2000" (Atlanta, Ga.: Centers for Disease Control, Nov. 28, 2003).
    [http://www.cdc.gov/mmwr/preview/mmwrhtml/ss5212a1.htm#tab4].

21. D. Sullivan, "Self-Injury: Poorly Understood Problem," Sept. 5,
    2000. [http://www.cnn.com/2000/HEALTH/09/05/
    self.mutilation.wmd/].

22. K. Arenson, "At N.Y.U., Not All Want to Talk About Deaths, But
    Reminders Are Never Far Away," *New York Times*, Oct. 21, 2003.
    [http://www.nytimes.com/2003/10/21/nyregion/21NYU.html].

23. News Channel 8, "College Acknowledges Responsibility in Stu-
    dent's Suicide," July 25, 2003. [http://www.news8.net/news/
    stories/0703/96196.html].

24. S. Hall, "Lethal Chemistry at Harvard," *New York Times Magazine*,
    Nov. 29, 1998, pp. 120–125.

25. American College Health Association, *National College Health
    Assessment: Reference Group Report*.

26. Centers for Disease Control, National Center for Chronic Disease
    and Health Promotion, "Youth Risk Surveillance: National College
    Health Risk Survey."

27. J. Grunbaum and others, "2001 Youth Risk Behavior Surveillance,"
    MMWR Surveillance Summary 51:4 (2001): 1–62.

28. National Institute of Mental Health, *In Harm's Way: Suicide in America* (Bethesda, Md.: National Institute of Mental Health, Apr. 2003). [www.nimh.nih.gov/publicat/harmaway.cfm].

29. National Institute of Mental Health, *In Harm's Way*.

30. American College Health Association, *National College Health Assessment: Reference Group Report*.

31. Jed Foundation and National Mental Health Association, *Safeguarding Your Students Against Suicide* (New York: Jed Foundation and National Mental Health Association, 2002).

PART TWO

1. R. Gallagher, *National Survey of Counseling Center Directors 2002* (Pittsburgh, Pa.: International Association of Counseling Services, 2002).

2. E. Hoover, "More Help for Troubled Students," *Chronicle of Higher Education*, Dec. 5, 2003, p. A25.

CHAPTER FIVE

1. M. Kitzrow, "The Mental Health Needs of Today's College Students: Challenges and Recommendations," *NASPA Journal* 41:1 (Fall 2003): 165–183.

2. R. Kessler, C. Foster, W. Saunders, and P. Stang, "Social Consequences of Psychiatric Disorders," *American Journal of Psychiatry*, 152:7 (1995): 1026–1032.

3. F. Post, "Creativity and Psychopathology: A Study of 291 World-Famous Men," *British Journal of Psychiatry* 165 (1994): 22–34.

4. K. Kelly, "Lost on the Campus," *Time*, Jan. 15, 2001, pp. 51–53.

5. R. Gallagher, *National Survey of Counseling Center Directors 2002* (Pittsburgh, Pa.: International Association of Counseling Services, 2002).

6. P. Joffe, "An Empirically Supported Program to Prevent Suicide Among a College Population" (paper presented at the Twenty

Fourth Annual National Conference on Law and Higher Education, Clearwater Beach, Fla., Feb. 16, 2003).

7. A. J. Schwartz and L. C. Whitaker, "Suicide Among College Students: Assessment, Treatment, and Intervention," in S. J. Blumenthal and D. J. Kupfer (eds.), *Suicide over the Life Cycle: Risk Factors, Assessment, and Treatment of Suicidal Patients* (Washington, D.C.: American Psychiatric Press, 1990).

8. Kitzrow, "The Mental Health Needs of Today's College Students: Challenges and Recommendations."

9. "What's in a Pill?" *Psychology Today* (May 2002): 4.

10. A. Sanoff, P. Glastris, P. Ellis-Simons, and J. Rachlin, "The Freshman Year: Unkind, Ungentle," *U.S. News and World Report,* Apr. 17, 1989, p. 56.

11. Sanoff, Glastris, Ellis-Simons, and Rachlin, "The Freshman Year: Unkind, Ungentle."

12. R. Hartigan, "On the Edge on Campus," *U.S. News & World Report,* Feb. 18, 2002, p. 41.

13. Hartigan, "On the Edge on Campus."

14. B. Gose, "Elite Colleges Struggle to Prevent Student Suicides," *Chronicle of Higher Education,* Feb. 25, 2000, pp. 95–98.

15. American Foundation for Suicide Prevention. "The College Screening Project: A Program to Identify and Treat Depressed Students Who May Also Be at Risk for Suicide," n.d. [http://www.afsp.org/whats-new/collegescreen.htm].

CHAPTER SIX

1. American College Health Association, *National College Health Assessment: Reference Group Report* (Baltimore, Md.: American College Health Association, 2002).

2. American College Health Association, *National College Health Assessment.*

3. E. Hallowell, *Worry* (New York: Ballantine Books, 1998), pp. 25–26.

4. American Psychiatric Association, *Diagnostic and Statistical Manual of Mental Disorders*, 4th ed. (Washington, D.C.: American Psychiatric Association, 2000).

5. National Advisory Council of the National Institute on Alcohol Abuse and Alcoholism, Task Force on College Drinking, "Meeting Summary," Apr. 3, 2002. [http://www.niaaa.nih.gov/about/min4–02-text.htm].

6. National Institute of Mental Health, *Anxiety Disorders Research at the National Institute of Mental Health* (Bethesda, Md.: National Institute of Mental Health, Dec. 7, 2000). [www.nimh.nih.gov/publicat/anxresfact.cfm].

7. American Psychiatric Association, *Diagnostic and Statistical Manual of Mental Disorders*.

8. American Psychiatric Association, *Diagnostic and Statistical Manual of Mental Disorders*.

9. D. Sontag, "A Suicide at M.I.T.," *New York Times Magazine*, Apr. 28, 2002, p. 60.

CHAPTER SEVEN

1. National Association of Anorexia Nervosa and Associated Disorders, "Facts About Eating Disorders," n.d. [http://www.anad.org/site/anadweb/content.php?type=1&id=6982].

3. E. Hallowell, *Worry* (New York: Ballantine Books, 1998).

APPENDIX B

1. S. Caulfield, "Depression on College Campuses: A New Challenge for Student Health Services and Counseling Centers." *The Student Health Spectrum Fall 2001 Leadership Forum*. 2001.

2. J. Rosack, "Prescription Data on Youth Raise Important Questions." *Psychiatric News*, Feb. 7, 2003, p. 52.

3. L. Neergaard, "Parents Cite Pros, Cons of SSRI Drugs." Boston.com. [http://www.boston.com/yourlife/health/children/

articles/2004/02/03/parents_cite_pros_cons_of_ssri_drugs/].
Feb. 2, 2004.

4. C. J. Tere, S. E. McCabe, C. J. Boyd, and S. K. Guthrie, "Illicit
Methylphenidate Use in an Undergraduate Student Sample:
Prevalence and Risk Factors." *Pharmacotherapy* 23:5 (2003):
609–617.

5. J. Foreman, "St. John's Wort: Less Than Meets the Eye." *Boston
Globe*, Jan. 10, 2000, p. C-1.

About the Authors

Richard Kadison is the chief of the Mental Health Service at Harvard University Health Services. He is a board-certified child and adult psychiatrist who has worked for twenty-five years in the student health field at various schools, including Harvard University, Wellesley College, Mount Ida College, and Pine Manor College. Dr. Kadison specializes in treating patients with eating disorders, a problem that plagues college campuses, and has started several eating disorder programs throughout New England. He is married and is the proud father of Will, his five-year-old son. Dr. Kadison lives in Massachusetts.

Theresa Foy DiGeronimo is an award-winning author of many successful books, including *How to Talk to Teens About Really Important Things* and other titles in the Jossey-Bass How to Talk series. She is an adjunct professor of English at William Paterson University in New Jersey.

Index

A

Abdul-Jabbar, K., 52

Abilify (aripiprazole), 257

Abortion, 17

Academic pressures, 35–36; and alcohol, 114; and grades, 36–38; and work habits, 38–39

Acquaintance rape, 82, 83

ACT, 36

Acting white, 52

Active Minds on Campus, 234–235

Adderall, 116–117

Adubato, S., 189, 190

African Americans, 96

Aging Well (Vaillant), 11

Akathesia (restlessness), 247

Al-Anon Family Group Headquarters (Web site), 117

Alateen groups, 117

Alcohol: academic problems and, 114; as interpersonal issue, 30–31; and link with sex and emotional disorders, 19–20; and male response in developing relationships, 33; and sexual assault, 21; and substance abuse, 112–115

Alcoholics Anonymous (AA), 112, 190; World Services (Web site), 117

Allen, I., 49–50

Alprazolam, 251–252

Altom, J., 147

Ambien (zolpidem), 253

American Association of Suicidology (Web site), 151

American College Health Association, 16, 31, 33, 38, 147, 149; survey results, 240–241

American Council for Drug Education (Web site), 118

American Foundation for Suicide Prevention (AFSP; Web site), 151, 179, 180

American Journal of Psychiatry, 131

Americans with Disabilities Act, 165

Amitriptilene, 245

Amphetamines, 255–257

Anorexia Nervosa, 131–133, 221; symptoms of, 199. *See also* Eating disorders

Anthony (case), 66–67

Antianxiety medication, 244, 250–251

Anticonvulsants, 254–255

Antidepressants, 244–251; side effects of, 246–247; use of, 249–251

Antihistamines, 253

Anti-intellectualism, 51–54

Antipsychotic medications, 257–258

Anxiety: and body image, 24; disorders, 119–125; financial, 66; one-year prevalence of, disorders in adults, 125*fig*.4.1; over sexual orientation, 24–26

Anxiety Disorders Association of America (Web site), 125

Anya (case), 9–10

Aripiprazole, 257
Armitage, R., 105
Ashley (case), 125–130
Asian American students, 56–59, 96
Asian parents' syndrome, 57
Assault, alcohol and, 114
Association of Independent
    Consumer Credit Counseling
    Agencies (AICCCA), 75
Association of Recovery Schools, 205
Atemoxetine, 255
Athletes, 40–43
Ativan (lorazepam), 251–252
Attention deficit disorder, 255–257
Augsburg College (Minnesota), 205
Autonomy, 12, 47

B
Barbiturates, 253
Beautiful Mind, A (cinema), 163
Ben (case), 84–85
Benadryl (diphenhydramine), 253
Bensodiazepines, 251–253
Better Sleep Council (Web site), 109
Binge-eating disorder, 136–138,
    221–222
Biological clock, 105–106
Bipolar disorder, 97–99, 244, 246,
    251, 254. *See also* Depression
"Black Students' School Successes:
    Coping with the 'Burden of Acting
    White'" (*Urban Review*), 52
Bobst Library (New York University),
    146
Body dysmorphic disorder, 136, 145
Body image, 22–23; male, 24. *See also*
    Relationships; Sexuality
Bohler, S., 146
"Booty runs," 17
Borderline personality disorder, 145
Boston Globe, 247, 258
Bradley (case), 13
Brandy (case), 68–69
Brigham and Women's Hospital
    (Boston), 107
Broward Community College, 79
Brown, F., 106–107
Bulimia Nervosa, 131, 132, 134–136,
    221; symptoms of, 199–200

Buproprion, 250
Burning, 144
Buspar (buspirone), 251–252
Buspirone, 251–252

C
Campus violence, 77–79
Campusblues.com, 180, 234
Care, coordination of, 176–177
Case Western Reserve University
    (Cleveland, Ohio), 78
Catawba College, 78–79
"Catawba College Shooting"
    (*Salisbury Post*), 78–79
Catherine (case), 72
Celexa (citalopram), 246
Center for Health Policy Studies
    (Washington, D.C.), 24
Center for Substance Abuse
    Prevention (Web site), 118
Center for Wellness and Health
    Communication, 108–109
Centers for Disease Control, 95, 96;
    Abortion Surveillance (2000), 141;
    Surveillance Report (2002),
    141
Checklist: college, for counseling
    review, 261–263; counseling
    service, 263–266; of questions
    concerning role of parents, 204–209
Chickering Insurance, 244
Chlamydia, 141
Chlordiazepoxide, 251–252
Chlorpromazine, 257
Churchill, W., 163
Circadian clock, 106
Citalopram, 246
Clozapine, 257
Clozaril (clozapine), 257
Clubbing, 17
Cocaine, 115
College Board, 66
College Screen Project (American
    Foundation for Suicide
    Prevention), 179
"College Shooting Spree" (WBAL),
    78
"College Students Report More
    Stress, Depression, Suicidal

Thoughts" *(Knight Ridder/Tribune News Service)*, 99

Columbine High School, 77–79

Communication: close, 46–47; and new way of communicating, 185–193; skills, modeling, 187–189; tips for good, 193–194. *See also* Parents, expectations of; Parents, role of

Community outreach, 174–175

Competition. *See* Pressures

Concentration problems, 248, 250

Confidentiality, rules of, 202–204

Connectedness, 186–187, 225–227

Coping mechanisms, 33, 116, 138, 141, 146

Counseling services, improving, 177–178

Culture, problems of, 48–59; and anti-intellectualism, 51–54; and discrimination, 49–51; and family expectations, 54–55; and family hopes, 51–54; and prejudice against Asian students, 56–59

Cutting, 142–146

Cycling moods, 98

D

Dalmane (flurazepam), 253

Dan (case), 21–21, 69

Dana College (Nebraska), 205

Darbamazepine, 254

Darrell (case), 92–95

Date rape, 17, 82

Delayed sleep syndrome, 106

Delta sleep, 104

Denial, 232

Depakoat (Valproic acid), 254

Dependence, alcohol and, 115

Depression, 92–101, 244; biologic, 248; and bipolar disorder, 97–99, 244; and body image, 23, 24; and dysthymia, 97–99; epidemic of, 93–95; and sexual orientation, 24–26; stigma about, 101; symptoms of, 96–97, 197

Depression and Bipolar Support Alliance (Web site), 101

Desipramine, 245

Desyryl (trazodone), 250, 253

Developmental issues: and gender, 32–33; and identity development, 8–16; and interpersonal issues, 26–31; and relationships and sexuality, 17–26

Dexedrine, 255

Dexroamphetamine, 115

Diagnostic and Statistical Manual of Mental Disorders (DSM), 96–97, 131–132, 134

Diazepam, 250–251

Dietary Supplement Health and Education Act, 259

Diphenhydramine, 253

Discrimination, 49–51. *See also* Culture, problems of; Race

Divorce, children of, 67–69

Donahue, S., 73

Dopamine, 257

Doxepin, 245

Drug use, 17; as interpersonal issue, 30–31

Drunk driving, 114

Dumbing-down phenomenon, 52

Dysthymia, 97–99. *See also* Depression

E

Eastern Asia, 61

Eating disorders, 63, 125–138, 248; and anorexia nervosa, 131–133; and binge-eating disorder, 136–138; and body image, 24; and bulimia nervosa, 134–136; and eating on campus, 130–131

Eating Disorders (National Institute of Mental Health), 131

Ecstasy, 17

Effexor (venlafaxine), 246

Eisenberger, N. I., 13

Elavil (amitritilene), 245

Electrolyte imbalances, 135–136

Emory University, Atlanta, Georgia, 179

Emotional disorder, 19–21. *See also* Relationships: and meeting potential partners

England, 247

Erin (case), 27–28

Exercise, 39, 218–219
Expectations: family, 54–55; parental, 43–48
Extracurricular pressures, 40–43

F

Facts About Anxiety Disorders (National Institute of Mental Health), 125
Facts on Tap (Phoenix House), 118, 235
Family: expectations of, 54–55; hopes of, 55–56; togetherness, 46–47
"Family Guide to Keeping Youth Mentally Healthy and Drug Free" (Center for Substance Abuse Prevention), 118
Federal Drug Administration, 247, 249
Federal Student Aid, 77
Female sexuality, 22–23
Ferrum College (Virginia), 146–147, 163
Financial worries, 65–76; and children of divorce, 67–69; and loans, 70–71; and need for financial return, 74–76; and peer approval, 67–69; and uncertain economic times, 71–73; and working student, 69–70
Flores, R., 78, 160
Florida, 79
Flurazepam, 253
Fluvoxamine, 246, 250
Follow-up care, 175–176
Food, 39, 63
Fordham, S., 52
"Fraternity Brawl Results in Critical Injuries" (CNN), 78
Freedom from Fear (Web site), 125
Frentzel, M., 146–147, 163
Frink, R., 79

G

Gabapentin, 254–255
Gallagher, R., 171
Gender, 21, 33; and alcohol abuse, 112–113; and eating disorders, 131, 221–222; and sexuality, 139–140; and suicide, 150

Generalized anxiety disorder, 123, 124; symptoms of, 198–199. *See also* Anxiety
Geodon (ziprasidone), 257
Germany, 63
Geta (case), 44–45
GHB, 82
Ginko biloba, 258
Glamour magazine, 23
Glenn (case), 109–112
Glory days, lost, 14–15. *See also* Identity development
Gluckman, M., 146
Gonorrhea, 141. *See also* Sexually transmitted disease
Grades: obsession with, 36–38; and parental expectations, 44–45; and work habits, 38–39
"Graduate Nabbed in Case Western Shooting" (Philly Burbs), 78
Guilt, 66

H

Hallowell, N., 186, 231
Harvard University, 70, 71, 73, 147, 160, 165, 168, 263; Business School, 61–62; Center for Wellness and Health Communication, 108–109; Eating Disorder Center (Web site), 138; Health Services, 49–50; Law School, 45; Medical School, 107, 108; School of Public Health, 24, 168; Sexual Assault Prevention and Response, 85; Student Mental Health Advocacy and Awareness Group, 168
Hawking, S., 163
Health problems, alcohol and, 114
Heiligenstein, E., 116
Help, resistance to, 64
Herbs, 258–259
Heroine, 115
High-risk college drinking consequences, 113*fig.4.1*
HIV/AIDS, 17, 141
Ho, T., 160
Home connection, 13
Homosexuality, 24–26
Honesty, 201–202

HOTLINE: 1-800-SUICIDE (Web site), 151
Hypnotics, 252–254; key points about, 252–254

I

Identity development, 8–16; and changes in plan, 15–16; and glory days, 14–15; and living changes, 9–10; and personal connections, 11–13
Imipramine, 245
Independence, 12
Indian students, 62
Indonesian students, 62
Informality, classroom, 62
Insomnia, 248
Institute of International Education, 60–62
International students. *See* Students, international
Internet sex, 140
Interpersonal issues, 26–31; and alcohol and drug abuse, 30–31; and learning to share, 27–28; and overnight guests, 30; and psychological disorders, 28–29. *See also* Developmental issues, normal
Intimacy, 21
Investment Company, 70
Invulnerability attitude, 141
Ipecac, 135
Iraq, war in, 79–80
Irena (case), 54–55
Irtazapine, 250

J

Jannine (case), 50–51
Jed Foundation, 180–182, 234
Jenkins, Y., 50–51
Jim (case), 80–81
Joffe, P., 174
Johns Hopkins University, 179

K

Kansas State University, 95, 99
Kara (case), 214–217, 237
Karen (case), 9, 10–11
Kashif (case), 52–53

Katlyn (case), 29
Kaufman, P., 57
Kaylee (case), 84–85
Keith (case), 102–103
Kisha (case), 12
Kleptomania, 145
Knight Ridder/Tribune News Service, 99
Korea, 63
Krueger, S., 112

L

Lamictal (lamotrigine), 251, 254–255
Lamotrigine, 251, 254–255
Language deficit, 57–58
Larry (case), 42–43
Laxatives, 135
Learning styles, 59–62
Legal issues, for international students, 63–64
Librium (chlordiazepoxide), 251–252
Light, R., 218
Lithium carbonate, 254–255
Livingston College, 78–79
Loans, 70–71
Lorazepam, 251–252
Louisiana Technical College, 78, 160
LSD, 115
Luvox (fluvoxamine), 246, 250

M

Mackes, M., 71
Madrid, terrorist bombing in, 79–80
Making the Most of College (Light), 218
Manic-depressive psychosis, 247, 254. *See also* Bipolar Disorder
MAOs. *See* Monoamine oxidase inhibitors
Mara (case), 19–20
Marijuana, 115
Marijuana Anonymous (Web site), 118
Marine, S., 85
Mark (case), 14–15
Massachusetts Institute of Technology (MIT), 112, 147, 165, 173, 179, 203
Matt (case), 74
Max (case), 47
Maya (case), 29

MDMA (Ecstasy), 115
Medication, 237; everything you need to know about, 243–260; self, 116
Melatonin, 105, 106, 258
Memory retention, 105
Mental Health: Culture, Race, and Ethnicity (U.S. Department of Health and Human Services), 230
Mental health issues, normalizing, 188–189
Mental Health Net (Web site), 181
Mental health services: college institution benefits from, 162–164; and funding adequate staffing, 171–173; individual student benefits from, 157–159; recommendations for creating strong, 167–177; student body benefits from, 159–161; why some schools do not have, 164–166
Mental health, tips for, 22
Methadone, 115
Methamphetamine, 115
Methylphenidate, 255–257
Microaggressions, 51
Middle Eastern students, 62, 80
Minorities, 230; and depression, 96
Monet, C., 163
Monoamine oxidase inhibitors (MAOs), 250
Mood stabilizers, 254–255
Mozart, W. A., 163
Muslim students, 62–63
MyStudentBody, 234

N

Narcotics Anonymous (Web site), 118
Nash, J. F., Jr., 163
National Association for Equal Opportunity in Higher Education, 54
National Association of Anorexia Nervosa, 138
National Association of Colleges and Employers (NACE), 71
National Center for Chronic Disease and Health Promotion (Centers for Disease Control), 96

National Center for Education Statistics, 57, 71
National Center for Post Traumatic Stress Disorder (PTSD), 86, 125
National Center for Victims of Crime, 79
National Clearinghouse for Alcohol and Drug Information, 118
National College Health Assessment: Reference Group Executive Summary (American College Health Assessment), 31, 38, 149, 184, 241
National College Health Association, 18
National Council on Alcoholism and Drug Dependency (Web site), 117
National Council on Sexual Addiction and Compulsivity, 139
National Depression Screening Week, 168, 217
National Eating Disorders Association, 138
National Families in Action (Web site), 118
National Foundation for Credit Counseling, 75
National Foundation for Depressive Illness (Web site), 101
National Institute of Mental Health (NIMH), 123, 125, 137; Web site, 138, 181
National Institute on Alcohol Abuse and Alcoholism (NIAAA), 113; Web site, 117
National Lampoon's Animal House (cinema), 115
National Mental Health Association (NMHA), 181, 234
National Organization of People of Color Against Suicide (Web site), 151
National Sleep Foundation (Web site), 109
National Student Loan Survey (2002), 71
National Survey of Counseling Center Directors, 171
National Women's Study, 83
Native Americans, 96

Natural medications, 243, 258–259
Nefazodone, 250
Nellie Mae survey, 70
Neurontin (gabapentin), 254–255
New York Times Magazine, 203
New York University, 146
non-REM (NREM), 104, 105
Norpramin (desipramine), 245
North Carolina, 78–79
Nutrition, 220–222

O

Obsessive compulsive disorder
   (OCD), 28–29, 119–123. *See also*
   Anxiety disorders
Obsessive Compulsive Foundation
   (Web site), 125
OCD. *See* Obsessive compulsive
   disorder
Off-campus resources, 176–177
Ogbu, J., 52
Olanzepine, 257
Omega 3 fatty acids, 258
*Open Doors 2003: International
   Students in the US* (Institute of
   International Education), 60–61
Opiates, 115
Outsidetheclassroom.com, 234
Overnight guests, 30
Oxazepam, 251–252
Oxcarbazine, 254–255

P

Pakistani students, 62, 186–187
Panic disorder, 123. *See also* Anxiety
   disorders
Parents, expectations of, 43–48; for
   close communication and family
   togetherness, 46–47; and emotional
   or mental problems, 48; to share
   same goals, 45–46
Parents, Family and Friends of
   Lesbians and Gays (PFLAG), 26
Parents, role of: and awareness,
   184–185; and being proactive with
   college, 200–204; checklist of
   questions concerning, 204–209;
   and communication, 185–193; and
   crisis action plan, 209–211; and

encouraging problem-solving skills,
   194–196; and listening, 189–191;
   and modeling strong
   communication skills, 187–189;
   and recognizing limits, 212; and
   warning signs, 196–200
Paroxetine, 246
Pat (case), 25–26
Patience, 189–190
Patterson, K., 99
Paxil (paroxetine), 246
PCP, 115
Peer pressure, 18, 73–74. *See also*
   Relationships; Sexuality
Personal connections, breaking,
   11–13. *See also* Connectedness;
   Identity development
PFLAG. *See* Parents, Family and
   Friends of Lesbians and Gays
   (PFLAG)
Pharmaceutical industry, 95
Pharming, 116
Phobias, 123, 124. *See also* Anxiety
   disorders
Phoenix House (Web site), 118
Pillsbury Corporation, 130
Plagiarism, 62
Plans, change in, 15–16. *See also*
   Identity development
Plath, S., 163
Police involvement, alcohol and, 115
Posttraumatic stress disorder (PTSD),
   83, 123. *See also* Anxiety disorders
Pregnancy, 17
Pressures, student: academic, 35–40;
   cultural, 48–59; extracurricular,
   40–43; and international students,
   59–64; parental, 43–48; and peer
   pressure, 18, 73–74; racial, 48–59
"Preventing Campus Suicide" (Jed
   Foundation), 182
Prevention, 151–152; student
   education to promote, 167–171
PRIDE Surveys (Web site), 118
Princeton Review, 162
Princeton University, 155
Proactivity, 200–204, 233–235
Problem-solving skills, 194–196
Property damage, alcohol and, 114

Prozac, 94, 100, 121, 122, 175, 245
Psychological disorders, 28–29
Psychology Today, 100
Psychotropic medications, 244
PTSD. *See* Posttraumatic stress
   disorder
Purging, 134–136. *See also* Bulimia
   Nervosa

Q

Quetiapine, 257

R

Race, 48–59; and absence of role
   models, 56; and anti-
   intellectualism, 51–54; and
   discrimination, 49–51; and family
   expectations, 54–55; and family
   hopes, 55–56; and prejudice against
   Asian students, 56–59
Reaching out, 229–230
Rebound, 253
Relationships, 17–26; and gender
   differences, 21; and meeting
   potential partners, 17–18; and peer
   pressure, 18
REM (rapid eye movement), 104,
   105
Remeron (mirtazapine), 250
"Report: Minorities Lack Proper
   Mental Health Care" (CNN), 96
Respiridone, 257
Restoril (temazepam), 253
Risperdal (respiridone), 257
Ritalin (methylphenidate), 116–117,
   243, 255–257
Rockland-Miller, H., 172
Rohypnol, 82
Role models, 56
Roth, G., 130
Rutgers University, 78, 205

S

Safe sex, 17
Salary Survey, 71
Same-sex couples, 22
Sasha (case), 119–122
SAT, 36, 57
Satcher, D., 230
Satow, D., 180, 234

Satow, P., 180, 234
Sawyer, D., 192–193
Schwartz, A. J., 174
Sedation, 252
Selective serotonin reuptake
   inhibitors (SSRIs), 95, 100,
   244–247, 249, 252
Self-Abuse Finally Ends (SAFE; Web
   site), 146
Self-esteem, 139
Self-injury: as coping mechanism,
   146–144; reason for, 145–146; as
   secret act, 144–145
"Self-Injury: Poorly Understood
   Problem" (CNN), 146
Self-mutilation. *See* Self-injury
Serax (oxazepam), 251–252
Seroquel (quetiapine), 257
Sertaline, 246
Serzone (nefazodone), 250
Sexual assault, 21, 81–86; alcohol
   and, 114, 138–142
Sexual Assault Prevention and
   Response (Harvard University), 85
Sexual dysfunction, 21, 246–247,
   250
Sexuality, 17–26, 138–142; and
   confusion over sexual orientation,
   24–26; and consequences of
   promiscuity, 140–141; female, and
   body image, 22–23; and gender
   differences, 21, 139–140; link with
   alcohol, 19–21; and meeting
   potential partners, 17–18; and peer
   pressure, 18; and sexual activity, 18;
   and sexual freedom, 17
Sexually transmitted disease (STD),
   17, 141
Sharing, learning to, 27–28
Shin, E., 163, 173, 203
Shin, W., 147
Silvie, T., 78, 160
Sinequan (doxepin), 245
Skolnik, J. D., 146
Sleep disorders, 102–109, 248; and
   confusing biological clock,
   105–106; and high cost of sleep
   deprivation, 106–108; and sleeping,
   222–225; and slow-wave sleep, 105;
   and stages of sleep, 104–105;

symptoms of, 197–198; warning
signs of, 106

Sleep medications, 102–103, 244,
252–254

Social fears, 76–87; and campus
violence, 77–79; and post-9/11
terror, 79–81; and sexual assault,
81–86

Social isolation, 11–12

Social phobia, 124. *See also* Anxiety
disorders

Sonata (zaleplon), 253

Speak from the Heart (Adubato),
189–190

Specific phobia. *See also* Anxiety
disorders

SSRIs. *See* Selective serotonin
reuptake inhibitors (SSRIs)

St. John's Wort, 243, 258

St. Luke's Roosevelt Hospital (New
York, New York), 102

STD. *See* Sexually transmitted
disease

Steven (case), 28

Stickgold, R., 108, 223

Stimulants, 255–257

Stone Center (Wellesley College), 33

Strattera (atemoxetine), 255

"Student Guide to Funding Your
Education" (Federal Student Aid),
77

Student Mental Health Advocacy
and Awareness Group (Harvard
University), 168

"Student Slain in College Shooting"
(CBS), 78

Students, international: daily life
dilemmas of, 63; effects of terrorism
on, 62–63; and learning styles,
59–62; and legal issues, 63–64; and
resistance to help, 64

Students, working, 69–70

Styron, W., 163

Substance abuse, 109–118; and
alcohol abuse, 112–115; and drug
abuse, 115–118; symptoms of, 198

Suicide: attempts, and alcohol, 114;
incidents of, 146–147; shocking
statistics concerning, 147–148;
students at high-risk for, 148–151;

and symptoms of suicidal thinking,
200

"Suicide Among College Students:
Assessment, Treatment, and
Intervention" (Schwartz and
Whitaker), 174

Suicide attempts, alcohol and, 114

Suicide Prevention Advocacy
Network (Web site), 151

Sullivan, D., 146

Suzan (case), 69

Suzanne (case), 23

Syphilis, 141. *See also* Sexually
transmitted disease

T

Tadesse, S., 160

Task Force on College Drinking
(National Institute on Alcohol
Abuse and Alcoholism), 113

Tegretol (carbamazepine), 254

Temazepam, 253

Terrorist attacks of September 11,
2001, 62–64, 74, 77, 79–81, 86

Texas A&M, 179

Texas Tech University, 205

Therapy, 188

Theresa (case), 51

Thorazine (Chlorpromazine), 257

"Three Professors Killed at University
of Arizona" (CNN), 78

Time management, 227–229

Topamax (topiramate), 254–255

Topiramate, 254–255

Torfranil (imipramine), 245

Tourette syndrome, 145

Trazodone, 250, 253

Trichotillomania, 145

Tricyclic antidepressants, 245, 250

Trileptal (oxcarbazine), 254–255

"Two Die in Community College
Shooting" (Click10), 78–79

U

Ulifeline.com (Jed Foundation), 180,
234

"Understanding Insomnia: Scope,
Severity, and Solutions"
(SynerMed Communications), 102

United Negro Fund, 54

United States Department of Health
and Human Services, 81
United States Department of Justice,
81
United States health care system, 168
United States Public Health Service,
96
University of Arizona, 78, 160, 180,
234
University of California, Berkeley, 57
University of California, Los Angeles,
13
University of Chicago, 107
University of Cincinnati, 23
University of Idaho, Student
Counseling Center, 158
University of Illinois, 174
University of Maryland, 78, 178
University of Massachusetts,
Amherst, 172, 263
University of Michigan, 105
University of Nevada, Reno, 179
University of Pittsburgh, 171
University of Rochester, 179
University of South Carolina, 179
University of Texas, Austin, 205
University of Wisconsin, 116
Unsafe sex, alcohol and, 114
Urban Review, 52
U.S. News & World Report, 162

V
Vaillant, G., 11
Valerian, 258
Valium (diazepam), 251–252
Valproic acid, 254
Van Couter, E., 107
Van Couter Lab (University of
Chicago), 107
Vandalism, alcohol and, 114

Venlafaxine, 246
Violence Against Women Survey
(U.S. Department of Justice), 81, 82
Violence, campus, 77–79

W
Wallace, M., 163
Wang, L.-C., 57–59
WebMD.com, 181
Wechsler, H., 168
Wellbutrin (buproprion), 250
Wellesley College, 33, 192–193
"What's in a Pill?" (*Psychology Today*),
100
Whitaker, L. C., 174
Wilinski, J., 78
Winkelman, J., 107
Withers, T., 78
Worry (Hallowell), 186, 231
Worry, productive *versus* toxic,
231–232
Wright-Swadel, B., 71–73

X
Xanax (alprazolam), 251–252

Y
Youth Risk Behavior Survey (2001),
149
"Youth Risk Surveillance: National
College Health Risk Survey"
(Centers for Disease Control), 96

Z
Zaleplon, 253
Zammitt, G., 102
Ziprasidone, 257
Zoloft (sertraline), 126, 246
Zolpidem, 253
Zyprexa (olanzepine), 257